NAMING ACHILLES

NAMING ACHILLES

David Shive

New York   Oxford
OXFORD UNIVERSITY PRESS
1987

Oxford University Press

Oxford   New York   Toronto
Delhi   Bombay   Calcutta   Madras   Karachi
Petaling Jaya   Singapore   Hong Kong   Tokyo
Nairobi   Dar es Salaam   Cape Town
Melbourne   Auckland

and associated companies in
Beirut   Berlin   Ibadan   Nicosia

Copyright © 1987 by David Shive

Published by Oxford University Press, Inc.,
200 Madison Avenue, New York, New York 10016

Oxford is a registered trademark of Oxford University Press

Library of Congress Cataloging-in-Publication Data

Shive, David
Naming Achilles.

Bibliography: p.
Includes index.
1. Homer—Style.   2. Homer—Characters—Achilles.
3. Homer. Iliad.   4. Oral-formulaic analysis.
5. Oral tradition—Greece.   6. Achilles (Greek
mythology) in literature.   I. Title.
PA4176.S55 1987   883′.01   86-18250
ISBN 0-19-504860-1

246897531

Printed in the United States of America
on acid-free paper

à mes professeurs
et
à mes étudiants

Preface

Homeric oral poetry is in crisis. Milman Parry's masterly theory accounted for Homer's characteristic inconsistencies and inconcinnities. Adam and Anne Parry's vital revision of that theory addressed the timely need to account for Homer's rediscovered consistencies and concinnities.[1] Oralists now join non-oralists in discerning such subtle delicacies as Milman Parry would have deemed illusory in Homer and appropriate only in the literary refinement of self-conscious Hellenistic and Roman epic. Homeric oral poetry has become indistinguishable from Homeric literate poetry: any poetic device that is now characteristic of literate composition might have been developed and deployed by oral technique—and so may be demonstrative of orality.[2] Transcendently oral to the oralist, to the non-oralist Homer has transcended traditional orality. Is there a fine line between preeminently oral and residually oral?

Although other aspects of Milman Parry's momentous theory have not gone unopposed and unrevised, his two fundamental tenets, *extension* and *economy,* are thought and said to be unassailable. Even Norman Austin concedes:

> Hardly any scholar remains a rigid Parryist today; even so, those of us who came to Homer after Parry are Parryists of one shape or another, uneasy with the rigidity of Parry's conclusions yet unable to escape the implications of the overwhelming evidence of the formulaic system.[3]

This is an attempt to assail Parry's still overwhelming evidence.

Je tiens à remercier HRH Prince Philip et Bernard Knox et ma famille.   D.S.

*The Center for Hellenic Studies, The Phillips Collection
and Georgetown University, Washington, D.C.*
June 1985

Contents

NAMING ACHILLES

Ce que vous dites-là,
se dit par tout le monde,
et est imprimé en mille
endroits: cependant rien
n'est moins vray que
cette belle oeconomie.

Charles Perrault

I

The Formula:
Parry and His Predecessors

Formulae are repetitions.[1] The history of the formula derives from the problem of repetitions. The ancients no doubt noticed the recurrent phrases in the *Iliad* and *Odyssey*—they are notable and can scarcely escape notice.[2] They were not problematic, however, until modern times.

Michel de Montaigne is commonly praised and blamed for being a founder of modernity. His dictum bore centuries of repetition: "La redicte est par tout ennuyeuse, fut ce dans Homere."[3] Houdar de la Motte dilated upon censure of Homer's repetitions:

> On me diroit en vain, qu'une grande partie de ces répétitions sont courtes. Je répondrois que les plus courtes reviennent aussi plus souvent, et que par là, elles ne déparent pas moins tout l'ouvrage que les plus longues. Rien n'est plus ennuyeux, par exemple, que ces refrains dans les combats de l'Iliade: *la terre retentit horriblement du bruit de ses armes, il fut précipité dans la sombre demeure de Pluto.* J'en dis autant de ces longues épithetes, et de ces attributs attachés aux Dieux et aux Héros; quant même il seroit vrai que ces attributs n'étoient pas moins essentiels pour désigner les personnes que les noms propres: encore n'a-t'on pas raison de le prétendre. Homere se passe souvent de ces attributs; ils n'étoient donc pas nécessaires et il ne lui restoit d'autre raison de les employer que sa propre négligence.[4]

At first, such petulant attacks as this doubtless evoked dismay and disbelief. But Homer lost the pristine primacy acknowledged by Dante: *poeta sovrano.* He suffered torment in our scholarly Inferno.

F. A. Wolf determined that Homer was a nonliterate bard in a nonliterate age.[5] The beginnings of literacy were given to the seventh century and Homer to the tenth. It seemed certainly beyond the powers of man (primitive or modern) to compose, memorize, and perform poems of epic length without recourse to writing. And even if the feat were feasible, the tenth century had no time or place to perform them and no way to preserve them. Κλέα ἀνδρῶν of several hundred lines are all that one could reasonably expect from the Dark Ages. Much poetry therefore implies many nonliterate bards, each with a small repertoire. Homer must have been superior to the common lot of bards: his name became renowned and eventually also generic or eponymous for the best heroic lays. The most memorable lays were memorized. In the seventh and sixth centuries some of this orally transmitted poetry was transcribed and fixed in texts. Finally Pisistratus compiled and composed our *Iliad* and *Odyssey,* gathering dispersed and disparate κλέα of Achilles and Odysseus and fashioning these into monumental epics, as a mason builds a wall with stones that he hammers and mortars.

After Wolf, Homerists set about analyzing the *Iliad* and *Odyssey* in an attempt to distinguish Homer's holograph from the mostly inferior digressions of his imitators and editors. When these poetasters and versemongers slavishly imitated Homer's phraseology, the tell-tale result was the recurrent phrase.

"Homerus non tam pauper fuit ingenio ut bis diceret idem" was the fallacious axiom of the discerpters.[6] For example, the simile of the stalled stallion that breaks his tether and romps over the plain occurs at VI 506–11 and at XV 263–68.[7] The conviction that the great Book VI is to be attributed to the great Poet is confirmed by the particular aptness of the simile as a description of Paris, whereas a lesser poet in a lesser lay must have copied the lines and applied them less aptly to Hector.[8] Again, Homer's admirable verse for a charioteer,

XVI 776

κεῖτο μέγας μεγαλωστί, λελασμένος ἱπποσυνάων,

was borrowed for xxiv 40 and unadmirably applied to Achilles—no charioteer.[9] If Homer had composed the ending of the *Odyssey,* he might well have invented a line to do justice to Achilles, as he had done for the charioteer Cebriones. Inept repetition of Homer's words was the contribution of Homer's successors, the Homeridae, for whom the Poet's vignettes and similes became models for analogy and imitation—formulae, as it were. Although their theory won general acceptance, the Analysts failed to convince each other of what in particular was Homer's and what not.

The Unitarians, on the other hand, made the *Iliad* and *Odyssey* the measure of Homer, rather than the *Aeneid* or Dictys or Ossian or whatever might meet critical standards for authentic epic poetry. In this they convicted the Analysts of historical anachronism and subjective judgment (of which they themselves were scarcely less culpable). Unitarians assumed that Homer wrote Homer and may have nodded occasionally. It was demonstrated that single works by single authors had such inconsistencies and inconcinnities as the Analysts decried in Homer, and that the *Iliad* and *Odyssey,* on the other hand, had such consistencies and concinnities as the Analysts would praise in single works by single authors.[10]

As some attributed everything to Homer and some attributed something to Homer, it remained for some to attribute nothing to Homer. Seemingly *par esprit de contradiction* or *par goût du paradoxe,* the abbé d'Aubignac was of opinion that Homer (like Orpheus) was a mythic figure and could not be reprimanded for the abysmal lot of rhapsodies that were foisted upon him.[11] This was the time of the great *Querelle des anciens et des modernes,* in which the age of Louis Le Grand was measured against Greece and Rome.[12] Jean de La Fontaine might be compared with Aesop; but Homer had to be debased considerably to bring him into line with Chapelain (*La Pucelle*), Saint Amant (*Moïse sauvé*), Godeau (*Saint Paul*), Louis Le Laboureur (*Charlemagne*), Carel de Sainte-Garde (*Childebrand*), and Desmarets de Saint-Sorlin (*Clovis*). A satirical *Battle of the Books,* rather than scholarly refutation, seems a suitable reply to that fantastic idea. Eloquent rhetoric was the favored mode of argumentation in the *Querelle:* contentiousness is often impatient of scientific rigor.

The ideas proclaimed, however, would later find scholars and scholarship to substantiate them. Consider Charles Perrault:

> Ce Poëte, pour faciliter sa versification, a commencé par équiper tous ses Héros & tous ses Dieux, de plusieurs épithetes de differentes longueurs, pour finir ses vers pompeusement & commodément. Achille

est divin, il est un Dieu, il est semblable à un Dieu; il est bien botté, il est bien coiffé, il a les pieds legers; & tout cela non point selon le cas dont il s'agit, mais selon qu'il reste plus ou moins de place à remplir pour achever le vers. Junon a des yeux de boeuf, ou a les bras blancs, est femme de Jupiter, ou fille de Saturne, suivant le besoin de la versification, & nullement par rapport aux aventures où elle intervient. Le plus souvent ces épithetes vaines & vagues, non seulement ne conviennent point au fait qui est raconté, mais y sont directement opposées. Il est dit, par exemple, qu'Achille aux pieds legers, ne bougeoit du fond de son vaisseau; que Venus qui aime à rire, pleuroit amérement; il donne à la mere d'Irus, le plus vilain de tous les Gueux, l'épithete de venerable, aussi franchement qu'à Thetis la mere d'Achille, parce que cette épithete orne le vers, & jointe avec le mot de mere en fait heureusement la fin, qui est la partie du vers la plus mal aisée à faire. Une seconde commodité tres grande, c'est qu'il se sert, suivant le besoin, de sept ou huit particules qui ne signifient rien, & qui emplissent admirablement le nombre des sillabes requis pour composer le vers. Et pour troisiesme commodité, il employe indifféremment toutes sortes de dialectes; ce qui lui fournit des sillabes longues ou breves, selon l'exigence de la versification.[13]

Richard Bentley, it would seem, proposed to compose the French quarrel with English compromise.[14] Homer is granted historicity— but in the eleventh century, where the distinction between history and legend must then have been gratuitous. Homer is allowed to have composed merry Iliadic and Odyssean songs and rhapsodies— although it was five hundred years before these were revised and redacted into epic poems (the intervening years being blank). One scholar's verisimilitude is specious speculation to the next. Coercive arguments are required: Wood's inductions and Vico's deductions.

Giambattista Vico originated a philosophy of history and social development.[15] He disagreed with the prevailing view that man's nature is constant—that ancient man, medieval man, and modern man are essentially alike and differ only in inessentials. Vico discovered historical perspective. Essentials evolve; inessentials may remain unchanged. The *Iliad* is essentially different from the *Aeneid*. Although both are ostensibly hexametric heroic epics, even the meanings of hexameter, hero, and epic have changed. For early Greeks, epic was a natural pervasive mode of human expression. Homer never existed, except in the minds of those who suppose that a poem must have been written by a poet because poems are written by poets elsewhere and otherwise. Compare must now yield to contrast. Likenesses are illusory, differences are decisive. So thought Vico.

The problem is how to know that of which we can have no experience, since we live in a changed world. Contrasts can be imagined that are merely imaginary. Dislike of the present harks back to a dissimilar past: a Utopia or Erewhon nowhere to be found in history. Pride in progress disdains the primitive past; it primps the present by disparaging the past.

Homer's original genius for Robert Wood consists (so to speak) in being free from the eighteenth century: the refinements and affectations of a learned age.[16] Homer is the poet of Nature—which is likely to be situated near Utopia. The thoughts and language of Nature are always true and clear and memorable. The secret to the state of Nature is nonliteracy: writing undermines memory, clarity, and truth.

This is precisely the opinion that Socrates expresses at the end of the *Phaedrus.* Theuth of Naucratis, an Egyptian god, recommends his invention of letters to Thamous, king of Egyptian Thebes (274e4–7):

"τοῦτο δέ, ὦ βασιλεῦ, τὸ μάθημα," ἔφη ὁ Θεύθ,
"σοφωτέρους Αἰγυπτίους καὶ μνημονικωτέρους παρέξει·
μνήμης τε γὰρ καὶ σοφίας φάρμακον ηὑρέθη."

Thamous, in defense of oral tradition, foretells the true effect of writing (275a1–5):

"τοῦτο γὰρ τῶν μαθόντων λήθην μὲν ἐν ψυχαῖς
παρέξει μνήμης ἀμελετησίᾳ, ἅτε διὰ πίστιν
γραφῆς ἔξωθεν ὑπ' ἀλλοτρίων τύπων, οὐκ ἔνδοθεν
αὐτοὺς ὑφ' αὑτῶν ἀναμιμνῃσκομένους."

It is foolish to expect writing to retain anything σαφὲς καὶ βέβαιον (275c6). Truth must be entrusted to a living oral tradition: τὸν τοῦ εἰδότος λόγον ... ζῶντα καὶ ἔμψυχον (276a8). Wood seems to have translated Plato's myth into history.[17]

The fortunate advantages of Homer's nonliteracy and oral tradition might even have produced many Homers (Vico), rather than just one original genius Homer (Wood). Although Wood cannot be expected to have read Vico, he might well have replied that literacy has not produced many Shakespeares nor Italian philosophers many a *pax Romana*.[18]

Apart from this, Wood could have been a disciple of Vico. He practiced Vico's historical perspective:

> We proposed to read the *Iliad* and *Odyssey* in the countries where Achilles fought, where Ulysses travelled, and where Homer sung. ...
>
> A review of Homer's scene of action leads naturally to the consideration of the times, when he lived; and the nearer we approach his country and age, the more we find him accurate in his picture of nature. ...
>
> We should approach, as near as possible, to the time and place, when and where he wrote [*sic*].[19]

With Homer his guide, the English gentleman gingerly visited Homer's world: winds and waters, country and travels, religion and manners, language and learning. Wood's archeological insights came to fruition in Schliemann, his linguistic insights in Parry.

Most important for the present study is Wood's explanation of Homer's repetitions:

> When the sense was catched from the sound, and not deliberately collected from paper, simplicity and clearness were more necessary. Involved periods and an embarrassed style were not introduced, till writing became more an art, and labour supplied the place of genius. The frequent repetition of entire passages (for which Homer is censured) was not only more natural, but less observable, therefore less offensive; action, tone, and pronunciation were more essentially concerned in every composition of genius, and all poetry was dramatic; and so far might be ranked among the mimetic arts.[20]

James Beattie had expressed the same opinion several years before Wood:

> Let it be observed too, that Homer composed his immortal work at a time when writing was not common: when people were rather hearers than readers of poetry, and could not often enjoy the pleasure even of hearing it; and when, consequently, the frequent repetition of certain words and phrases, being a help to memory, as well as to right apprehension of the poet's meaning, would be thought rather a beauty than a blemish. The same thing is observable in some of our old ballads.[21]

Both Beattie and Wood considered repetitions to be useful in oral-aural poetry. It remained for Parry to demonstrate precisely how they were used: to turn repetitions into traditional formulae and series of them into oral verse. From useful, they became essential.

Milman Parry is to be acclaimed above all for inventing an operational model to show how it was possible for a nonliterate bard (Wood's and Wolf's Homer) to compose and perform long poems like the *Iliad* and *Odyssey;* and for testing the model on contemporary nonliterate songs in Yugoslavia. Milman Parry's work is considered an exemplary instance of rigorous scientific method in the field of literary criticism.

The elements of Parry's solution to the Homeric Question are discoveries of other scholars. Parry discovered the sum of the parts.

Parry builds directly on the work of Heinrich Düntzer, whom he mentions in the foreword to *L'Epithète traditionnelle* as the only one who "deals in serious fashion with the technique of the use of the fixed epithet."[22] Referring to Düntzer's essay "On the Interpretation of Fixed Epithets in Homer," Parry comments:

> Düntzer saw how the questions of the meaning of the epithet and of its use according to its metrical value were interrelated, and in this essay he prepared the way for his study of the influence of metre on Homeric style. The relation which he thus established between these two problems was undoubtedly the most important step since Aristarchus towards the understanding of the fixed epithet in Homer. "What I wish above all to show," he wrote (510), "is the capital fact that in the epithet the poet makes no reference whatever to the matter of the sentence, that he in no way represents the changing aspect of things by means of epithets relevant to the immediate situation."[23]

Parry's traditional epithet is, most simply, a defense of Düntzer's convenient fixed epithet:

> They attacked the weak points of his argument by calling attention to the equivalent forms in Homeric diction which Düntzer himself believed to be incompatible with his theory. Having made only a cursory examination of the matter, he had no notion of the extent to which the influence of metre was able to create systems of epithets, nor had he proofs in sufficient abundance to allow him to discount these equivalent elements. Yet we can now see that the objections made by Düntzer's adversaries have little weight next to his own proof.[24]

Parry's fortifications of Düntzer's theory are two: systems and analogies. Parry organized Düntzer's convenient fixed epithets into systems of convenient noun-epithet formulae, in which equivalent epithets (ἀγλαός, ἄλκιμος) and equivalent formulae (δόρυ χάλκεον, δόρυ μείλινον) are significantly rare; and these few equivalents are excusable because they can be attributed to the master fabricator of all formulaic diction: analogy. The usage and disusage of generations of bards (quasi natural selection: hence Wade-Gery's famous characterization of Parry as the Darwin of Homeric scholarship) determined which of the equivalents survived and became unique. This, in short, is Parry's thesis.

My thesis is that Parry might have found many equivalent epithets and formulae in his systems, if his methods had been more scientific; and that the working of analogy means that traditionally accepted unique formulae and Düntzer's fundamental principle of convenience are not working, analogy being more likely a sign of literary creation than of nonliterate evolution.

Antoine Meillet was Parry's most important *maître* in Paris. In the introductory chapter of *L'Epithète traditionnelle* Parry quotes Meillet's astonishing insight:

> Homeric epic is entirely composed of formulae handed down from poet to poet. An examination of any passage will quickly reveal that it is made up of lines and fragments of lines which are reproduced word for word in one or several other passages. And even lines, parts of which are not found in another passage, have the character of formulae, and it is doubtless pure chance that they are not attested elsewhere. It is true, for example, that A 554
>
> ἀλλὰ μάλ' εὔκηλος τὰ φράζεαι ἄσσ' ἐθέλῃσθα,
>
> does not appear again in the *Iliad* or anywhere in the *Odyssey;* but that was because there was no other occasion to use it.[25]

L'Epithète traditionnelle is Parry's attempt to prove the veracity of "our general impression":

> But this analysis is the only way we have of finding out how far the style of the *Iliad* and the *Odyssey* is due to tradition. It is our only way of giving some precision to our general impression of Homeric style, the impression formulated by M. Meillet in the passage quoted above.[26]

After analysis, Parry concludes that full proof eludes him:

> It is not yet definitely established to what extent the diction of Homer, taken as a whole, is formulaic and traditional. The complexity of the ideas of the epos, and the comparatively small amount of poetry which we possess, render impossible the complete analysis of a technique of composition which must be as varied as the thought it is designed to express. Only in the case of the ornamental epithets does an abundance of material render possible a quantitative analysis which indicates that they are probably all traditional. ...
>
> Should we, then, extend to the whole of Homeric diction the conclusion which we were able to draw from the study of the noun-epithet formulae in the nominative case of the seven principal heroes—that not one of them appears to be original? Obviously it is not possible to give a certain answer to this question.[27]

Having failed of certainty here, Parry turned to proof by analogy with contemporary nonliterate oral poetry. Here again, Parry had Meillet to thank for the insight:

> My first studies were on the style of the Homeric poems and led me to understand that so highly formulaic a style could be only traditional. I failed, however, at the time to understand as fully as I should have that a style such as that of Homer must not only be traditional but also must be oral. It was largely due to the remarks of my teacher M. Antoine Meillet that I came to see, dimly at first, that a true understanding of Homeric poems could only come with a full understanding of the nature of oral poetry.[28]

Before Parry had set out to test his model in Yugoslavia, he had the assurance of A. van Gennep that Serbian epic was composed of formulae. Parry wrote in 1932:

> In a society where there is no reading and writing, the poet, as we know from the study of such peoples in our own time, always makes his verse out of formulas. He can do it in no other way. Not having the device of pen and paper which, as he composed, would hold his partly formed thought in safe-keeping while his unhampered mind ranged where it would after other ideas and other words, he makes his verses by choosing from a vast number of fixed phrases which he has heard in the poems of other poets.

Here Parry cites van Gennep in a footnote:

> Cf. A. van Gennep on Serbian epic (*La Question d'Homère*, Paris,

1909, p. 52): "Les poésies des guslars sont une juxtaposition de clichés, relativement peu nombreux et qu'il suffit de posséder. Le développement de chacun de ces clichés se fait automatiquement, suivant des règles fixes. Seul leur ordre peut varier. Un bon guslar est celui qui joue de ses clichés comme nous avec des cartes, qui les ordonne diversement suivant le parti qu'il en veut tirer."[29]

The following year, Parry was in Yugoslavia to do for van Gennep and Slavic epic what he had already done for Meillet and Homeric epic: verify an insight. In Greek epic it was the lack of much extant hexameter verse that frustrated his attempts to prove all diction to be traditional repetitive formulae. In Slavic epic there is at least as much material as one has patience to hear. One misses, however, the friendly Ebeling, Prendergast, Dunbar, Gehring, and Schmidt to sort it all out. Parry did, in fact, find some repeated phrases, declared them formulae, and proclaimed: *"oral poetry is formulaic and traditional"* in his first publication in comparative literature.[30] Parry was overwhelmed, but not merely sentimentally:

> When ones hears the Southern Slavs sing their tales he has the overwhelming feeling that, in some way, he is hearing Homer. This is no mere sentimental feeling.[31]

This essay, "Whole Formulaic Verses in Greek and Southslavic Heroic Song," might have followed and contrasted with the chapter on "Epic Poems of Non-traditional Style" in *L'Epithète traditionnelle*. The characteristic possession of traditional formulae allows Homer and all oral poetry to be analyzed in the same way:

> While my earlier studies gave too little place to the nature of oral poetry as such, nevertheless, they gave me the method which I have followed in my study of Southslavic oral poetry.[32]

The next thing that became evident, however, was that, although repetition of phrases in Slavic epic was not rare, it was certainly not the general rule, nor the principal compositional technique. Parry expresses it thus:

> There existed for the Greek heroic songs a fixity of phrasing which is utterly unknown in the Southslavic [compared with] an entire identity of formulas [in the *Iliad* and *Odyssey*].[33]

This was a crisis for formulae. Parry could (1) abandon formulae, (2) soften them, or (3) retain them and renounce the analogy with Slavic oral poetry. Was there a choice? Only the second allowed him to save the combined theories of formularity and orality. The structural formula (e.g., νόον ἔγνω, θεὸν ἔγνω) of *soft* Parryism complemented the fixed formula of *hard* Parryism: both evinced oral poetry.

Another major influence on Parry was Mathias Murko:

> It happened that a week or so before I defended my *thèses* for the doctorate at the Sorbonne Professor Mathias Murko of the University of Prague delivered in Paris the series of conferences which later appeared as his book *La Poésie populaire épique en Yougoslavie au début du XXᵉ siècle.* I had seen the poster for these lectures but at the time I saw in them no great meaning for myself. However, Professor Murko, doubtless due to some remark of M. Meillet, was present at my *soutenance* and at that time M. Meillet as a member of my jury pointed out with his usual ease and clarity this failing in my two books [oral poetry]. It was the writings of Professor Murko more than of any other which in the following years led me to the study of oral poetry in itself and to the heroic poems of the South Slavs.[34]

Murko's book provides little more than introduction to the subject: thirty-one pages of text, followed by twenty-one pages of eighty-two photographs—a touristic portrayal of Bardland. If these images do not mitigate undue enthusiasm, a caveat is fairly issued to the eager visitor:

> En Amérique les ouvriers serbes et croates chantent toutes portes closes, de peur des moqueries. En tout cas, pour les admirateurs des beaux poèmes relatifs à la vieille histoire serbe, il vaut mieux ne pas les entendre chanter. ... Un Français admirateur de la poésie populaire serbe, étant allé entendre les chants à Cetinge, ne put les écouter pendant longtemps et s'en alla.[35]

Nevertheless, the report of epic formulae and oral improvisation must have allured Parry:

> Les chanteurs retiennent ces chants si longs grâce aux répétitions épiques bien connues, utilisées par exemple pour les messages, et à divers clichés destinés à célébrer les beautés féminines, les héros, les costumes, les chevaux, les armes, les duels, etc.
> Ce qui m'a le plus frappé c'est le magnifique débit des chanteurs. Se représente-t-on ce que c'est que de chanter de longs poèmes, sans errer sur le fond, en vers poétiques irréprochables, avec la rapidité la plus

grande? Cela n'est possible qu'à des chanteurs qui n'apprennent pas par coeur, mot à mot les poèmes, mais qui les recréent à nouveau chaque fois, en une brillante improvisation grâce à leur science de la langue et de la poésie.[36]

Parry intended to study these elements in greater detail and precision than Murko had, and also to apply them to Homer.

A final influence on Parry was that of Marcel Jousse, whose book *Le Style oral rythmique et mnémotechnique chez les verbo-moteurs* was published in Paris in 1925 when Parry was studying for his doctorate.[37] Parry declares this book to be "valuable as an attempt to set forth the psychological basis of oral poetic style."[38] Parry benefited by the addition of anthropological and psycholinguistic depth to his own theory of traditional poetry. The following summary reveals Parry's debt and drift:

Le rôle de la mnémotechnique, c'est-à-dire de l'habitude et de l'association imitative, et du mécanisme, domine tout le développement du style. ... La tendance à l'automatisme neutralise dans une large mesure la spontanéité et la personnalité du sujet parlant. Il faut faire une large place dans la langue à tout ce qui est mécanique et "déterminé" si l'on peut dire: association, appels, évocations, imitations, formules, groupes, clichés.[39]

When Homer was Parry's *traditional* poet, he was still essentially a subject for Hellenists and for the classical educated man. When Homer became Parry's *oral* poet, he was turned over to the experts of the world's multifarious oral poetries.

To prove that there were one or many, and to show what passages were taken whole from the tradition and which were made anew out of single formulas or verses, we must turn to the study of other oral poetries where the processes of composition can be studied in actual practice and in a greater body of poetry than we have for the Greek epic. When, by the exact analysis of oral poems in reference to their tradition, we have grasped in detail just how the oral poet works, and what it is that makes a poem good or bad in the judgment of himself and his hearers, we shall then, but only then, be able to undertake to study the authorship of the *Iliad* and *Odyssey,* and to try to apportion that which is due to the tradition and that which is due to the author.[40]

If oral poetry had been found to be everywhere the same and simply defined and easily distinguished from non-oral poetry (as

Parry had thought), then his case for an oral Homer could have been quickly decided (as, for example, by counting easily identified formulae). Nonuniformity, however, appears to be no less pervasive in oral than in literate poetry. Thus R. Finnegan:

> A main point in this discussion has been the denial of a clear-cut differentiation between oral and written literature. Throughout the book I have rejected the suggestion that there is something peculiar to "oral poetry" which radically distinguishes it from written poetry in nature, composition, style, social context, or function.[41]

Comparative oral poetry, therefore, cannot determine whether Homer represents peculiarly Hellenic oral poetry or a significant difference in kind from oral poetry. The less distinct oral poetry is, the less it can be distinguished from literate poetry. It was Parry's systematic fixed formulae that clearly set Homer off from Apollonius and Vergil. A knowledge of *hard* formulae is still effective in distinguishing these poets. *Soft* formulae have tended rather to confound them again.

Reading Parry in the light of scholarship in Paris in the 1920s leaves one with the impression that he was somewhat less than original, but at least up to date.[42] Parry himself clearly disclosed the points of his own originality:

> But no one had yet tried to see just to what extent the style was formulaic, nor to show how the technique of the formulas functioned for the composition of poetry, nor to show how such a technique of formulas by its complexity must be the work not of one man, but of many and of many years.[43]

Parry believed that he had proved that all Homer's name-epithet phrases were traditional formulae. The proof depends upon these phrases falling nicely into systematic tables of principal types of metrical diction that are defined by economy and extension. Alexander Shewan had noticed Homer's "economy of phraseology" before Parry.[44] Andrew Lang, referring to repetitions in Scottish ballads, remarks:

> How like is all this to the higher criticism of Homeric *Wiederholungen!* In fact, ballad poetry and Homeric poetry have stocks of formulae open to every maker. Not to use them would be not to play the game.[45]

The same point was often made:

> The manipulation of the Homeric phrase is simply an admirable illustration of the economy of means of expression which is characteristic of early poetry.[46]

> Among the characteristic features of Greek epic poetry nothing is more marked than the freedom with which it allows the repetition of language already used. Favourite epithets or phrases, lines or half-lines, and even long descriptive passages, recur as often as the poet has occasion for them. Sometimes we almost feel that the Homeric singer is not using a language of his own, but is ringing the changes on a stock of traditional verbiage, some of which has even ceased to convey a clear meaning. If this were so it would be impossible, generally speaking, to draw conclusions regarding the comparative originality, and hence the earlier or later date, of identical passages. All would be equally derived from a conventional storehouse, accumulated in pre-Homeric times.[47]

> The repeated verses furnish no indication of the relative antiquity of the Iliad and the Odyssey, a traditional description may fit better now in one poem now in another, but this does not prove as far as they are mutually concerned imitation or dependence.[48]

> Scholarship has always admitted, although in rough and imprecise terms, that Homer's diction is made up to a greater or lesser extent of formulae.[49]

Parry, however, wanted to go beyond economy to parsimony of phraseology and niggardliness. Parry wanted systems of unique formulae—one for each useful metrical shape, one for each essential idea. Parry (I think and shall attempt to show) achieved this, not by a careful reading and scrutiny of the texts of the poems, but by narrow dependence on Ebeling, Schmidt, and the concordances.[50] There is, in fact, less economy (especially in the principal types of noun-epithet formulae) but more extension (especially in the unprincipal types of noun-epithet formulae) than Parry mustered. If the edifice of Parry's systematic diction is crazy, then all the epics lodged therein are imperiled.

It is convenient for Parry to assume the existence of innumerable bards between Troy and Homer with daily compositional performances. If, however, there were few poets and monthly or yearly concerts in the Dark Ages, then a strong systematic tradition of oral formulaic poetry would not arise, and formulaic diction and epic would be as (un)systematic and (un)traditional as Homer's. "We are not mistaken in believing that Homer's audience had previously heard many another epic poem."[51] Parry's evidence for the number of bards and epic performances is the nature of the diction—which is itself the critical question. This study examines the critical question.

Homer repeats himself and does not repeat himself. III 39 is the same as XIII 769:

Δύσπαρι, εἶδος ἄριστε, γυναιμανές, ἠπεροπευτά,

which is not the same as XI 385:

τοξότα, λωβητήρ, κέρᾳ ἀγλαέ, παρθενοπῖπα,

although the same man is rebuked in all three cases:

δῖος Ἀλέξανδρος, Ἑλένης πόσις ἠϋκόμοιο.

Moreover, Hector can rebuke Paris without either formula:

VI 325–26
τὸν δ' Ἕκτωρ νείκεσσεν ἰδὼν αἰσχροῖς ἐπέεσσι·
δαιμόνι', οὐ μὲν καλὰ χόλον τόνδ' ἔνθεο θυμῷ.

Nor does Helen require a formula to rebuke Paris:

III 426–28
ἔνθα κάθιζ' Ἑλένη, κούρη Διὸς αἰγιόχοιο,
ὄσσε πάλιν κλίνασα, πόσιν δ' ἠνίπαπε μύθῳ·
ἤλυθες ἐκ πολέμοι· ὡς ὤφελες αὐτόθ' ὀλέσθαι.

If Helen had repeated the formulaic line,

Δύσπαρι, εἶδος ἄριστε, γυναιμανές, ἠπεροπευτά,

should we have thought her unmannerly, or just formulaically determined? Such usage would sort well with Penelope's *heavy hand*. Homer's repetitions have received much attention; failure to repeat is also Homeric and deserves much attention. Of course, even in a casual reading of Homer one is aware of repetitions; one must read the texts quite carefully in order to notice avoided parallels. Here, possibly, may be found the poet's originality: the rejection of formulae.

Alexander Pope began the preface to his translation of the *Iliad* with the declaration: "Homer is universally allowed to have had the greatest *invention* of any writer whatever."[52] Aimé Puech, who supervised Parry's *thèses,* began the preface to his own book on the *Iliad* with the same idea: "Les Grecs ont admiré comme nous dans l'*Iliade* la variété et la puissance de l'invention." [53]

Milman Parry, on the other hand, made Homer singularly uninventive:

> The principles which Parry formulated, taken at their face value, seem to offer virtually no room for poetic originality of any kind or, for that matter, for any real development of the tradition itself.[54]

L'Epithète traditionnelle set out to answer

> the question of capital interest: what portion of Homeric diction is to be attributed to the tradition and what portion to the poet? ...
> [and] the question of supreme importance—what portion of them [formulae] must derive from the tradition and what portion from the originality of a particular poet.[55]

Parry answers the question unequivocally in regard to epithets:

> Traces of originality remain, perhaps; but of an originality that does no more than rearrange the words and expressions of the tradition without important modifications. The poet's greatest originality in the handling of epithets would have been to use some noun-epithet formulae a little more or a little less frequently than other poets. All the epithets of the *Iliad* and the *Odyssey* we call "Homeric." But the entire investigation which we have just carried out has not turned up a single epithet which can be called "Homeric" as the epithets of Pindar have the right to be called "Pindaric." ...
> Should we, then extend to the whole of Homeric diction the conclusion which we were able to draw from the study of the noun-epithet formula in the nominative case of the seven principal heroes— that not one of them appears to be original?[56]

Parry finds the extension irresistible: the whole theory of traditional formulaic poetry depends on there being traditional formulaic verbs and adverbs to go with traditional formulaic nouns and adjectives in corresponding cola.

> The categoric nature of these conclusions concerning the traditional character of noun-epithet formulae suggests that they should be extended to most other formulae. ...

In our earlier book, we were more than once led to make the observation which we must now make again concerning the formulary element in the Homeric poems: as one proceeds from the sure ground of expressions whose frequency is a demonstration of their formulary character, and often of their traditional character as well, one inevitably arrives at a point where all the expressions appear to be formulae, but no one of them is incontrovertibly a formula.[57]

F. M. Combellack has recently studied "Homer the Innovator" from a Parryan perspective. He is willing to attribute to Homer's deliberate artistry στεροπηγερέτα Ζεύς and μεγάθυμος Ἀχιλλεύς:

> These two passages represent, I think, the kind of innovation which must be sought out by anyone who hopes to show that Homer was a conscious innovator in this aspect of style. ...
> What we need, if our case for novelty in the use of formulas is to be anything but a guess, are passages in which Homer employs an unusual phrase in a context where the normal formula would otherwise fit but where it might seem for one reason or another less suitable.[58]

Combellack cites his two fine examples but doubts that there are many more, or a significant number to affect Parry's assessment of Homer:

> Enough convincing examples have been collected to make a reasonably good case for the belief that once in a while Homer did indulge in deliberate innovations of this sort. Further study may well reveal other instances. But it seems to me that possibly the most impressive feature of all the activity in this field is the almost unbelievably small number of convincing examples so far produced. I do not feel very hopeful that the ultimate total will be great enough to enable even Homer's least critical champions to claim that he shows this kind of novelty oftener than, say, once in a thousand lines.[59]

Another scholar might look at the same two examples of deliberate artistry and not doubt but that there must be more and perhaps a sufficient number to affect Parry's assessment of Homer. What "incantation of the heroic" is sacrosanct if not νεφεληγερέτα Ζεύς and πόδας ὠκὺς Ἀχιλλεύς? What "habitual movement of the voice" is inevitable if not νεφεληγερέτα Ζεύς and πόδας ὠκὺς Ἀχιλλεύς? What inconcinnity (like inconsistency) is expected of formulaic poetry if not νεφέλην νεφεληγερέτα Ζεύς and πόδας ὠκὺς Ἀχιλλεύς ἐς πόδας ἐκ κεφαλῆς? To Combellack it is

all but certain that this was a kind of innovation in which he either had very little interest or had very little ability.⁶⁰

To another scholar, στεροπηγερέτα Ζεύς and μεγάθυμος Ἀχιλλεύς seem best explained by Homer's evident interest and ability in deliberate artistry. The outstanding quality and persuasive perspicuousness of these two examples encourages one to search for a sufficient quantity of other examples that might satisfy even Homer's highly critical champions.

Parry found in all Homer only one nontraditional phrase: Ἥρης χρυσοπεδίλου. He attributes it not to Homer but to "a poet who had lost the sense of the ancient heroic rhythm."⁶¹ Parry believes that Homer or "the author or authors of these two poems faithfully maintain the tradition of bardic diction."⁶² Homer is the ideal, inscrutable, traditional bard. For Parry's historicism, a man equals his historical circumstance: Homer and traditional poetry are equivalent terms. "Traditional poetry is uninventive" implies that "Homer is uninventive."

In the following chapters, Parry's economical and extensive systematic diction for Achilles will be put to the test of the texts of the *Iliad* and *Odyssey*. Expressions for Achilles gleaned from the texts are presented according to grammatical case and metrical shape.⁶³ I contend that Homer's Homeric diction is significantly different from Parry's Homeric diction. Only a thorough review of the evidence—both Parry's and Homer's—will allow one to evaluate the fundamental principles of extension and economy.

II

Unique and Equivalent Formulae for Achilles: Nominative Case

Αὐτός, ἥρως, and υἱός are the expressions that Homer uses to identify Achilles in the nominative case when only the sixth foot is available. Ἕζετο δ᾽ αὐτός looks as if it could have been a useful phrase, since heroes often get up to speak, speak, and then sit down. It occurs only once:

I 245–46

 ὣς φάτο Πηλεΐδης, ποτὶ δὲ σκῆπτρον βάλε γαίῃ
 χρυσείοις ἥλοισι πεπαρμένον, ἕζετο δ᾽ αὐτός.

*Ἕζετο δ᾽ ἥρως seems a valid phrase, built on the model of ἤλυθεν ἥρως (iii 415) or *ἤλυθε δ᾽ ἥρως, or happening to resemble them.[1] It has an epic look but is not in Homer. Greek grammar would suggest that Homer chose the word αὐτός at I 246 because Achilles did two things, and Greek has a penchant for setting two things in opposition: here, the scepter on the one hand and himself on the other. Αὐτός brings out the contrast, as in

III 195–96

 τεύχεα μέν οἱ κεῖται ἐπὶ χθονὶ πουλυβοτείρῃ
 αὐτὸς δὲ κτίλος ὣς ἐπιπωλεῖται στίχας ἀνδρῶν.[2]

The context is relevant here because it must supply two contrastive elements. Systematic diction, on the contrary, needs a convenient heroic phrase to express the essential idea *he* (the hero, Achilles) *sat down*. If this was the function of ἕζετο δ᾽ αὐτός, it might have been quite useful. On the other hand, bards of heroic epic might be expected to have preferred the more heroic phrase *ἕζετο δ' ἥρως. One might well suppose that this was indeed the traditional formula and that Homer was untraditional and unheroically grammatical and Aristarchean.

Μήτηρ τε καὶ υἱός is the sort of phrase that one expects to be formulaic in any language, in poetry and prose, written and oral. Homer has it only once:

XXIV 141–42

ὡς οἵ γ' ἐν νηῶν ἀγύρει μήτηρ τε καὶ υἱὸς
πολλὰ πρὸς ἀλλήλους ἔπεα πτερόεντα ἀγόρευον.

It resembles another phrase that has an even better claim to formularity and does recur in Homer: μήτηρ τε πατήρ τε.[3] One may be quite content with μήτηρ τε καὶ υἱός at **XXIV** 141 and still not discount the possibility of Homer's ever considering ἥρως or αὐτός in place of υἱός: αὐτός because he *himself* has just spoken, ἥρως because he is the exemplary hero, and either one because it was traditional formulaic diction for Achilles in the sixth foot.

Formularity might also have made an even greater change in the couplet. One wonders how Homer resisted the temptation of hastily composing

* ὡς οἵ γ' ἐν νηῶν ἀγύρει Θέτις ἀργυρόπεζα
ἠδ' Ἀχιλεὺς μεγάθυμος.[4]

If Homer is a faithful representative of traditional diction, the ready formula signifying Thetis after the hephthemimeris must have been Θέτις ἀργυρόπεζα. Homer often repeats a formula and sometimes with dubious propriety; but his failure to repeat himself may indicate that the influence of the hexameter and of sheer repetition was less awesome for him than for more tradition-bound bards, and that he had interest and skill in finding alternative expressions.

Ἥρως cannot be replaced by υἱός or αὐτός in the following passage:

XXIII 824–25

αὐτὰρ Τυδεΐδῃ δῶκεν μέγα φάσγανον ἥρως
σὺν κολεῷ τε φέρων καὶ ἐϋτμήτῳ τελαμῶνι.

Moreover, here ἥρως designates Achilles although he has been absent from verse since he introduced the contest.[5] For these reasons ἥρως, and not αὐτός or υἱός, was probably the normal way of referring to Achilles in the sixth foot.[6] Homer, therefore, may be demonstrating independence of diction by using the other expressions whenever they suit him. If Homeric diction were more systematic (extensive and economical), Homer might have had and used three expressions beginning one with a vowel another with a single consonant and another with a double consonant, instead of three beginning with a vowel, which is characteristic of unformulaic literate poetry. Ἥρως would satisfy all the lines cited and illustrate formulaic insouciance in regard to unformulaic prosaic precision.

If the expression for Achilles needs to be one breve longer and follows the fifth trochee, Ἀχιλλεύς is the obvious element of traditional versification. It falls there 158 times in the *Iliad*, 65 times without a directly preceding epithet. Homer is steadfastly traditional in this regard, with one exception:

XXIII 896–97

δῶκε δὲ Μηριόνῃ δόρυ χάλκεον· αὐτὰρ ὅ γ᾽ ἥρως
Ταλθυβίῳ κήρυκι δίδου περικαλλὲς ἄεθλον.[7]

Ἀχιλλεύς and ὅ γ᾽ ἥρως are equivalent.[8] One might defend ὅ γ᾽ ἥρως by pointing out that it belongs to a more complex formula, αὐτὰρ ὅ γ᾽ ἥρως, which occurs seven times in the *Iliad*. But αὐτὰρ Ἀχιλλεύς occurs seventeen times in the *Iliad* and therefore may be considered the traditional way of expressing the idea *but Achilles*. Αὐτὰρ ὅ γ᾽ ἥρως is necessary when the hero's name or patronymic does not fit the metrical space after αὐτάρ,[9] or when the hero has just recently been named.[10] Αὐτὰρ Ἀχιλλεύς once follows a sentence in which Achilles is named in an oblique case (XX 423), although it never follows a sentence in which Achilles, even as a pronoun, is the subject. Αὐτὰρ ὅ γ᾽ ἥρως might have been *ἀλλ᾽ Αἰνείας at V 308 and *αὐτὰρ Τεῦκρος at VIII 268: the poet possibly avoided a spondee in the fifth foot, or he used αὐτὰρ ὅ γ᾽ ἥρως because it was the accepted way of expressing this idea. On the contrary, αὐτὰρ Ἀχιλλεύς is dactylic and Homer's way of expressing this idea. The same applies to Odysseus and doubtless to other names that are bacchiacs.[11]

Homer might have used αὐτὰρ ὅ γ᾽ ἥρως often and unambiguously

in place of αὐτὰρ Ἀχιλλεύς: any inconcinnity might have been
attributed to the use of formulae.[12] The first clause in the following
statement of Homeric usage suits the simplified diction of traditional
style, but the rest better suits an idiosyncratic poet. Αὐτὰρ ὅ γ' ἥρως is
standard for all heroes, except those whose names are bacchiacs, in
which case that name follows αὐτάρ, unless that hero also figures in
the preceding sentence, in which case αὐτὰρ ὅ γ' ἥρως is used if the
hero was subject and either phrase if the hero was mentioned in an
oblique case.[13] The simplicity of traditional diction supposedly has
one phrase for one idea (αὐτὰρ ὅ γ' ἥρως); Homer's simplicity is to
favor unsystematically the hero's common name (αὐτὰρ Ἀχιλλεύς).
Αὐτὰρ ὅ γ' ἥρως might have been traditional and αὐτὰρ Ἀχιλλεύς
Homeric; but even if both were traditional, the poet's preference for
one or the other is undetermined.

If the expression for Achilles must fill the last two feet of the
hexameter, δῖος Ἀχιλλεύς and ὠκὺς Ἀχιλλεύς are regularly used. Δῖος
avoids hiatus or lengthens a preceding syllable; ὠκύς shortens a
preceding syllable or avoids lengthening it. Metrical necessity,
however, does not account for them entirely.

First, since nu-ephelkystikon, no less than δῖος, avoids hiatus, the
poet can easily show a preference for δῖος or —ν ὠκύς, which become
equivalent epithets when nu is available. Homer has δῖος Ἀχιλλεύς
every time;[14] another poet might have had —ν ὠκὺς Ἀχιλλεύς or both
expressions.

Second, since Homer allows overlengthening, δῖος and ὠκύς are
equivalent epithets after a long closed syllable.[15] Homer has

XIX 40
   αὐτὰρ ὁ βῆ παρὰ θῖνα θαλάσσης δῖος Ἀχιλλεύς

where another poet might have avoided overlengthening with ὠκὺς
Ἀχιλλεύς.

Third, it is possible to choose between δῖος Ἀχιλλεύς and δαίμονι
ἶσος. The latter refers to Achilles four times in the Iliad, all within a
short space of text—as if they might be related. The first instance of
δαίμονι ἶσος for Achilles is in his first duel with Hector:

XX 445–48
   τρὶς μὲν ἔπειτ' ἐπόρουσε ποδάρκης δῖος Ἀχιλλεὺς
   ἔγχεϊ χαλκείῳ. τρὶς δ' ἠέρα τύψε βαθεῖαν.

ἀλλ' ὅτε δὴ τὸ τέταρτον ἐπέσσυτο δαίμονι ἶσος
δεινὰ δ' ὁμοκλήσας ἔπεα πτερόεντα προσηύδα.

This should be compared with his shout at the trench:

XVIII 228

τρὶς μὲν ὑπὲρ τάφρου μεγάλ' ἴαχε δῖος Ἀχιλλεύς.

It is hoped that no one will claim as canonical that δῖος Ἀχιλλεύς traditionally follows τρίς, as δαίμονι ἶσος follows τὸ τέταρτον. A flexible use of formulae would no doubt permit

* τρὶς μὲν ὑπὲρ τάφρου μεγάλ' ἴαχε δαίμονι ἶσος

and

* ἀλλ' ὅτε δὴ τὸ τέταρτον ἐπέσσυτο δῖος Ἀχιλλεύς.

The former line would do very well at XVIII 228; the subject is unambiguous and δαίμονι ἶσος hardly differs from δῖος Ἀχιλλεύς in meaning. The latter line in place of XX 447 would more likely be praised and blamed for the repetition of δῖος Ἀχιλλεύς within three lines than for failure to repeat the whole-line formula

ἀλλ' ὅτε δὴ τὸ τέταρτον ἐπέσσυτο δαίμονι ἶσος.[16]

Δαίμονι ἶσος stands as a pronoun for δῖος Ἀχιλλεύς.[17]

The second instance of δαίμονι ἶσος for Achilles is after a simile that likens him to fire:

XX 493

ὣς ὅ γε πάντῃ θῦνε σὺν ἔγχεϊ δαίμονι ἶσος.[18]

This should be compared with the similar line,

XXII 326

τῇ ῥ' ἐπὶ οἷ μεμαῶτ' ἔλασ' ἔγχεϊ δῖος Ἀχιλλεύς.

Again, an exchange of formulae produces acceptable lines:

* τῇ ῥ' ἐπὶ οἷ μεμαῶτ' ἔλασ' ἔγχεϊ δαίμονι ἶσος
* ὣς ὅ γε πάντῃ θῦνε σὺν ἔγχεϊ δῖος Ἀχιλλεύς.

The context does not require one or the other; δαίμονι ἶσος and δῖος Ἀχιλλεύς are practically synonymous and equivalent formulae. If δαίμονι ἶσος adds nothing to the sentence other than a convenient subject, then Homer is free and forced to choose between δῖος

Ἀχιλλεύς and δαίμονι ἶσος. Traditional style, therefore, does not fully determine the use of even so common a phrase as δῖος Ἀχιλλεύς.

The third instance of δαίμονι ἶσος for Achilles occurs thirty lines later when he jumps into the river:

XXI 15–18

ὣς ὑπ' Ἀχιλλῆος Ξάνθου βαθυδινήεντος
πλῆτο ῥόος κελάδων ἐπιμὶξ ἵππων τε καὶ ἀνδρῶν.
Αὐτὰρ ὁ διογενὴς δόρυ μὲν λίπεν αὐτοῦ ἐπ' ὄχθη
κεκλιμένον μυρίκῃσιν, <u>ὁ δ' ἔσθορε δαίμονι ἶσος.</u>

Compare with this the following passage:

XXII 99–103

ὤ μοι ἐγών, εἰ μέν κε πύλας καὶ τείχεα δύω,
Πουλυδάμας μοι πρῶτος ἐλεγχείην ἀναθήσει,
ὅς μ' ἐκέλευε Τρωσὶ ποτὶ πτόλιν ἡγήσασθαι
νύχθ' ὕπο τήνδ' ὀλοήν, ὅτε τ' ὤρετο <u>δῖος Ἀχιλλεύς.</u>

The examples clearly show the nominal use of δῖος Ἀχιλλεύς and the pronominal use of δαίμονι ἶσος. After being mentioned by name, Achilles is soon referred to as ὁ διογενής and ὁ δαίμονι ἶσος, whereas thoughtless formulaic diction might have produced less natural lines:

ὣς ὑπ' Ἀχιλλῆος Ξάνθου βαθυδινήεντος
πλῆτο ῥόος κελάδων ἐπιμὶξ ἵππων τε καὶ ἀνδρῶν.
*Αὐτὰρ ὁ Πηλεΐδης δόρυ μὲν λίπεν αὐτοῦ ἐπ' ὄχθη
*κεκλιμένον μυρίκῃσιν, ὁ δ' ἔσθορε δῖος Ἀχιλλεύς.

On the other hand, at XXII 103 δαίμονι ἶσος would be vague because it lacks an antecedent. There is more to good style than the use of traditional formulae. The existence of pronominal expressions makes the use of nominal expressions facultative.

The fourth instance of δαίμονι ἶσος for Achilles follows his speech to the river god:

XXI 227

ὣς εἰπὼν Τρώεσσιν <u>ἐπέσσυτο δαίμονι ἶσος.</u>

A similar line follows another speech of Achilles:

XVIII 343

ὣς εἰπὼν ἑτάροισιν <u>ἐκέκλετο δῖος Ἀχιλλεύς.</u>

In these examples, the distinction is not between nominal and pronominal forms; either a noun or a pronoun can refer to a hero who has just made a speech. Instead, what is *daimonic* is contrasted with what is not. Heroes rush, charge, and leap *daimonically* in the *Iliad;* no one commands δαίμονι ἶσος.[19] Δῖος Ἀχιλλεύς, on the other hand, is not restricted to any particular kind of action. Homer uses δαίμονι ἶσος when Achilles is doing something *daimonic* and when a pronominal expression makes for better style than a repeated name does. But these are precisely the sorts of nice distinctions that one expects from unformulaic poets. Formulaic bards should rather find it inconvenient and pointless to have to choose between two expressions for Achilles that have the same meter. To choose between two expressions is to distinguish the qualities of each: each has its proper context. Homer's use of the formulae δαίμονι ἶσος and δῖος Ἀχιλλεύς is not utterly regardless of context. Homer, wanting or having to make Achilles subject after the diaeresis, does not automatically sing δῖος Ἀχιλλεύς. Even here there is some choice and therefore some individuality.

Homer has three expressions signifying Achilles and following the hephthemimeral caesura: πόδας ὠκὺς Ἀχιλλεύς, κλυτὸς (ὠκὺς) Ἀχιλλεύς, and μεγάθυμος Ἀχιλλεύς. In three ways, they fail to fulfill the systematic criteria of extension and economy. First, none of the formulae begins with a vowel. This should indicate that there was no need for such a formula. Without it, however, the bard has to commit the metrical fault of overlengthening:

XXIV 751

ἄλλους μὲν γὰρ παῖδας ἐμοὺς πόδας ὠκὺς Ἀχιλλεύς.

If overlengthening is reprehensible, then so is the failure of traditional diction to provide a means of avoiding it. It can hardly have been much trouble and might even have been a pleasurable exercise for bards to compose, for the sake of metrical convenience, at least a passable phrase, if not a grand locution worthy of repeated use. In an instant, a Homerist can come up with several phrases:

* ὠκὺς πόδας ἥρως

* ὠκὺς πόδ' Ἀχιλλεύς

* ἀγαθὸς πόδ' Ἀχιλλεύς

*ἀγαλείος Ἀχιλλεύς
*ἴφθιμος Ἀχιλλεύς.[20]

As the epithet is shortly to be vacuous and a thing of indifference, perhaps it need not be sublime, lest the audience should marvel at it and so miss the tale.[21] Of course, there may have been such a formula in traditional diction, but Homer forgot it or preferred πόδας ὠκὺς Ἀχιλλεύς. At any rate, theory and practice appear to be at variance.

Second, the phrase beginning with two consonants is not regularly used to lengthen a short syllable:

XI 112
εἶδεν, ὅτ' ἐξ Ἴδης ἄγαγεν πόδας ὠκὺς Ἀχιλλεύς.[22]

Nu with πόδας ὠκὺς Ἀχιλλεύς is preferred to κλυτὸς (ὠκὺς) Ἀχιλλεύς, whereas δῖος Ἀχιλλεύς was preferred to —ν ὠκὺς Ἀχιλλεύς.[23] Paragogic *nu* allows but does not determine the choice: the words in the formulae make the difference. Κλυτὸς (ὠκὺς) Ἀχιλλεύς, however, is indispensable when *nu* cannot be drawn in, as for example at viii 3 (with Achilles substituted for Odysseus):

*ἂν δ' ἄρα διογενὴς ὦρτο κλυτὸς (ὠκὺς) Ἀχιλλεύς.[24]

If metrical needs are paramount, the formula κλυτὸς (ὠκὺς) Ἀχιλλεύς is guaranteed.[25] Homer's one use of it is peculiar, if not dubious:

XX 319–20
βῆ ῥ' ἴμεν ἄν τε μάχην καὶ ἀνὰ κλόνον ἐγχειάων,
ἷξε δ' ὅθ' Αἰνείας ἠδ' ὁ κλυτὸς ἦεν Ἀχιλλεύς.[26]

Κλυτός looks like an independent generic epithet or a supplement of the preceding pronoun-article.[27] The noun-epithet formula is unapparent. It also looks as if κλυτός might have been θρασύς if κλόνον had been θρόνον.[28] This, however, is the sort of nicety that one expects from unformulaic poets. Traditional bards, on the other hand, are supposed to compose verses of common formulae. But if there is nothing more than this to versification, one could easily improve on Homer. The following lines surpass Homer's in simplicity, rapidity, and plainness; for they make use of a familiar formula:

*ἷξε δ' ὅθ' Αἰνείας ἦεν καὶ δῖος Ἀχιλλεύς

ἷξε δ' ὅθ' ἦν Ἀγχισιάδης ἠδ' ὠκὺς Ἀχιλλεύς
ἷξε δ' ὅθ' Αἰνείας μεγάθυμος ἴδ' ὠκὺς Ἀχιλλεύς.

Paradoxically, Homer would have composed better formulaic epic if he had been able to read a concordance; for he could have eschewed Unparallel-Homer. As it is, the formula κλυτὸς (ὠκὺς) Ἀχιλλεύς may be unique, equivalent, or nonexistent.

Third, the single occurrence of μεγάθυμος Ἀχιλλεύς spoils the uniqueness of πόδας ὠκὺς Ἀχιλλεύς:

XXIII 168–69

δημὸν ἑλὼν ἐκάλυψε νέκυν μεγάθυμος Ἀχιλλεύς
ἐς πόδας ἐκ κεφαλῆς, περὶ δὲ δρατὰ σώματα νήει.

At first glance, it would seem obvious that μεγάθυμος Ἀχιλλεύς is an *ad hoc* phrase that avoids the inconcinnity of repeated πόδας and the absurdity of Achilles' being *foot-swift from head to foot.*[29] The idea of inconcinnity, however, supposes that Homer revised his text, and therefore that the *Iliad,* as we have it, is not the record of improvised composition-performance. For this technique requires that a preceding line should be composed before a succeeding line, and therefore, if the repetition is to be avoided (although neither bard nor audience should have noticed it), the succeeding rather than the preceding πόδας would have been expressed differently.[30] The idea of absurdity supposes that Achilles *great-hearted from head to foot* is somehow less absurd than Achilles *foot-swift from head to foot.*[31] Alternatively, μεγάθυμος Ἀχιλλεύς was a formula of traditional diction and long equivalent to πόδας ὠκὺς Ἀχιλλεύς. If, moreover, it signified the *great anger* of Achilles (at least until indifference made μεγάθυμος insignificant), it may be as old as the idea of the *Iliad* and the first story of the *anger* of Achilles.[32] Nevertheless, neither as *ad hoc* phrase nor as traditional phrase does it conduce to systematic simplicity.

Πόδας ὠκὺς Ἀχιλλεύς, κλυτὸς (ὠκὺς) Ἀχιλλεύς, and μεγάθυμος Ἀχιλλεύς make a poor case for economy and extension. Analogy is called to the defence and pleads extenuating circumstance.[33] Μεγάθυμος Ἀχιλλεύς, for example, may be condoned because the bewildered bard somehow had in mind μεγάθυμος Ἀγήνωρ and somehow forgot about πόδας ὠκὺς Ἀχιλλεύς.[34] In rebuttal, three objections may be lodged.

First, μεγάθυμος Ἀγήνωρ is only presumed to be a unique formula itself. But Agenor's formulae may be just as muddled as those of Achilles; the scarcity of lines about Agenor may conceal πολύβουλος Ἀγήνωρ, πολύϊππος Ἀγήνωρ, πόδας ὠκὺς Ἀγήνωρ, and others. Μεγάθυμος Ἀγήνωρ, which only occurs twice, may well be an analogical formation from μεγάθυμος Ἀχιλλεύς, which might have occurred frequently in lost epic about the hero famous for his megathymia.[35]

Second, it is incredible that a traditional bard should be oblivious of πόδας ὠκὺς Ἀχιλλεύς, even for a moment. A monk might just as soon forget his Paternoster or Britannia forget to rule the waves. Formulaic poetry is made possible by memory of familiar formulae; if Homer's memory of πόδας ὠκὺς Ἀχιλλεύς was faulty, he must have had great trouble composing the *Iliad* and *Odyssey*. Remedial analogy would have been in operation constantly. The use of analogy is concurrent with the disuse of systematic formulae. Alternatively, Homer regularly chose from equivalent noun-epithet formulae and had no need for long and simple systems.

Third, analogy is not so well suited to defend oral composition as it is to defend literate composition. It is lightly assumed that if a phrase resembling μεγάθυμος Ἀχιλλεύς can be found, then oral composition is assured and the lapse of simplicity is venial. A formulaic bard can compose a new phrase only by substituting a word into an old phrase taken as a model. A literate poet, apparently, would never do this; he always creates *ex nihilo* phrases that do not resemble those of other poets. These logical categories represent the extremes of imitation and originality; they are, however, nullities.[36]

Surely the operation of analogy is absolutely fundamental to literate composition, as to the development of language generally. Successful phrases are reused and reworked; art is constantly imitating art. An analogical formation may be the work of either an oral or a literate poet. A typical formulaic bard, however, might be expected to yield to systematic formulae and sing πόδας ὠκὺς Ἀχιλλεύς, whereas a typical unformulaic poet might readily yield to analogy and write μεγάθυμος Ἀχιλλεύς. A formulaic bard has fair recourse to analogy when there is a lacuna in traditional diction; a literate poet can fairly ignore the systematic simplicity of πόδας ὠκὺς Ἀχιλλεύς. Analogy does not make μεγάθυμος Ἀχιλλεύς patent formulaic improvisation.

If the expression for Achilles is to follow the tritotrochaic caesura, there is a muddle of phraseology and a disregard of nice systematization. Ποδάρκης δῖος Ἀχιλλεύς is the only regularly recurring phrase, and it is marred by overlengthening.[37] It would seemingly have been so easy to repair the fault with

*ποδάρκης ὠκὺς Ἀχιλλεύς

or

*Διὶ φίλος ὠκὺς Ἀχιλλεύς

or

*πελώριος ὠκὺς Ἀχιλλεύς

or

*δαΐφρων ὠκὺς Ἀχιλλεύς.[38]

Homer kept to ποδάρκης δῖος Ἀχιλλεύς even when a paragogic *nu* would have allowed him to exchange it for a faultless formula beginning with a vowel:

*ἀμύμων ὠκὺς Ἀχιλλεύς
*ἀρήϊος ὠκὺς Ἀχιλλεύς
*Ἀχιλλεὺς ἰσόθεος φώς
*Ἀχιλλεὺς ὄρχαμος ἀνδρῶν
*Ἀχιλλεὺς ὄζος Ἄρηος.[39]

Seventeen of the twenty-one instances of ποδάρκης δῖος Ἀχιλλεύς could have been avoided in this way.[40]

Homer did indeed use that alternative twice, as follows. Polydamas, in oratorical style, withholds an unmistakable name to gain emphasis or to repel the thought:

XIII 745–47

δείδω μὴ τὸ χθιζὸν ἀποστήσωνται Ἀχαιοὶ
χρεῖος, ἐπεὶ παρὰ νηυσὶν ἀνὴρ ἆτος πολέμοιο
μίμνει, ὃν οὐκέτι πάγχυ μάχης σχήσεσθαι ὀΐω.

A contrasting line occurs in a narrative passage, where the familiar formula is used instead of the rhetorical figure:

II 688

κεῖτο γὰρ ἐν νήεσσι ποδάρκης δῖος Ἀχιλλεύς.

Ἀνὴρ ἆτος πολέμοιο no doubt would have been effective here and elsewhere, but eventually familiarity would have weakened its effect somewhat and made it formulaic. This phenomenon is hardly peculiar to oral poetics: Vergil's clamor rising to the very stars is rather worn and weary.[41]

Ἀνὴρ ἆτος πολέμοιο may derive from Ἄρης ἆτος πολέμοιο.[42] It is not however the sort of analogical formation that results from a confusion and fusion of elements from separate set phrases. The absence of ποδάρκης δῖος Ἀχιλλεύς is intentional, not casual. The substitution of ἀνὴρ ἆτος πολέμοιο is meaningful, not gratuitous. A minute change in a formula (Ἄρης to ἀνήρ) causes Achilles to be identified with Ares and war itself. The formula is not fixed, but flexible, for an inventive poet. The phrasing of formulae is not always a matter of insensitivity and indifference. If ἀνὴρ ἆτος πολέμοιο (like στεροπηγερέτα Ζεύς and μεγάθυμος Ἀχιλλεύς) is an untraditional phrase used for special effect in its line, it testifies to original artistry.

It may be argued, however, that ἀνὴρ ἆτος πολέμοιο is indeed the traditional formula designating Achilles after the tritotrochaic caesura and beginning with a vowel, and that therefore a traditional poet would certainly have used it to shorten a preceding long vowel or to avoid lengthening a short vowel followed by a consonant, circumstances that never arose in the *Iliad* or *Odyssey*.[43] Even so ἀνὴρ ἆτος πολέμοιο is neither unique nor specific. The metrical equivalent ἀρήϊος (ὠκὺς) Ἀχιλλεύς is at least unrhetorical and unambiguous and therefore more suitable to represent Achilles simply, as a systematic noun-epithet formula.

Presumably, one inessential epithet or the other can be replaced by an essential element of the sentence, as in the following verse:

XVI 166
ῥώοντ᾽· ἐν δ᾽ ἄρα τοῖσιν ἀρήϊος ἵστατ᾽ Ἀχιλλεύς.

If the verb of the previous sentence had not suffered enjambement, there would have been space for ἵστατ᾽ in the first hemistich and therefore space for ὠκύς in the second hemistich. It is more common for a verb to fill the place of ἀρήϊος: the result is ὠκύς or δῖος Ἀχιλλεύς. The ease with which a phrase can lose an inessential epithet is perhaps an indication of its formularity. Ἀνὴρ ἆτος πολέμοιο is immutable; ἀρήϊος (ὠκὺς) Ἀχιλλεύς is quite versatile and therefore more useful.[44]

On the other hand, systems of formulae should perhaps include phrases, like ἀνὴρ ἆτος πολέμοιο, that are suited for pronominal and oblique reference.[45] Ἀρήϊος (ὠκὺς) Ἀχιλλεύς at XIII 746 would not have rhetorical effect; ἀνὴρ ἆτος πολέμοιο at XVI 166 might have referred to Patroclus.

At any rate, even ἀρήϊος (ὠκὺς) Ἀχιλλεύς is not required at XVI 166: equivalents abound. Consider these:

*ἐν δ᾽ ἄρα τοῖσιν ἀμύμων ἵστατ᾽ Ἀχιλλεύς
*ἐν δ᾽ ἄρα τοῖσι ποδώκης ἵστατ᾽ Ἀχιλλεύς.

For ποδώκης may be substituted ποδάρκης, πελώριος, δαΐρων, and Διὶ φίλος. The poet had to hand at least seven epithets. Ποδώκης would have been standard for Achilles; but the poet, perhaps unaware of the insensitivity and indifference accruing to ornamental epithets, was unwilling to let it be heard twice in two lines.[46] If ἀρήϊος (ὠκὺς) Ἀχιλλεύς was the traditional systematic counterpart of ποδάρκης δῖος Ἀχιλλεύς, it was the obvious alternative phrase in this predicament. If ἀρήϊος (ὠκὺς) Ἀχιλλεύς was not a traditional phrase, ἀρήϊος was one of many localized generic epithets and either the first to come to mind or selected advisedly.[47]

A similar line is the following:

XVIII 234
μυρόμενοι· μετὰ δέ σφι ποδώκης εἵπετ᾽ Ἀχιλλεύς.

Again, this is only one of at least seven ways to compose the line:

*μετὰ δέ σφι πελώριος εἵπετ᾽ Ἀχιλλεύς
*μετὰ δέ σφιν ἀρήϊος εἵπετ᾽ Ἀχιλλεύς.

Epithetic substitutions are ἀμύμων, δαΐφρων, Διὶ φίλος, and ποδάρκης. Ποδάρκης always needs δῖος Ἀχιλλεύς and is therefore less versatile than (ποδώκης) (δῖος) Ἀχιλλεύς, which regularly gives up one of its epithets to accommodate an essential word in the sentence. The remaining lines employ generic epithets, which might traditionally be expected to yield precedence to the distinctive epithet, ποδώκης.

On the contrary, the generic epithet Διὶ φίλος is used instead of the distinctive ποδώκης on three occasions:

XVI 168–69
Πεντήκοντ᾽ ἦσαν νῆες θοαί, ᾗσιν Ἀχιλλεύς
ἐς Τροίην ἡγεῖτο Διὶ φίλος· ἐν δὲ ἑκάστῃ

XVIII 202–203

ἡ μὲν ἄρ' ὣς εἰποῦσ' ἀπέβη πόδας ὠκέα *Ἶρις,*
αὐτὰρ Ἀχιλλεὺς ὦρτο Διὶ φίλος· ἀμφὶ δ' Ἀθήνη

XXIV 471–72

. . . . γέρων δ' ἰθὺς κίεν οἴκου,
τῇ ῥ' Ἀχιλεὺς ἵζεσκε Διὶ φίλος· ἐν δέ μιν αὐτὸν.[48]

In the second example, the reason for Διὶ φίλος is obvious. In traditional formulaic verse, *foot-swift Achilles* could apparently follow *foot-swift Iris* without demur and even without notice. Here, as in the case of ἀρήϊος cited above, the poet demonstrates his sensitivity to the particular music and meaning of an ornamental epithet. In the excitement over irrational uses of ornamental epithets, no one reckoned the number of failures to use an ornamental epithet irrationally. The former are conspicuous; the latter are not. A theory of composition must account for these as well as those.

The same justification of Διὶ φίλος applies to the first example above as to the second. At XVI 165 Achilles is *foot-swift.* In the next line therefore ποδώκης yields its place to ἀρήϊος. Moreover, it is not *foot-swift Achilles* that leads the *swift ships* of the preceding line. Variety serves the passage well. Three times *foot-swift Achilles* and *swift ships,* far from being unnoticeable, might well have created a false emphasis on swiftness. Homer apparently cared and dared to discard ornamental fixed epithets as though they were neither fixed nor ornamental.

The same justification does not apply to the third example of Διὶ φίλος. One might hypothesize that traditional diction called for Διὶ φίλος to follow Ἀχιλλεύς, and ποδώκης to precede Ἀχιλλεύς. On the other hand, *foot-swift* does follow *knights,* and *dear to Zeus* does precede the *knight Phyleus:*

XXIII 262

Ἱππεῦσιν μὲν πρῶτα <u>ποδώκεσιν</u> ἀγλά' ἄεθλα

II 628

Φυλεΐδης, ὃν τίκτε <u>Διὶ φίλος</u> ἱππότα <u>Φυλεύς.</u>

Analogy, therefore, would eventually produce *ἵζεσκε Διὶ φίλος ὠκὺς Ἀχιλλεύς* and *Ἀχιλεὺς ἵζεσκε ποδώκης.* At any rate, this distinction between ποδώκης and Διὶ φίλος is pointless in formulaic poetry; for it does not facilitate versification. Coincidental misapplication of epithets would be a more likely alternative if *foot-swift* could have been easily misremembered. If any phrase should have been memorable, indeed inevitable, it was *foot-swift Achilles*. Casual disuse of it shows insensitivity to traditional diction.

There remains the possibility that the poet preferred Διὶ φίλος to ποδώκης because it conveyed his meaning better. Without having to assert that every ornamental epithet always expresses precise particular meaning, one may suppose that some choice among equivalent epithets was possible and occasionally even desirable. The poet must have been well aware that there existed metrically equivalent epithets for Achilles. In most cases, the distinctive epithet fell into place cursorily, almost carelessly; and it was heard cursorily, almost carelessly. Poets somehow knew then what are now among the elements of style: not to depend on adjectives to make a story, but to compose with nouns and verbs.[49] In some cases, however, the poet was careful to notice which epithet avoided illogicality or inconcinnity and therefore better suited the context and improved the sense.

In this same example, consider the alternatives to Διὶ φίλος: ποδάρκης, ποδώκης, δαΐφρων, πελώριος, —ν ἀρήϊος, —ν ἀμύμων, —ν ἀνὴρ ἆτος πολέμοιο, —ν ἀνὴρ ἠΰς τε μέγας τε, —ν ἀνὴρ ἀγαθὸς καὶ ἐχέφρων. Homeric diction and versification is perhaps not so thrifty and simple as one had hoped. Of course, neither an oral nor a literate Homer would have had or taken time to ponder many possibilities. The first word that came to mind would have been the distinctive *foot-swift,* and Achilles sitting swift-footed might normally have been acceptable. It is the sort of phrase, however, that could be found inconsistent or insufficient. Even long use of such a phrase does not guarantee it eternity; for its inadequacies may become apparent to a poet at any time. Consistency can easily be established with a metrically equivalent epithet. Sufficiency can be established beyond consistency if the poet uses an epithet sufficient to convey a special meaning. Διὶ φίλος solves the problem of inconsistency, but it also makes sufficient sense in Homer's story of Achilles.[50]

If Homer chose Διὶ φίλος for either of these reasons, it becomes one more example of deliberate artistry in the *Iliad*. If, on the other hand, Homer's phraseology for Achilles after the feminine caesura fails to demonstrate his originality but merely repeats genuine traditional diction, then it is a marvellous muddle and no simple system for easy versification.

Quite the contrary, if the nominative expression for Achilles is to follow the penthemimeral caesura, Homer shows the utter simplicity of a void. After some spade work, however, archaeologic reconstruction restores phrases that may be authentic traditional formulae. Nevertheless, in the search for a unique formula, these too are lamentably equivalent. Four verses constitute all the help that Homer offers in this matter:

II 875

   ἐν ποταμῷ, χρυσὸν δ' Ἀχιλεὺς ἐκόμισσε δαΐφρων

IV 512

   οὐ μὰν οὐδ' Ἀχιλεύς, Θέτιδος πάϊς ἠϋκόμοιο

XVI 860

   τίς δ' οἶδ' εἴ κ' Ἀχιλεύς, Θέτιδος πάϊς ἠϋκόμοιο

XXI 233

   ἦ, καὶ Ἀχιλλεὺς μὲν δουρικλυτὸς ἔνθορε μέσσῳ.

The first line is odd and probably unformulaic. Not only does Ἀχιλεὺς ∪ ∪ – ∪ δαΐφρων fail to recur, but even Ἀχιλεύς after the penthemineral caesura is unparalleled.[51] Moreover, there is no epithet that can take the place of the verb: nominative singular, ending in a short open vowel. A flexible formula can substitute an essential verb for an inessential epithet when necessary, but in this phrase it would always be necessary to find an essential verb to fill the meter between Ἀχιλεύς and δαΐφρων. If traditional diction had a vocalic noun-epithet formula for Achilles after the penthemimeris, this was not it, nor even a close analogue. Nor need it have been; for far from being difficult to formulate a suitable phrase destined for indifference, one need not even be particularly clever to invent several:

   *ἀγαθὸς πόδας ὠκὺς Ἀχιλλεύς

   *ἥρως πόδας ὠκὺς Ἀχιλλεύς

   *Ἀχιλεὺς δουρικλυτὸς ἥρως

*Ἀχιλεὺς ἠΰς τε μέγας τε

*Ἀχιλεὺς ἀτάλαντος Ἄρηι.

It seems reasonable to suppose that the poet could have used such a phrase with a verb legged on in the next verse—if he had wanted. Instead, he prosaically conjoined subject and verb, and then found that he had space to append an expletive epithet. It seems possible, in this case, to read the poet's mind. The cause of the unfamiliar diction is manifest: the familiar diction of the previous line. The poet avoided repeating an epithet:

ἀλλ' ἐδάμη ὑπὸ χερσὶ ποδώκεος Αἰακίδαο

*ἐν ποταμῷ, χρυσὸν δὲ ποδώκης αἴνυτ' Ἀχιλλεύς.

Composing cursorily, the poet came to the main caesura.[52] This is notoriously followed by *foot-swift Achilles:* ποδάρκης δῖος Ἀχιλλεύς (when nothing essential need be interposed, otherwise ποδώκης – ᴗ Ἀχιλλεύς) the consonantal noun-epithet formula for Achilles following the tritotrochaic caesura. The poet jibbed at the repetition. This demonstrates and proves Homer's sensitivity in the use of epithets— which might be one of the differences between Homer and the lesser bards or even between literate and oral poetry.[53] Some in Homer's audience learned this sensitivity; others doubtless remained indifferent to ornamental epithets and praised Homer for other reasons.

Not only did Homer abstain from *ποδώκης αἴνυτ' Ἀχιλλεύς, but he also disregarded other formulaic hemistichs:

*χρυσὸν δ' ἐκομίσσατο δῖος Ἀχιλλεύς

*χρυσὸν δὲ λάβεν πόδας ὠκὺς Ἀχιλλεύς

*χρυσὸν δὲ δαΐφρων αἴνυτ' Ἀχιλλεύς

*χρυσὸν δ' Ἀχιλεὺς μεγάθυμος ἀπηύρα

*χρυσὸν δ' εἷλεν μεγάθυμος Ἀχιλλεύς

*χρυσὸν δ' εἷλε κλυτὸς ὠκὺς Ἀχιλλεύς.[54]

If Homer had adopted one of these phrases, its formulaic family could easily be traced in Homeric usage, and it could therefore be regarded as a traditional phrase, rather than Homer's invention. Ἀχιλεὺς ᴗ ᴗ – ᴗ δαΐφρων, on the other hand, is a foundling with no family in Homer—although one could be invented. Δαΐφρων and its vocalic congener ἀμύμων could facilitate versification by making vocative and nominative formulae for heroes at the end of a verse:

*Τεῦκρε δαΐφρον, Τεῦκρος ἀμύμων
*Μενέλαε δαΐφρον, Μενέλαος ἀμύμων.[55]

These epithets accommodate second declension names ending in a trochee. Ἀχιλεύς/Ἀχιλλεύς, being a third declension noun ending in an iamb or spondee, does not fit the pattern and therefore could have no place in this system. Epithets able to accommodate such a name and form such a system are easily found:

*.. Ἀχιλλεῦ δῖε
*.. Ἀχιλλεὺς ἥρως
*.. Ἀχιλεῦ θεοειδές
*... Ἀχιλεὺς ἀγαπήνωρ
*.. Ἀχιλλεῦ δουρικλειτέ
*.. Ἀχιλλεὺς ἰσόθεος φώς
*.. Ἀχιλεῦ πεπνύμενα εἰδώς
*....................................... Ἀχιλεὺς ἠΰς τε μέγας τε
*....................... Ἀχιλεῦ θεόφιν μήστωρ ἀτάλαντος
*........................... Ἀχιλεὺς ἐπιείκελος ἀθανάτοισι.

These are the sorts of phrases that one expects from a systematic formulaic poet. Homer has none of these.

Another hypothetical system is this:

*........................... Ἀχιλεὺς ∪ ∪ − ∪ ∪ − −
*........................... Ἀχιλεὺς ∪ ∪ − ∪ ∪ δῖος (ἥρως)
.... Ἀχιλεὺς ∪ ∪ − ∪ δαΐφρνω (ἀμύμων)
*........................... Ἀχιλεὺς ∪ ∪ − μεγάθυμος (ἐῢς ἥρως)
*........................ Ἀχιλεὺς ∪ ∪ δουρικλειτός (ἰσόθεος φώς)
*........................... Ἀχιλεὺς ἠΰς τε μέγας τε (ἀτάλαντος Ἄρηι).

If Homer's hemistich derives from this system, he had no further use for the system in the *Iliad* and *Odyssey*. It is especially adapted to accommodate essential words of various lengths between Ἀχιλεύς and a final epithet when the whole phrase must follow the penth-emimeris and begin with a vowel, a circumstance that occurs once in

Homer. In normal practice, the essential word is followed by various lengths of a contiguous noun-epithet formulae ending the verse.

If Ἀχιλεὺς δαΐφρων is a formula and its formulaic system authentic, then all noun-epithet phrases are bound to be formulae and the poet had in his mind an astonishing number of formulaic systems. It is, however, quite easy to invent whole systems of formulae on the spot; for any anomalous phrase in Homer can be elaborated into a formulaic system. It must be even easier, therefore, to compose an unformulaic phrase and let scholars build a system round it.

The two lines that have Θέτιδος πάϊς ἠϋκόμοιο after the penthemimeral caesura would seem to offer the requisite formula to extend and enhance Achilles' formulaic labyrinth. These are the lines:

IV 512

οὐ μὰν οὐδ' Ἀχιλεύς, Θέτιδος πάϊς ἠϋκόμοιο

XVI 860

τίς δ' οἶδ' εἴ κ' Ἀχιλεύς, Θέτιδος πάϊς ἠϋκόμοιο.

Here, however, the formula is Ἀχιλεύς Θέτιδος πάϊς ἠϋκόμοιο after the trithemimeral caesura. Θέτιδος πάϊς ἠϋκόμοιο never shows that it is sufficient to represent Achilles without the preceding name: it is always appositional.

Furthermore, Ἀχιλεύς was not an optional and occasional adjunct to Θέτιδος πάϊς ἠϋκόμοιο, because the long closed syllable at the juncture would have been disapproved.[56] The juxtaposition of Ἀχιλεύς and Θέτιδος is as unlikely as the correction of its metrical fault is easy:

*οὐ μὰν οὐδ' αὐτός, Θέτιδος πάϊς ἠϋκόμοιο

*τίς δ' οἶδ' εἴ κ' αὐτός, Θέτιδος πάϊς ἠϋκόμοιο.

Since a poet would not choose to join Ἀχιλεύς and Θέτιδος they must already have been joined in the poet's inherited diction and sanctioned by habitual use.[57] The fixed formula preserves overlengthening—which in turn reveals the fixed formula.[58]

Moreover, the long fixed formula is to be blamed for the enjambement of the verb. If the poet had not got carried away by the flow of the formula, he would have been able to express his idea in a single line:

*οὐ μὰν οὐδ' Ἀχιλεὺς ἄρα μίσγεται ἐν παλάμῃσι

*οὐ πολεμίζει νῦν γε ποδάρκης δῖος Ἀχιλλεύς

*οὐ πολεμίζει κεῖνος ἀνὴρ ἆτος πολέμοιο

*τίς δ' οἶδ εἴ κ' Ἀχιλεὺς ἀπὸ θυμὸν ὀλέσσας φθήῃ

*τίς δ' οἶδ εἰ φθήῃ κε ποδάρκης δῖος Ἀχιλλεύς

*τίς δ' οἶδ εἰ φθήῃ κεν ἀρήιος ὠκὺς Ἀχιλλεύς.[59]

Formulaic composition would benefit in three ways if Ἀχιλεύς, Θέτιδος πάϊς ἠϋκόμοιο was not a traditional formula: unnecessary enjambement and overlengthening could be avoided and a formula for Achilles after the penthemimeris could be enlisted.

Nevertheless, these three considerations are beside the point if Ἀχιλεύς, Θέτιδος πάϊς ἠϋκόμοιο is Homer's own significant phrase. All along, it has been supposed that the phrase merely fills space and gets the poet to the end of the verse without the effort involved in saying anything significant. If the phrase is read in context, however, it makes excellent sense. It is easy to conceive, then, that Homer intended it to make sense. The alternative is coincidence. If there were in Homer only few occasions when such a judgment between intention and coincidence had to be made, the latter would have a stronger case than it does. As it stands, there is reason to demur.

Here is the verse in context. Hector's last retort to Patroclus may be paraphrased as (XVI 860): "Patroclus, why foresee death for me? Who knows but Achilles, goddess-born and half divine that he is and I am not, may perish before?" Without the concessive clause, there is no sense of predicament nor hint of desperation, which lead to recognition of fate and heroic resignation—the very gist of the tragic. There then remains only infatuation: "Talk not of death to me. I am just as good as he."

With Achilles withdrawn from battle, the tug of war is stretched even. So Apollo encourages (IV 512): "Have at them, Trojans, nor yield to Argives, whose skin is not stone or iron and invulnerable to bronze butchery. No, you are no longer fighting Achilles, whom some say Thetis made invulnerable. While he is sulking in his hut, take heart."[60] If the allusion to invulnerability is disallowed, there remains a verbose way of saying little: "Have at the Argives. They are not indomitable without Achilles." If this is what the poet meant, he could have expressed himself more simply in familiar formulae. Some easy verses have been suggested; poets could doubtless compose others and better ones. The fact that the poet has many ways of expressing himself supports belief in the significance of his chosen phrase.

Ἀχιλεύς, Θέτιδος πάϊς ἠϋκόμοιο is not uncontestably a traditional formula differing only in length, not in significance, from the unepitheted name. If Homer did compose the phrase and if he was unconcerned with overlengthening and enjambement, he might still have made it by joining Ἀχιλεύς to a traditional formula: Θέτιδος πάϊς ἠϋκόμοιο. But if Θέτιδος πάϊς ἠϋκόμοιο was a traditional formula, a traditional bard probably would have allowed it to stand on its own to represent Achilles, and if metrically necessary, αὐτός or κεῖνος could have lengthened the formula. If Θέτιδος πάϊς ἠϋκόμοιο was a traditional formula, Homer probably was not a traditional bard; if Homer was a traditional bard, Θέτιδος πάϊς ἠϋκόμοιο probably was not a traditional formula.

The fourth and last line that gives hope of discovering the formula for Achilles after the penthemimeris is

XXI 233

ἦ, καὶ Ἀχιλλεὺς μὲν δουρικλυτὸς ἔνθορε μέσσῳ.

Not much could be simpler than composing *δουρικλυτὸς ὠκὺς Ἀχιλλεύς by combining two elements that are already formulaic: the localized epithet δουρικλυτός and the familiar phrase ὠκὺς Ἀχιλλεύς. If epithets are insignificant vocables that merely lengthen a noun by filling some metrical space, it is no trouble to extend a simple progression of noun-epithet formulae:

$$\text{.. } Ἀχιλλεύς$$
$$\text{.. } ὠκὺς \ Ἀχιλλεύς$$
$$\text{.. } πόδας \ ὠκὺς \ Ἀχιλλεύς$$
$$* \text{.................................... } ποδάρκης \ ὠκὺς \ Ἀχιλλεύς$$
$$* \text{................................ } δουρικλυτὸς \ ὠκὺς \ Ἀχιλλεύς.$$

Such a system is easy for artificer, apprentice, and artisan to institute, incorporate, and implement. If Homer had been a professional bard of this school, he would have sung

*ἦ, θόρε δ' ἐν μέσσῳ δουρικλυτὸς ὠκὺς Ἀχιλλεύς.

Homer's is a more complicated versification. He refers to Achilles most often with a pronoun: ὁ, ὅδε, αὐτός, οὗτος, (ἐ)κεῖνος, also ἀνήρ, ἥρως. Achilles' name in the nominative has two forms and five metrical placements: Ἀχιλεύς after the first, second, or third half-foot; Ἀχιλλεύς after the first or fifth trochee. There is also a choice of patronymics: Πηλεΐδης, Πηλῆος υἱός, Πηλέος υἱός (of Achilles' other patronymics, Πηλεΐων and Πηληϊάδης occur only in oblique cases, and Αἰακίδης in the nominative refers only to Peleus). Moreover, each of these many ways of referring to Achilles is extended and varied and fitted into verse with the help of epithets and appositives. Homer, therefore, might have expressed the idea of the verse in as many ways as he could name Achilles. One alternative to Homer's verse has been mentioned; here are six more:

*ἦ, καὶ ὁ γ' ἔνθορεν αἶψ' ἐν μέσσῳ (δῖος Ἀχιλλεύς)

*ἦ, καὶ κεῖνος μὲν δουρικλυτὸς ἔνθορε μέσσῳ

*ἦ, θόρε δ' ἥρως αἶψ' ἐν μέσσῳ (δῖος Ἀχιλλεύς)

*ἦ, καὶ δὴ μέσσῳ ἔνθορ' ἀνὴρ (ἆτος πολέμοιο)

*ἦ, καὶ μὴν Ἀχιλεὺς δουρικλυτὸς ἔνθορε μέσσῳ

*ἦ, καὶ Πηλεΐδης δουρικλυτὸς ἔνθορε μέσσῳ.

In such a system of versification, *δουρικλυτὸς ὠκὺς Ἀχιλλεύς would be the formula that uses the basic Ἀχιλλεύς and fills the line after the penthemimeris. Others of the fundamental ways of referring to Achilles might also have a formula that fills the line after the penthemimeris:

*μεγάθυμος Πηλέος υἱός

*Πηλῆος υἱὸς μεγάθυμος

*δουρικλυτὸς ἄλκιμος ἥρως

*κεῖνος, πόδας ὠκὺς Ἀχιλλεύς.[61]

Moreover, even these might have multiple equivalents:

*δουρικλυτὸς ἄλκιμος ἥρως

*μεγάθυμος φαίδιμος ἥρως

*δουρικλυτὸς ὠκὺς Ἀχιλλεύς

*μεγάθυμος δῖος Ἀχιλλεύς.

A cursory look at Homer's evidence reveals the possible formulae Θέτιδος πάϊς ἠϋκόμοιο and *δουρικλυτὸς ὠκὺς Ἀχιλλεύς. If merely their equivalence was problematical, they would be no worse off than all the other various equivalent formulae for Achilles. But a closer look shows that if they are formulae, then Homer is not a good index of formulaic diction; for he could easily have used them as formulae for Achilles after the penthemimeris, but he did not. If, on the other hand, Homer is accepted as an exact index of formulaic diction, then they are not formulae, and there is a void for Achilles after the penthemimeris. It seems extraordinary that never in the *Iliad* or *Odyssey* is Achilles the subject to a predicate that is located before the penthemimeris, although this hemistich and main caesura are prominent elements of versification. Indeed, far from being classified as one of the *principal types* of noun-epithet formulae, in Achilles' case it cannot even be classified as one of the *less frequent types*.[62]

Since a formula for Achilles never follows the penthemimeris as subject to a predicate preceding the penthemimeris, the opposite would seem to be the obvious and necessary alternative: a noun-epithet formula for Achilles filling two-and-a-half feet and ending at the penthemimeris, followed by a predicate. But Homer did not compose such a line either, although it even involves one of the *principal types of noun-epithet formulae of gods and heroes in the nominative case*.[63] Again, there is a void in Homer's formulaic diction. Again, composing suitable phrases to fill the void is child's play:

    *Πηλεΐδης (δ') Ἀχιλεύς
    *διογενὴς (δ') Ἀχιλεύς
    *αἰχμητὴς (δ') Ἀχιλεύς
    *δῖος Πηλεΐδης
    *δῖος δ' Αἰακίδης
    *διογενὴς (δ') ἥρως
    *αἰχμητὴς (δ') ἥρως
    *δουρικλειτὸς ἀνήρ
    *Πηλεΐδης (δ') ἥρως
    *ἥρως Πηλεΐδης
    *ἥρως (δ') Αἰακίδης.[64]

Homer, on the other hand, identifies Achilles before the penthemimeris in these ways:

$- \cup \cup -$ Ἀχιλεύς

$- \cup$ Ἀχιλλεύς $-$

$-$ Ἀχιλεὺς $\cup \cup -$

$- \cup \cup$ Πηλεΐδης

Πηλεΐδης $\cup \cup -$

$- \cup \cup$ οὗτος ἀνήρ

$- \cup \cup -$ αὐτός

$- \cup \cup -$ κεῖνος

κεῖνος ὁ $- \cup \cup -$

$- \cup$ ὁ διογενής

$- \cup$ ὁ $- \cup \cup -$

$- \cup \cup - \cup \cup -$.[65]

Homer never has recourse to a noun-epithet formula to fill the hemistich. This, of course, is uncharacteristic of traditional formulaic style, where facile versification and facile ornamentation mean facile epithets. If διογενὴς 'Οδυσεύς, ῞Εκτωρ Πριαμίδης, Ζεὺς ὑψιβρεμέτης and Πάλλας Ἀθηναίη are indications of traditional formulaic poetry, then the lack of such formulae for Achilles, Nestor, Hera, and Ares is contradictory evidence. It would seem that a formulary bard must have had and used such a noun-epithet formula for Achilles. Coming first in the line, it would always be easy to versify, so that many verses with Achilles as subject might have begun with *Πηλεΐδης Ἀχιλεύς. It might also, after a full sentence and verse, be added paratactically in enjambement—both conveniently and stylishly. A thrifty poet would use it constantly; in comparison, Homer's variety makes him look like a spendthrift. The following are examples of Homer's lines that a formulary bard might have sung with noun-epithet formulae.

XXIV 587-90

τὸν δ' ἐπεὶ οὖν δμῳαὶ λοῦσαν καὶ χρῖσαν ἐλαίῳ
ἀμφὶ δέ μιν φᾶρος καλὸν βάλον ἠδὲ χιτῶνα,
αὐτὸς τόν γ' Ἀχιλεὺς λεχέων ἐπέθηκεν ἀείρας,
σὺν δ' ἕταροι ἤειραν ἐϋξέστην ἐπ' ἀπήνην.

Αὐτὸς τόν γ' Ἀχιλεὺς never recurs. The hemistich essentially names

Achilles; but so would *Πηλεΐδης Ἀχιλεύς. The formula has, moreover, the heroic embellishment of an epithet and avoids a third pronominal reference to Hector in three lines.[66] Most importantly, however, the formula trips off the tongue lightly and spares the effort required to compose prosaic words. What might be said for Homer's hemistich is that, if *Πηλεΐδης Ἀχιλεύς is a traditional insensitive formula, then αὐτός can be taken as emphatic by an audience indifferent to epithets. In oral poetry, however, the nuance of meaning hardly repays the time and effort expended by the expeditious bard. Αὐτὸς τόν γ᾽ Ἀχιλεύς looks suspiciously like simple prose; it can hardly be paraphrased more simply.

Homeric style can be so plain and artless (*unkunstsprachlich*) that only the meter makes it poetry. Homer may well have been able to paraphrase a whole epic in prosaic verse.

XXIV 59–61

αὐτὰρ Ἀχιλλεύς ἐστι θεᾶς γόνος, ἣν ἐγὼ αὐτὴ
θρέψα τε καὶ ἀτίτηλα καὶ ἀνδρὶ πόρον παράκοιτιν,
Πηλέϊ, ὅς περὶ κῆρι φίλος γένετ᾽ ἀθανάτοισι.

Homer's first line is quite plain and unstylized; it could be thought a paraphrase for a more stylized line:

*Πηλεΐδης Ἀχιλεύς γε θεᾶς γόνος
*Πηλεΐδης (δ᾽) Ἀχιλεὺς θεῖον γένος.[67]

These are a few of the abundant examples of Homer's failure to compose with noun-epithet formulae:

XXIV 511

αὐτὰρ Ἀχιλλεὺς κλαῖεν ἑὸν πατέρ᾽, ἄλλοτε δ᾽ αὖτε
*Πηλεΐδης δ᾽ Ἀχιλεὺς πατέρα κλαῖ᾽, ἄλλοτε δ᾽ αὖτε[68]

XXIII 208

ἀλλ᾽ Ἀχιλεὺς Βορέην ἠδὲ Ζέφυρον κελαδεινὸν
ἐλθεῖν ἀρᾶται
*Πηλεΐδης δ᾽ Ἀχιλεὺς Βορέην Ζέφυρόν τε δυσαὴν
ἐλθεῖν ἀρᾶται

XVIII 316, XXIII 17

τοῖσι δὲ Πηλεΐδης ἁδινοῦ ἐξῆρχε γόοιο
*Πηλεΐδης δ᾽ Ἀχιλεὺς ἁδινοῦ ἐξῆρχε γόοιο

XXIV 631

αὐτὰρ ὁ Δαρδανίδην Πρίαμον θαύμαζεν Ἀχιλλεύς

*Πηλεΐδης δ᾽ Ἀχιλεὺς Πρίαμον θαύμαζεν ἄνακτα.⁶⁹

Homer had no need of *Πηλεΐδης Ἀχιλεύς. What need had he then of διογενὴς ᾽Οδυσεύς? This formula occurs four times; but Homer could doubtless have got on well without it by composing unformulaic lines like the ones that disdain *Πηλεΐδης Ἀχιλεύς. Surely, Homer was not about to abandon formulaic diction; but neither did he abandon himself to it, as a slavish amanuensis. Homer's style is both formulaic and unformulaic; the disuse of *Πηλεΐδης Ἀχιλεύς no less than the use of διογενὴς ᾽Οδυσεύς, is characteristic of the *Iliad* and *Odyssey*.

Achilles receives the same treatment before the tritotrochaic as before the penthemimeral caesura. There is no noun-epithet formula for the poet's convenience and the hero's embellishment. This is Homeric diction:

– ∪ Ἀχιλλεὺς αὐτός

– ∪ ∪ Πηλέος υἱός

– ∪ Ἀχιλλεὺς – ∪

– Ἀχιλεὺς ∪ ∪ – ∪

Πηλεΐδης ∪ ∪ – ∪

– ∪ ∪ – ∪ ∪ αὐτός

– ∪ ∪ – ∪ ∪ κεῖνος

αὐτός ∪ – ∪ ∪ – ∪

κεῖνος ∪ – ∪ ∪ – ∪

– ∪ ὁ – ∪ ∪ – ∪

– ∪ ∪ – ∪ ∪ – ∪.

Homer might have spared himself the use of either Ἀχιλλεὺς αὐτός or Πηλέος υἱός, which are equivalent when they follow any open syllable or a short closed syllable.⁷⁰ The expressions are interchangeable in all three instances in Homer—if the audience is insensitive to synonyms:

XXIII 491

εἰ μὴ Ἀχιλλεὺς αὐτὸς ἀνίστατο καὶ φάτο μῦθον

XXIII 734

εἰ μὴ Ἀχιλλεὺς αὐτὸς ἀνίστατο καὶ κατέρυκε

XXI 139

τόφρα δὲ Πηλέος υἱὸς ἔχων δολιχόσκιον ἔγχος.

Homer, however, seems to have been capable of such sensitivity that Ἀχιλλεύς was eschewed at XXI 139 after Ἀχιλλῆα in the previous line. One might think that the line was written just above and Homer was looking back rather than always looking ahead as extempore composers have to do.

Homer's invention, moreover, could hardly fail to come up with a full noun-epithet formula or even several:

*Πηλεΐδης μεγάθυμος

*Πηλεΐδης πτολίπορθος

*Πηλεΐδης πόδας ὠκύς

*δῖος Πηλέος υἱός

*ἥρως Πηλέος υἱός

*ἥρως δουρικλειτός.[71]

Composing formulae is so simple that composing equivalencies is inevitable.

Such a phrase would be convenient opposite a predicate that follows the tritotrochaic caesura. It could also name the subject of a predicate expressed in the previous verse or enhance a subject already identified by a pronoun and thereby advance the poet to the caesura. Such versification is notoriously facile:

I 306

Πηλεΐδης μὲν ἐπὶ κλισίας καὶ νῆας ἐΐσας / ἤϊε

*Πηλεΐδης μεγάθυμος ἐπὶ κλισίας τε νέας τε / ἤϊε   '

I 54

τῇ δεκάτῃ δ' ἀγορήνδε καλέσσατο λαὸν Ἀχιλλεύς

*τῇ δεκάτῃ δ' ἀγορήνδε καλέσσατο λαὸν Ἀχαιῶν

*Πηλεΐδης μεγάθυμος.

I 7

Ἀτρεΐδης τε ἄναξ ἀνδρῶν καὶ δῖος Ἀχιλλεύς

might have been turned round and composed in several ways:

*Πηλεΐδης μεγάθυμος ἰδ' Ἀτρεΐδης Ἀγαμέμνων

*Πηλεΐδης μεγάθυμος ἄναξ τ' ἀνδρῶν Ἀγαμέμνων

*Πηλεΐδης Ἀχιλεὺς καὶ ἄναξ ἀνδρῶν Ἀγαμέμνων

*Πηλεΐδης Ἀχιλεὺς εὐρυκρείων τ' Ἀγαμέμνων.[72]

The poet also might have expanded each hemistich into a full line and turned out a couplet:

διογενὴς Πηλῆος υἱὸς πόδας ὠκὺς Ἀχιλλεύς

ἥρως τ' Ἀτρεΐδης εὐρυκρείων Ἀγαμέμνων.

One can surmise therefore that Homer had a hand in turning his own phrase. I 7 or one of its variants might have fallen into place after

I 258

οἱ περὶ μὲν βουλὴν Δαναῶν, περὶ δ' ἐστὲ μαχέσθαι

e.g.,

*Πηλεΐδης μεγάθυμος ἄναξ τ' ἀνδρῶν Ἀγαμέμνων.

A formulary bard and a garrulous Nestor might have been allowed the epexegesis; Homer chose to forgo any expansion.

It remains to consider the whole-verse formula for Achilles in the nominative case. There are those who imagine that composing formulae is a difficult task and that producing two formulae in a lifetime is all that can reasonably be expected (since Vergil himself did not, therefore could not, create formulae).[73] If traditional diction supplied a unique formula, it was rather to elude an *embarras du choix*. Here are some two hundred and twenty.

*Πηλεΐδης μεγάθυμος	ἀρήϊος ὠκὺς Ἀχιλλεύς
*Πηλεΐδης πτολίπορθος	ἀμύμων ὠκὺς Ἀχιλλεύς
*Πηλεΐδης πόδας ὠκὺς	Ἀχιλλεὺς ἰσόθεος φώς
*δῖος Πηλέος υἱὸς	Ἀχιλλεὺς ὄρχαμος ἀνδρῶν
*ἥρως Πηλέος υἱὸς	Ἀχιλλεὺς ὄζος Ἄρηος
*ἥρως δουρικλειτὸς	ἀνὴρ ἆτος πολέμοιο
*δῖος Ἀχιλλεὺς αὐτὸς	ἀνὴρ ἠΰς τε μέγας τε
*κεῖνος Ἀχιλλεὺς δῖος	ἀνὴρ ἀγαθὸς καὶ ἐχέφρων

*Πηλείδης Ἀχιλεύς	Θέτιδος πάϊς ἠϋκόμοιο
*διογενὴς Ἀχιλεύς	ἀγαθὸς πόδας ὠκὺς Ἀχιλλεύς
*αἰχμητὴς Ἀχιλεύς	ἥρως πόδας ὠκὺς Ἀχιλλεύς
*δῖος Πηλείδης	Ἀχιλεὺς δουρικλυτὸς ἥρως
*δῖος δ' Αἰακίδης	Ἀχιλεὺς ἠΰς τε μέγας τε
*διογενὴς ἥρως	Ἀχιλεὺς ἀτάλαντος Ἄρηι
*αἰχμητὴς ἥρως	Ἀχιλεὺς μεγάθυμος ἀμύμων
*δουρικλειτὸς ἀνὴρ	μεγάθυμος δῖος Ἀχιλλεύς
*Πηλείδης ἥρως	βροτολοιγῷ ἶσος Ἄρηι
*ἥρως Πηλείδης	θεόφιν μήστωρ ἀτάλαντος
*ἥρως Αἰακίδης	ἐπιείκελος ἀθανάτοισι
*κεῖνος ὁ διογενὴς	δουρικλειτὸς μεγάθυμος.[74]
*Πηλέος υἱὸς ἐΰς	

The whole-verse formula is simply an extension of the formulae that fill the first hemistich. It functions by enjambement: a subject is added to a completed predicate, or the subject of the previous line is enlarged. This whole-verse formula also provides the weary poet with a respite from the rigors of composition, the provident poet with a moment's preparation, and the profuse poet with extravagant embellishment. Such masterly devices of formulaic composition might have found abundant use. Homer gives Achilles a whole-verse formula only twice:

I 488–89

αὐτὰρ ὁ μήνιε νηυσὶ παρήμενος ὠκυπόροισι
διογενὴς Πηλῆος υἱός, πόδας ὠκὺς Ἀχιλλεύς

XXII 131–32

ὣς ὅρμαινε μένων, ὁ δέ οἱ σχεδὸν ἦλθεν Ἀχιλεὺς
ἶσος Ἐνυαλίῳ κορυθάϊκι πτολεμιστῇ.

Metrically, the phrases are easily interchangeable:

αὐτὰρ ὁ μήνιε νηυσὶ παρήμενος ὠκυπόροισι
ἶσος Ἐνυαλίῳ κορυθάϊκι πτολεμιστῇ[75]

ὣς ὅρμαινε μένων, ὁ δέ οἱ σχεδὸν ἦλθεν Ἀχιλλεύς,
διογενὴς Πηλῆος υἱός, πόδας ὠκὺς Ἀχιλλεύς,
σείων Πηλιάδα μελίην κατὰ δεξιὸν ὦμον.[76]

Semantically, they would be equivalent if the one served automatically when Achilles was not named in the previous line and the other automatically when he was already named. Such parallel systems of nominal and pronominal or adjectival formulae apparently would have been as common in traditional diction as they would have been useful in oral composition.

If, however, ἶσος 'Ἐνυαλίῳ is in fact adverbial and describes how Achilles came, rather than an adjectival extension and embellishment of Achilles' name, then it was composed for its meaning and not added just to fill some metrical space.[77] In that case, the other formulaic line would be unique—an uncommon thing in Homeric diction. Its uniqueness, however, could then be attributed to the unique occurrence of a whole-verse formula for Achilles. With this exception, Homer was never so expansive in his expressions for Achilles: this cunning device was not for common use.[78] If Homer had been induced to expand I 7 into two whole-verse formulae, he might have corroborated the unique formula, but he might have composed one of the innumerable equivalents.

There is ample opportunity for frequent use of a perfunctory, whole-verse formula for Achilles.[79] Either Homer avoided using it and so failed to transmit it unequivocally, or there was no special verse uniquely sanctioned by tradition. If disuse of a formula had an effect opposite to that of continual use, then Homer's audience would have been as much at a loss as his audience is now to determine whether to construe the two lines as circumstantial or ornamental, Homeric or traditional.

III

Unique and Equivalent Formulae for Achilles: Genitive Case

If the idea *Achilles* is to be expressed in the genitive case and contained in the sixth foot of the hexameter, the bard has to use pronominal expressions, such as κείνου, τοῦδε, αὐτοῦ, and ἀνδρός, because neither name nor patronymic suits the meter.[1]

Likewise, if the expression had to be longer by one breve, the bard has recourse to ἐκείνου, ἄνακτος, and τοῦ ἀνδρός. Although Homer never refers to Achilles with one of these forms, the technique is exemplified by their application to Odysseus in the following lines:

xviii 354
 ἔμπης μοι δοκέει δαΐδων σέλας ἔμμεναι <u>αὐτοῦ</u>

xiv 163
 οἴκαδε νοστήσει, καὶ τίσεται ὅς τις <u>ἐκείνου</u>

xvii 255
 αὐτὰρ ὁ βῆ, μάλα δ' ὦκα δόμους ἵκανεν <u>ἄνακτος</u>.

No one could possibly suppose that one pronoun should be formulaic and unique for Odysseus and another for Achilles, or that Homer and traditional diction, lacking such a pronoun for Achilles, found it impossible to refer to that hero in the last two or three syllables of a line. The pronouns and common nouns must have been of general utility and particular meaning. The questions of formularity and equivalence arise only when the expressions of indirect reference are phrases parallel to noun-epithet formulae.

Homer has a single expression for Achilles in the verse's final foot-and-a-half: Ἀχιλῆος. Other expressions might have served for oblique references in the same meter: κείνοιο, αὐτοῖο, ἥρωος, τοῦδ' ἀνδρός.

XXIV 154–55

ὃς ἄξει ἧός κεν ἄγων Ἀχιλῆι πελάσσῃ.
αὐτὰρ ἐπὴν ἀγάγῃσιν ἔσω κλισίην <u>Ἀχιλῆος</u>

shows the sort of situation in which Homer often substitutes a pronominal expression rather than repeat the name:

*αὐτὰρ ἐπὴν ἀγάγῃσιν ἔσω κλισίην ἥρωος.

In this line, however, three persons are involved: Hermes, Priam, and Achilles. Clarity and directness call for a proper name; indirect expression is better only when the reference is unmistakable. Moreover, Ἀχιλῆος makes the fifth foot dactylic, whereas ἥρωος closes the verse with spondees. It would be rash, however, to assume that Homer neither would nor could under any circumstances prefer ἥρωος to Ἀχιλῆος. If Homer can hesitate in order to consider the propriety of direct and indirect expression, then Ἀχιλῆος is not the only and automatic means of denoting Achilles here.

There is little wonder, moreover, that Ἀχιλῆος should be a unique nominal expression for Achilles in this meter, as only an equivalent patronymic could possibly be a direct substitute for the hero's proper name. If final Ἀχιλῆος was a unique formula, it hardly owes this to a traditional oral diction, but to the uniqueness of names.

After the fourth diaeresis, the genitival form of Achilles is represented in the following ways in Homer:

Αἰακίδαο
Πηλεΐωνος
Πηλεΐδαο
παιδὸς ἑοῖο (ἑῆος)
υἷος ἑοῖο (ἑῆος)
τοῖο ἄνακτος
ἀνδρὸς ἑῆος.[2]

Achilles is Αἰακίδαο at the end of a verse and without a preceding epithet six times; this vocalic formula always follows a final consonant that must remain single or a final long vowel that must suffer correption. As a unique formula, it should also have tripped off a lolling tongue in the following two verses:

XVIII 138

    ὡς ἄρα φωνήσασα πάλιν τράπεθ' <u>υἱὸς ἑοῖο</u>

XIX 342

    τέκνον ἐμόν, δὴ πάμπαν <u>ἀποίχεαι ἀνδρὸς ἑῆος</u>.[3]

The naturalness of Thetis turning from *her son* did not escape Homer's notice. If Thetis had turned from *Aeacides*, the illogical use of a formula would imply the constraint of economical formulaic systems or the habit of professional patter. Logical use of formulae, therefore, implies that Homer sings in context and conveys particular meaning by his choice of formulae. In XIX 342, ἀνδρὸς ἑῆος must be either equivalent to Αἰακίδαο, which it replaces because the bard failed to recall the regular formula and was distracted by some analogy, or unequivalent to Αἰακίδαο, which it replaces because the poet is portraying Zeus as speaking rhetorically, not expositively. The example of υἱὸς ἑοῖο supports the latter interpretation. Both confusion and artistry impair formulaic thrift and automatic extempore composition.

Πηλείωνος and Πηλεΐδαο at the end of a verse contravene the principle of unique formulae. Elsewhere in the verse, the pair constitutes a convenient device to allow final and initial vowels or consonants to link without metrical fault. Distinct consonantal and vocalic forms of Peleides are unnecessary at the end of the line. One form of the patronymic is all the bard can need or want, and the tradition would already have chosen the superior expression.

Homer's evidence is tantalizing, but inconclusive:

XVII 191

    οἳ προτὶ ἄστυ φέρον κλυτὰ τεύχεα Πηλείωνος. / στὰς
    191 Πηλείωνος h N[1] V[16] v.1. in A: Πηλεΐδαο vulg.

XVII 208

    δέξεται Ἀνδρομάχη κλυτὰ τεύχεα Πηλείωνος. / ἢ

XXIV 465

    τύνη δ' εἰσελθὼν λαβὲ γούνατα Πηλείωνος, / καὶ

xxiv 23
τὸν προτέρη ψυχὴ προσεφώνεε Πηλεΐωνος· / Ἀτρεΐδη
23 πηλειδαο Pap[28].

A solution depends upon the proper reading of the first example.
Some will hold that Homer's lines have been correctly cited and that
the apparatus reveals rhapsodic aberration and troubled trans-
mission. On the other hand, Πηλεΐδαο is by far the best attested
reading at XVII 191, where Πηλεΐωνος looks like a scribal emend-
ation to make the hemistich conform to κλυτὰ τεύχεα Πηλεΐωνος
seventeen lines later, and where Πηλεΐωνος. / στάς makes a
cacophonous conjunction of sibilants that is easily avoided by
Πηλεΐδαο. Were scribes more formulaic than Homer?

For indirect reference to Achilles, the consonantal versions of υἷος
ἑοῖο (ἑῆος) and ἀνδρὸς ἑῆος are παιδὸς ἑοῖο (ἑῆος) and τοῖο ἄνακτος:

I 393
ἀλλὰ σύ, εἰ δύνασαί γε, περίσχεο <u>παιδὸς ἑῆος</u>

XVIII 71
ὀξὺ δὲ κωκύσασα κάρη λάβε <u>παιδὸς ἑοῖο</u>

XVIII 221–22
ὣς τότ' ἀριζήλη φωνὴ γένετ' <u>Αἰακίδαο</u>
οἳ δ' ὡς οὖν ἄιον ὄπα χάλκεον <u>Αἰακίδαο</u>[4]
222 Αἰακίδαο]αὐδήσαντος V¹ γρ. P³: τοῖο ἄνακτος N⁴ m. rec.

A formulaic bard with a unique formula Πηλεΐωνος might have
considered it sufficient to express the idea *Achilles* in all contexts in
the same way. Achilles would pray Thetis to preserve *Peleides* rather
than *her goodly son,* and Thetis would take in her hands the head of
Peleides rather than that of *her own son.*

Either there is equivalence of formulae again and Homer, having
lost track of Πηλεΐωνος had recourse to a random analogy; or there
were parallel formulaic systems of direct and indirect reference and
Homer suits the formulae to the context; or Homer is capable of
composing in unformulaic as well as in formulaic phrases and with
deliberate artistry. The first makes Homer semiprofessional and
doubtfully capable of an *Iliad* or *Odyssey;*[5] the second makes
Homer semidivine for formulae but doubtfully capable of extempore composition;[6] the third makes Homer semioriginal, that is,
capable of both oral and literate style.[7] At any rate, Homer's diction

for the genitival form of Achilles in the last two feet of the hexameter does not suit a simple notion of unpremeditated oral versification made from unique formular systems.

Homer has scant use for genitival Achilles after the hephthe-mimeral caesura — three instances without recurrence:

XX 324
καὶ τὴν μὲν προπάροιθε ποδῶν <u>Ἀχιλῆος</u> ἔθηκεν

XXI 553
ὤ μοι ἐγών· εἰ μέν κεν ὑπὸ <u>κρατεροῦ Ἀχιλῆος</u>

xi 557
ἶσον <u>Ἀχιλλῆος κεφαλῇ Πηληϊάδαο</u>.[8]

Formulaic material is not hard to invent:

*Ἀχιλῆος ἀγαυοῦ
*Ἀχιλῆος ἄνακτος
*Ἀχιλῆος ἑῆος
*Ἀχιλῆος δίου
*ἀγαθοῦ Ἀχιλῆος
*θείου Ἀχιλῆος
*δίου Ἀχιλῆος
*μεγάλου Ἀχιλῆος
*ξανθοῦ Ἀχιλῆος
κρατεροῦ Ἀχιλῆος.[9]

Theoretically, time and tradition refined many into three: κρατεροῦ Ἀχιλῆος, Πηληϊάδαο, Ἀχιλῆος (δίου). Only these were at Homer's disposal. He had one occasion to use the first and second, and he would have used the third once but the epithet is replaced by a vital verb. Practically, however, with so little need for such formulae and with so little effort to make them, they are more easily made than kept; for they must soon be lost to neglect and the operation of analogy.

After the tritotrochaic caesura, Homer is both thrifty and unthrifty with genitival Achilles. Ποδώκεος Αἰακίδαο is unique; ἀμύμονος Αἰακίδαο and Ἀχιλλῆος θείοιο are equivalent. All three appear to be simple extensions of proper names:

XX 94
ἦ κε δάμην ὑπὸ χερσὶν <u>Ἀχιλλῆος</u> καὶ Ἀθήνης

XIX 279
βὰν δ' ἐπὶ νῆα φέροντες <u>Ἀχιλλῆος θείοιο</u>

IX 184
ῥηϊδίως πεπιθεῖν μεγάλας φρένας <u>Αἰακίδαο</u>

II 860, 874
ἀλλ' ἐδάμη ὑπὸ χερσὶ <u>ποδώκεος Αἰακίδαο</u>

XVI 140
ἔγχος δ' οὐχ ἕλετ' οἶον <u>ἀμύμονος Αἰακίδαο</u>

XVI 854
χερσὶ δαμέντ' <u>Ἀχιλῆος ἀμύμονος Αἰακίδαο</u>.

*ἀντιθέου Ἀχιλῆος ἀμύμονος Αἰακίδαο
does not occur in the *Iliad* or *Odyssey* but presumably would occur if Homer had no other idea to express in this verse, or if he could emphasize the essential idea by extension.

Each of the equivalent formulae finds use only twice: ἀμύμονος Αἰακίδαο twice in XVI, Ἀχιλλῆος θείοιο twice in XIX. Parry ignores the patronymical formula; only Ἀχιλλῆος θείοιο appears on his tables of noun-epithet formulae for heroes in the genitive case.[10] The error of this practice is pointed up by the fact that their consonantal counterpart ποδώκεος Αἰακίδαο, which occurs ten times in Homer and is the unique way of expressing the essential idea *Achilles* in the given metrical form, is also ignored on the tables. There is more extension and less economy in Homeric diction than Parry shows. The tables are specifically designed to demonstrate the systematic results of the principles of extension and economy. Failure to include the patronymical formulae must vitiate their considerable authority and Parry's fundamental thesis.

One passage provides evidence for the deliberate use of Ἀχιλλῆος θείοιο:

XIX 295–98
οὐδὲ μὲν οὐδέ μ' ἔασκες, ὅτ' ἄνδρ' ἐμὸν ὠκὺς Ἀχιλλεὺς
ἔκτεινεν, πέρσεν δὲ πόλιν <u>θείοιο Μύνητος</u>,

κλαίειν, ἀλλά μ' ἔφασκες Ἀχιλλῆος θείοιο
κουριδίην ἄλοχον θήσειν, ἄξειν τ' ἐνὶ νηυσὶν.

If Ἀχιλλῆος θείοιο were just a unique convenient formula, its conjunction with θείοιο Μύντηος could be regarded as fortuitous. As it stands, either the poet is purposely playing with repetition, whether for sound or sense or both; or the traditional formula ἀμύμονος Αἰακίδαο has so little hold on him that analogy is apt to operate with very little provocation: θείοιο Μύντηος. Either way, the poet is rather oversensitive than insensitive to the epithet θείοιο, even as metrical filler.[11]

The only other occurrence of Ἀχιλλῆος θείοιο is seventeen lines before the verse in question. If the text is a record of oral composition, the equivalent phrase here shows that analogy is apt to operate without any provocation; for the epithet here is not particularly significant but serves to make a convenient noun-epithet formula. A writer, of course, could compose 297 before 279: Briseis' important speech before the connective narrative. It seems improbable that an extemporizing bard could have composed 279 while thinking ahead to the play on words at 297. Both uses should be coincidental occurrences of an automatic traditional formula.

On the contrary, ἀμύμονος Αἰακίδαο would seem an insignificant traditional formula and a missed opportunity for a significant formula:

XVI 139–44
εἵλετο δ' ἄλκιμα δοῦρε, τά οἱ παλάμηφιν ἀρήρει.
ἔγχος δ' οὐχ ἕλετ' οἶον ἀμύμονος Αἰακίδαο,
βριθὺ μέγα στιβαρόν· τὸ μὲν οὐ δύνατ' ἄλλος Ἀχαιῶν
πάλλειν, ἀλλά μιν οἶος ἐπίστατο πῆλαι Ἀχιλλεύς,
Πηλιάδα μελίην, τὴν πατρὶ φίλῳ πόρε Χείρων
Πηλίου ἐκ κορυφῆς, φόνον ἔμμεναι ἡρώεσσιν.

If the poet had chosen to say

*ἔγχος δ' οὐχ ἕλετ' οἶον ἀγαυοῦ Πηλεΐδαο

at 140, it would have enhanced the paronomasia. The familiar formula must have prevailed.[12] If both Ἀχιλλῆος θείοιο and ἀμύμονος Αἰακίδαο are traditional, then neither is a mere formula; for economy is lost and the poet can choose.

Although ποδώκεος Αἰακίδαο is a set phrase, it is not, however, set fast. In one instance it proves itself adaptable to a special need:

XX 89

οὐ μὲν γὰρ νῦν πρῶτα ποδώκεος ἄντ' Ἀχιλῆος / στήσομαι.

If ποδώκεος Αἰακίδαο were a fixed formula, an oral bard would have been obliged to compose *ποδώκεος Αἰακίδαο / στήσομαι ἄντα, for which there is a close parallel:

XVII 166–67

ἀλλὰ σύ γ' Αἴαντος μεγαλήτορος οὐκ ἐτάλασσας
στήμεναι ἄντα.

Not only the equivalent formulae Ἀχιλλῆος θείοιο and ἀμύμονος Αἰακίδαο but also the unique formula ποδώκεος Αἰακίδαο fails to function mechanically.

After the penthemimeral caesura, the genitival Achilles shows equivalence without any redeeming uniqueness:

Πηληϊάδεω Ἀχιλῆος
μεγαθύμου Πηλεΐωνος.[13]

The former figures in the tables as a unique formula;[14] the latter goes unreported although it occurs three times, presumably because it does not occur in Ebeling's lemma on Achilles or in the concordances under Ἀχιλ(λ)ῆος. Parry would hardly argue that Ἀχιλ(λ)ῆος and Πηλεΐωνος express different essential ideas: the former simply Achilles, and the latter vital genealogical information. The oversight spared him the trouble of dealing with many equivalencies.

The nominative equivalent pair πόδας ὠκὺς Ἀχιλλεύς and μεγάθυμος Ἀχιλλεύς has already been discussed, and the suggestion has been made that *megathymia* may be of particular significance to the theme of *anger* in the *Iliad*.[15] The use of μεγαθύμου Πηλεΐωνος corroborates belief in the poet's sensitivity to the latent meaning of the epithet. Socrates derives θυμός from θύω, to rage or seethe:

θυμὸς δὲ ἀπὸ τῆς θύσεως καὶ ζέσεως
τῆς ψυχῆς ἔχοι ἂν τοῦτο τὸ ὄνομα.[16]

θυμός can be a synonym of μῆνις and χόλος:

IX 636–37

.... σοὶ δ' ἄλληκτόν τε κακόν τε
θυμὸν ἐνὶ στήθεσσι θεοὶ θέσαν εἵνεκα κούρης

xiii 148

ἀλλὰ σὸν αἰεὶ θυμὸν ὀπίζομαι ἠδ' ἀλεείνω.

There is an apparent connection between these synonyms and Achilles' *megathymia:*

XVIII 225–26

.... ἐπεὶ ἴδον ἀκάματον πῦρ
δεινὸν ὑπὲρ κεφαλῆς μεγαθύμου Πηλεΐωνος/δαιόμενον

XIX 75

μῆνιν ἀπειπόντος μεγαθύμου Πηλεΐωνος

XVII 214

τεύχεσι λαμπόμενος μεγαθύμου Πηλεΐωνος.[17]

In the first passage, Achilles is both literally and figuratively fuming; Athena's fire is the divine manifestation of Achilles' rage.[18] In the second passage, Achilles renounces his anger against Agamemnon in order to vent his fury against Hector and the Trojans. One fury replaces another, and Achilles aptly remains μεγαθύμου.[19] This is a restatement of

XIX 66

θυμὸν ἐνὶ στήθεσσι φίλον δαμάσαντες ἀνάγκῃ,

each of us suppressing his own anger [θυμόν] because we must. The third passage appears to forecast Achilles' *great anger* against Hector. Πηληϊάδεω Ἀχιλῆος in any of these lines would identify rather than describe Achilles. The foregoing interpretation seems possible only if the poet was able to compose deliberately. Oral formulaic poetry could hardly maintain a strict difference in the use of the two formulae for very long: insensitivity and analogy would soon make them equivalent.

Two other lines suggest other formulae equivalent to these two:

XVI 686

νήπιος· εἰ δὲ ἔπος Πηληϊάδαο φύλαξεν

iv 5
τὴν μὲν Ἀχιλλῆος <u>ῥηξήνορος</u> υἱέϊ πέμπεν.

In fuller formulaic parlance, these might have been

*νήπιος· εἰ δὲ ἔπος <u>Πηληϊάδαο ἄνακτος</u>
πάντα φύλαξεν

*τὴν μὲν Ἀχιλλῆος <u>ῥηξήνορος Αἰακίδαο</u>
υἱέϊ πέμπεν.[20]

These might, in fact, be authentic formulae that Homer by chance failed to use in our performance of the *Iliad* and *Odyssey;* but even if they did not belong to traditional diction, analogy might soon have found a place for them.

Other forms of Achilles' name might also elicit equivalent formulae in this metrical position. The genitive of Achilles has eight forms in Homer:

Ἀχιλῆος
Ἀχιλλῆος
Αἰακίδαο
Πηλεΐωνος
Πηλεΐδαο
Πηλεΐδεω
Πηληϊάδαο
Πηληϊάδεω.

These eight could make the following postpenthemimeral name-epithet formulae. Ἀχιλῆος at the end of the line can make Πηληϊάδεω Ἀχιλῆος and perhaps *δουρικλειτοῦ Ἀχιλῆος; placed after the caesura it can make *Ἀχιλῆος ὑπερθύμοιο. Ἀχιλλῆος has little chance of making a graceful and useful phrase for this hemistich; for its meter suits it for use after the tritotrochaic or before the penthemimeral caesura. *Βασιλῆος Ἀχιλλῆος γε demonstrates the difficulty or trying to put it after the penthemimeris. Αἰακίδαο yields *μεγαλήτορος or *ῥηξήνορος Αἰακίδαο. Πηλεΐωνος yields μεγαθύμου Πελεΐωνος. Πηλεΐδαο would take the same epithet. Πηλεΐδεω, like Ἀχιλῆος, is better used elsewhere than in *μεγαθύμου Πηλεΐδεω γε. Πηληϊάδαο placed last gives *δίου or *μεγάλου or *κρατεροῦ Πηληϊάδαο; Πηληϊάδαο placed first gives *Πηληϊάδαο ἄνακτος. Πηληϊάδεω can take a name Πηληϊάδεω Ἀχιλῆος or an epithet *Πηληϊάδεω θείοιο or *βασιλῆος or *κρατεροῖο or *μεγαθύμου. The name falls naturally at the beginning or end of the hemistich, and the remaining space easily evokes a complementary epithet, which the poet may include in the line or exchange for a significant word that meets a present need.

Πηληϊάδεω Ἀχιλῆος may have been a traditional formula, but it was not a rigid impending monolith for Homer.

XXIV 431
ὄφρα κεν ἐς κλισίην <u>Πηληϊάδεω</u> ἀφίκωμαι

XXIV 155
αὐτὰρ ἐπὴν ἀγάγῃσιν ἔσω κλισίην <u>Ἀχιλῆος</u>

XXIV 122
ἷξεν δ᾽ ἐς κλισίην <u>οὗ υἱέος·</u> ἔνθ᾽ ἄρα τόν γε.

Κλισίην Πηληϊάδεω Ἀχιλῆος occurs twice and is twice shortened to κλισίην Πηληϊάδεω to accommodate a verb, which would have been expressed in the next line if the formula had commanded respect. XXIV 155 looks like a compressed version of the more amply formulaic

*ἀλλ᾽ ἐπεὶ ἐς κλισίην Πηληϊάδεω Ἀχιλῆος

followed by a verb. The very idea of compression seems out of keeping with that of oral formulaic style XXIV 122 makes mock of oral composition with traditional formulae. A professional bard could hardly avoid singing by force of habit

*ἷξεν δ᾽ ἐς κλισίην Πηληϊάδεω Ἀχιλῆος.

Homer, on the contrary, brought Thetis to the hut of *her son,* prevailing against formulaic simplicity with Homeric simplicity. Formulary bards might even be inclined to compose

*. . . . . αὐτὰρ Ἀχιλλεὺς
βῆ ῥ᾽ ἴμεν ἐς κλισίην Πηληϊάδεω Ἀχιλῆος

at XVI 221—and be forgiven for doing so, as under bardic duress. By comparison, Homer appears only semiformulaic.

Equivalence and adaptability of noun-epithet formulae are fundamental to Homeric composition. These qualities need not have been sought in themselves; they could have been avoided only by intentional, unnatural, systematic economy. Systems of unique and rigid formulae, if rigorously applied, could hardly produce more than doggerel. If this was the nature of pre-Homeric traditional poetry, then it is no wonder that Homer was preferred and preserved.[21]

On the other side of the penthemimeral caesura, Homer has the following expressions for Achilles:

– ∪ Ἀχιλλῆος
– ∪ Ἀχιλλῆος μεγαθύμου
– ∪ Ἀχιλλῆος ῥηξήνορος
– ∪ Ἀχιλλῆος ∪ ∪ – ∪ ∪ κυδαλίμοιο
ἀνδρὸς ἀριστῆος
ἀνδρὸς ∪ – ∪ ∪ –
τοίου – ∪ ∪ – ∪ ∪ ἀνέρος.

The first occurs seventeen times, the second twice, and the others once. The simple name is more used and useful than noun-epithet formulae.

The second and third, if traditional, may be equivalent for the formulary bard; he could have composed his essential idea as follows:

– ∪ Ἀχιλλῆος μεγαθύμου φαίδιμος υἱός
*– ∪ Ἀχιλλῆος ῥηξήνορος ἄλκιμος υἱός.

It would seem to have been easier for an oral bard to adapt the succeeding phrase to the ending of the fourth foot than to adapt the fourth foot to the beginning of the succeeding formula.[22]

Μενελάου κυδαλίμοιο is a formula of fourteen occurrences, after which *Ἀχιλλῆος κυδαλίμοιο might have been formed by analogy. Ἀχιλλῆος ∪ ∪ – ∪ ∪ κυδαλίμοιο and Ἀχιλλῆος ∪ ∪ – Πηληϊάδαο, however, can hardly be set formulae. If even principal types of formulae are wanting or unwanted (as genitival Achilles in this hemistich), it is unlikely that such anomalous types should be of sufficient use to qualify as formulae. Uncontiguous ornamental epithets imply composition by vocables, rather than by formulae. Equivalent epithets allow choice: Ἀχιλλῆος ∪ ∪ – ∪ ∪ κυδαλίμοιο or Πηλεΐωνος.

Ἀνδρὸς ἀριστῆος, which at least fills the metrical space, refers once to Achilles and also once to Teucer and twice to Odysseus. It is, therefore, a generic phrase of indirect reference for heroes.

Traditional diction probably had a hemistichal formula, or several:

*δίου Ἀχιλλῆος
*Πηλεΐδεω δίου
*Πηλεΐδεω κρατεροῦ.

Apparently, the best phrase would become unique and the others would be forgotten—only to be recalled at any time by any analogical mind.

Whether there was one or more, Homer availed himself of none. It is not that he had no occasion to use them; one need not be a professional bard to see how Homer's spare style can be made more amply formulaic. Homer's

XXI 46–47

. . . . δυωδεκάτῃ δέ μιν αὖτις
χερσὶν Ἀχιλλῆος θεὸς ἔμβαλεν, ὅς μιν ἔμελλε

forgoes the convenience and the nobility of epithets:

*. . . . . δυωδεκάτῃ δέ μιν αὖτις
δίου Ἀχιλλῆος θεὸς ἔμβαλε χερσὶ φίλῃσιν.

Homer adds an epithet *in extremis:*

XX 438–40

. . . . καὶ τό γ' Ἀθήνη
πνοιῇ Ἀχιλλῆος πάλιν ἔτραπε κυδαλίμοιο,
ἦκα μάλα ψύξασα,

whereas he might have composed tidily with contiguous epithets:

*. . . . . καὶ τό γ' Ἀθήνη
δίου Ἀχιλλῆος πάλιν ἔτραπε κούφῃ ἀϋτμῇ
ἦκα μάλα ψύξασα.

Homer's epanalepsis

XXIV 478

χερσὶν Ἀχιλλῆος λάβε γούνατα καὶ κύσε χεῖρας

seems ingenious and precious compared with an ingenuous unpremeditated noun-epithet formula,

*δίου Ἀχιλλῆος λάβε γούνατα καὶ κύσε χεῖρας.

Homer preferred prosaic vernacular to an artificial epithet:

I 240

   ἦ ποτ᾽ Ἀχιλλῆος ποθὴ ἵξεται υἷας Ἀχαιῶν

*δίου Ἀχιλλῆος ποθὴ ἵξεται υἷας Ἀχαιῶν.

Homer has a hemistich for indirect reference to Achilles:

XVII 202–3

. . . . σὺ δ᾽ ἄμβροτα τεύχεα δύνεις

ἀνδρὸς ἀριστῆος, τόν τε τρομέουσι καὶ ἄλλοι,

so that the characters can speak more rhetorically than they would
have spoken if diction were more thrifty:

*. . . . . . . σὺ δ᾽ ἄμβροτα τεύχεα δύνεις

δίου Ἀχιλλῆος, τόν τε τρομέουσι καὶ ἄλλοι.

Like the direct, the indirect expressions can be abbreviated to
accommodate other words:

XXIV 203–4

πῶς ἐθέλεις ἐπὶ νῆας Ἀχαιῶν ἐλθέμεν οἶος,

ἀνδρὸς ἐς ὀφθαλμούς, ὅς τοι πολέας τε καὶ ἐσθλούς,

although the noun-epithet formula might have been retained and
elongated:

*πῶς ἐθέλεις ἐπὶ νῆας Ἀχαιῶν ἐλθέμεν οἶος,

δίου Ἀχιλλῆος ῥηξήνορος εἰς ὀφθαλμούς.

And like the direct, the indirect expressions can be neglected for a
different way of phrasing the same idea:

XVII 164

τοίου γὰρ θεράπων πέφατ᾽ ἀνέρος, ὃς μέγ᾽ ἄριστος

*ἀνδρὸς ἀριστῆος θεράπων πέφατ᾽, ὃς μέγ᾽ ἄριστος

*δίου Ἀχιλλῆος θεράπων πέφατ᾽, ὃς μέγ᾽ ἄριστος.

If Homer is a traditional formulary bard, then either traditional diction put him to great trouble by not supplying the obvious formula, which he did not even venture to make by simple analogy; or traditional diction is easily disregarded because ideas are easily expressed in alternative ways.

Before the tritotrochaic caesura, Homer has a welter of possibilities:

Πηλεΐδεω Ἀχιλῆος
– ∪ ∪ – Ἀχιλῆος
– ∪ ∪ – Ἀχιλῆος ἀγαυοῦ
– ∪ ∪ – Ἀχιλῆος ἀμύμονος
– ∪ ∪ – Ἀχιλῆος ἀμύμονος Αἰακίδαο
– ∪ ∪ Πηλεΐωνος
– ∪ ∪ Πηλεΐωνος ἀγαυοῦ
– ∪ ∪ Πηλεΐωνος ὑπερθύμοιο
– ∪ ∪ Αἰακίδαο
– ∪ ∪ Αἰακίδαο δαΐφρονος
– ∪ ∪ Πηλεΐδαο
– ∪ ∪ Πηλεΐδαο ∪ – ∪ ∪ – θείοιο
χωομένου Ἀχιλῆος
ἀνδρὸς – ∪ ∪ – ∪
– ἀνδρὸς θείοιο
– ∪ ∪ τοιοῦδ᾽ υἷος
– ∪ ∪ – οὗ παιδὸς ἀμύμονος
– ∪ ∪ – αὐτοῖο
παιδὸς ἑοῦ ∪ ∪ – ∪.

At a glance, one would suspect that this goes beyond any economy of traditional formulae; for everything metrically possible provides an occasional resource, and no one phrase is of constant recourse. Only four occur more than twice: Ἀχιλῆος (5 ×), Πηλεΐωνος (3 ×), Πηλεΐδαο (3 ×), Πηλεΐδεω Ἀχιλῆος (3 ×).

Πηλεΐδεω Ἀχιλῆος has the look of an authentic traditional formula.[23] Homer, however, can lightly disregard it, as if convenient versification and habitual diction were facultative. He went to the trouble to compose a topical phrase:

IX 106-7

ἐξ ἔτι τοῦ ὅτε, διογενές, Βρισηΐδα κούρην
χωομένου Ἀχιλῆος ἔβης κλισίηθεν ἀπούρας.

A bard should not be dissatisfied with the ordinary familiar

*ἐξ ἔτι τοῦ ὅτε, διογενές, Βρισηΐδα κούρην
Πηλεΐδεω Ἀχιλῆος ἔβης κλισίηθεν ἀπούρας.[24]

Homer also expressed this same essential idea in one verse without either Πηλεΐδεω or χωομένου:

XIX 89

ἤματι τῷ ὅτ᾽ Ἀχιλλῆος γέρας αὐτὸς ἀπηύρων.

Πηλεΐδεω Ἀχιλῆος, on the other hand, can also be used with particular relevance:

XVII 194-97

. . . . ὁ δ᾽ ἄμβροτα τεύχεα δῦνε
Πηλεΐδεω Ἀχιλῆος, ἅ οἱ θεοὶ Οὐρανίωνες
πατρὶ φίλῳ ἔπορον· ὁ δ᾽ ἄρα ᾧ παιδὶ ὄπασσε
γηράς· ἀλλ᾽ οὐχ υἱὸς ἐν ἔντεσι πατρὸς ἐγήρα.

If it had suited him better, the poet could have used χωομένου Ἀχιλῆος or perhaps τεύχεα δῦνε/μαρμαίροντ᾽ Ἀχιλῆος.

The place of the epithet is often taken by a significant expression:

XX 341

αἶψα δ᾽ ἔπειτ᾽ Ἀχιλῆος ἀπ᾽ ὀφθαλμῶν σκέδασ᾽ ἀχλὺν

*Πηλεΐδεω δ᾽ Ἀχιλῆος ἀπ᾽ ὀφθαλμῶν σκέδασ᾽ ἀχλὺν

XXII 113

αὐτὸς ἰὼν Ἀχιλῆος ἀμύμονος ἀντίος ἔλθω

*Πηλεΐδεω Ἀχιλῆος ἀμύμονος ἀντίος ἔλθω.

The epithet must have some particular significance if it is, at any time, *not* the particular significance required by the poet. With substitution so easy and common, the epithet that holds a place must have been considered suitable, or at least satisfactory, for the context. Convenience is not a sufficient proof of an epithet's insignificance if another convenient expression can also be used.

Homer freely disregards convenient stylish noun-epithet formulae:

XVIII 32–33
Ἀντίλοχος δ' ἑτέρωθεν ὀδύρετο δάκρυα λείβων
χεῖρας ἔχων Ἀχιλῆος· ὁ δ' ἔστενε κυδάλιμον κῆρ
*Ἀντίλοχος δ' ἑτέρωθεν ὀδύρετο δάκρυα λείβων
Πηλεΐδεω Ἀχιλῆος ἔχων ἅμα χεῖρας ἀάπτους.

Moreover, he freely expresses a single idea in many different ways:

XX 79–80
Αἰνείαν δ' ἰθὺς λαοσσόυς ὦρσεν Ἀπόλλων
ἀντία Πηλεΐωνος, ἐνῆκε δέ οἱ μένος ἠΰ

XX 83–85
Αἰνεία, Τρώων βουληφόρε, ποῦ τοι ἀπειλαί,
ἃς Τρώων βασιλεῦσιν ὑπίσχεο οἰνοποτάζων
Πηλεΐδεω Ἀχιλῆος ἐναντίβιον πολεμίξειν

XX 87–88
Πριαμίδη, τί με ταῦτα καὶ οὐκ ἐθέλοντα κελεύεις,
ἀντία Πηλεΐωνος ὑπερθύμοιο μάχεσθαι

XX 97–98
τῶ οὐκ ἔστ Ἀχιλῆος ἐναντίον ἄνδρα μάχεσθαι·
αἰεὶ γὰρ πάρα εἷς γε θεῶν, ὃς λοιγὸν ἀμύνει

XX 112–13
οὐδ' ἔλαθ' Ἀγχίσαο πάϊς λευκώλενον Ἥρην
ἀντία Πηλεΐωνος ἰὼν ἀνὰ οὐλαμὸν ἀνδρῶν

XX 117–18
Αἰνείας ὅδ' ἔβη κεκορυθμένος αἴθοπι χαλκῷ
ἀντία Πηλεΐωνος, ἀνῆκε δὲ Φοῖβος Ἀπόλλων.

Compare the simplicity of expressing a single idea in a single way:

*Αἰνείαν δ' ἰθὺς λαοσσόος ὦρσεν Ἀπόλλων
Πηλεΐδεω Ἀχιλῆος ἐναντίβιον πολεμίξειν

*Αἰνεία, Τρώων βουληφόρε, ποῦ τοι ἀπειλαί,
ἃς Τρώων βασιλεῦσιν ὑπίσχεο οἰνοποτάζων,
Πηλεΐδεω Ἀχιλῆος ἐναντίβιον πολεμίξειν

*Πριαμίδη, τί με ταῦτα καὶ οὐκ ἐθέλοντα κελεύεις,
Πηλεΐδεω Ἀχιλῆος ἐναντίβιον πολεμίξειν

*Πηλεΐδεω Ἀχιλῆος ἐναντίβιον πολεμίζειν
οὐκ ἔστ'· αἰεὶ γὰρ πάρα εἷς γε θεῶν ἐπαμύντωρ
*οὐδ' ἔλαθ' Ἀγχίσαο πάϊς λευκώλενον Ἥρην
Πηλεΐδεω Ἀχιλῆος ἐναντίβιον πολεμίξων
*Αἰνείας ὅδ' ἔβη κεκορυθμένος αἴθωπι χαλκῷ
Πηλεΐδεω Ἀχιλῆος ἐναντίβιον πολεμίζειν.

Strict economy and habitude did not produce the *Iliad* and *Odyssey;*
Homer is clearly capable of variety and nuance of expression. Given
the opportunity to simplify the task of extempore composition with
the simple device of repetition, Homer often allows each context to
have its own particular expression.

When the context calls for an indirect expression to take the place
of a direct formula for Achilles, Homer provides an apt and
unrepeated phrase:

XVI 798–99
   ἀλλ' ἀνδρὸς θείοιο <u>κάρη χαρίεν</u> τε μέτωπον
   ῥύετ' Ἀχιλλῆος
   *Πηλεΐδεω δ' Ἀχιλῆος ἐρύετο καλὰ μέτωπα
   καὶ κεφαλήν

XIX 323–24
   ὅς που νῦν Φθίηφι τέρεν κατὰ δάκρυον εἴβει
   χήτεϊ <u>τοιοῦδ' υἷος</u>
   *<u>ὅς που νῦν Φθίηφι τέρεν κατὰ δάκρυον εἴβει</u>
   Πηλεΐδεω Ἀχιλῆος ὑπερθύμοιο χατίζων

XXIV 84–85
   . . . . ἡ δ' ἐνὶ μέσσῃς
   κλαῖε μόρον <u>οὗ παιδὸς ἀμύμονος</u>
   *. . . . . . . ἡ δ' ἐνὶ μέσσῃς
   Πηλεΐδεω Ἀχιλῆος ἔκλαιεν μόρσιμον ἦμαρ.

When Thetis comes to sit by Achilles, a formulaic line follows as
proof of oral poetry: yet it passes unnoticed that Homer uses no
single formulaic line for the simple recurrent idea *and Thetis sat by
Achilles:*

I 360–61
   καὶ ῥα πάροιθ' αὐτοῖο καθέζετο δάκρυ χέοντος,
   χειρί τέ μιν κατέρεξεν, ἔπος τ' ἔφατ' ἐκ τ' ὀνόμαζε

XXIV 126–27

ἡ δὲ μάλ' ἀγχ' αὐτοῖο καθέζετο πότνια μήτηρ,
χειρί τέ μιν κατέρεξεν, ἔπος τ' ἔφατ' ἔκ τ' ὀνόμαζε.

Lack of repetition is probably as characteristic of Homeric composition as repetition is. Concordances reveal the latter but not the former. The means of analysis determines what is found in Homer. The list of expressions for Achilles before the tritotrochaic caesura gives reason to believe that not all can reflect traditional diction. There are indeed not a few "passages in which Homer employs an unusual phrase in a context where the normal formula would otherwise fit but where it might seem for one reason or another less suitable."[25]

Homer uses no whole-verse formula for Achilles in the genitive case.

IV

Unique and Equivalent Formulae for Achilles: Dative Case

In the dative case also, Homer makes reference to Achilles with many names, nouns, and pronouns:

Ἀχιλλεῖ[1]	ἥρωϊ (ἥρῳ)	τῷ
Ἀχιλ(λ)ῆι	ἄνακτι	οἱ
Πηλεΐωνι	ἀνδρί	αὐτῷ
Πηλείδη	ἑταίρῳ (ἑτάρῳ)	τούτῳ
Πηληϊάδη	παιδί	(ἐ)κείνῳ
Αἰακίδη	υἱέϊ (υἱεῖ, υἷι)	τῷδε

With this lot and several epithets, it can hardly have been difficult to formulate diction; and it would have been difficult to elude equivalencies.

In the sixth foot, pronouns refer to Achilles:

XXI 248

δείσας· οὐδέ τ' ἔληγε θεὸς μέγας, ὦρτο δ' ἐπ' <u>αὐτῷ</u>

XX 335

ἀλλ' ἀναχωρῆσαι, ὅτε κεν συμβλήσεαι <u>αὐτῷ</u>

XXII 84–85

τῶν μνῆσας, φίλε τέκνον, ἄμυνε δὲ δήϊον ἄνδρα
τείχεος ἐντὸς ἐών, μηδὲ πρόμος ἵστασο <u>τούτῳ</u>.

Pronominal and other indirect expressions complicate oral diction and composition because a bard has to learn to express a thought not only in one way but in many. Let the essential idea *Scamander rose against Achilles* serve as an example. The sentence can be expressed in a whole line with both god and hero having proper names:

*ἀντίον ὦρτο Σκάμανδρος Ἀχιλλῆι πτολιπόρθῳ.

If the god's name has occurred recently, an indirect expression may be appropriate:

*ὦρτο δ' ἐπ' Αἰακίδῃ δῖος ποταμὸς βαθυδίνης.

If there is little space, the indirect expression will be a pronoun:

*ὦρτο δ' ἐπ' Αἰακίδῃ μεγαθύμῳ λαβρὸν ἐκεῖνος.

If there is no space, the subject will be implied in the verb:

*ὦρτο δ' ἐπ' Αἰακίδῃ μεγαθύμῳ Πηλεΐωνι.[2]

At the same time, it may be necessary for the object to be a name, a noun, a pronoun, or implicit. Homer's ὦρτο δ' ἐπ' αὐτῷ at XXI 248 is one of his many ways of expressing the idea. Fullness of expression is Homeric, but so is conciseness. Epic fullness unabated would have multiplied formulaic repetitions and expanded lines into couplets:

*δείσας· οὐδέ τ' ἔληγε θεός, ποταμὸς βαθυδίνης·
ὦρτο δ' ἐπ' Αἰακίδῃ δῖος ποταμὸς βαθυδίνης.

Pigres probably surpassed Homer in the use of traditional formulae. Homer uses great variety in naming gods and heroes. If oral formulaic poetry is essentially characterized by epic fullness and typical expression of ideas regardless of particular circumstances and ordinary speech, then Homer's complicated diction is something else.

If the expression for Achilles is to follow the fifth trochee, Homer calls Achilles Ἀχιλλεῖ, ἄνακτι, and ἑταίρῳ.

XXIII 792

ποσσὶν ἐριδήσασθαι Ἀχαιοῖς, εἰ μὴ Ἀχιλλεῖ.

Ἀχιλλεῖ never recurs, but Odysseus is twice 'Οδυσεῖ. If it was a traditional form, it might have occurred more often; if it was not, it need not have occurred at all. The traditional way of expressing the idea should have recommended itself and prevailed:

*ποσσὶν ἐριδήσασθαι Ἀχαιοῖς, πλὴν Ἀχιλῆος
*ποσσὶν ἐριδήσασθαι Ἀχαιοῖς, εἰ μὴ Ἀχιλλεὺς
ποσσὶ πειρήσαιτο
*ποσσὶν ἐριδήσασθαι Ἀχαιοῖς, εἰ μὴ ποσσὶν
αὐτὸς πειρήσαιτο ποδάρκης δῖος Ἀχιλλεύς,

or whatever it happened to be. Homer often expresses himself in ways that Schmidt's *Parallel-Homer* cannot recognize, although it seems easy to emend Homer with paralleled diction.

A traditional Ἀχιλλεῖ, on the other hand, would have been metrically convenient the five times that ἄνακτι and ἑταίρῳ stand for Achilles at the end of the verse. Metrical convenience, however, cannot choose the most appropriate expression for Achilles in any particular context; the poet cannot count on a mechanical versification of formulae.

As Ἀχιλλεῖ occurs only once, perhaps εἰ μὴ Ἀχιλλεῖ was a special phrase, an anomalous survival. The phrase, however, has more the look of plain talk than of special artificial diction: prose could hardly paraphrase the thought more simply.

Achilles is twice referred to as ἄνακτι:

XXIV 448–52

ἀλλ' ὅτε δὴ κλισίην Πηληϊάδεω ἀφίκοντο
ὑψηλήν, τὴν Μυρμιδόνες ποίησαν <u>ἄνακτι</u>
δοῦρ' ἐλάτης κέρσαντες· ἀτὰρ καθύπερθεν ἔρεψαν
λαχνήεντ' ὄροφον λειμωνόθεν ἀμήσαντες·
ἀμφὶ δέ οἱ μεγάλην αὐλὴν ποίησαν <u>ἄνακτι</u>.

In the first instance, ἄνακτι might have been Ἀχιλλεῖ; but Homer evidently would no more say *the hut of Peleus' son, which the Myrmidons made for Achilles* than a prose paraphrase would. Homer's verse is often good prose. In the second instance, either ἄνακτι or Ἀχιλλεῖ would be suitable. Since ποίησαν ἄνακτι is not a traditional formula (the phrase having been composed to suit the context above), this line might have been composed by glancing back three lines.

Achilles is called ἑταίρῳ in a repeated line:

I 345, IX 205, XI 616

ὣς φάτο, Πάτροκλος δὲ φίλῳ ἐπεπείθεθ' <u>ἑταίρῳ</u>.

If the essential idea is *Patroclus obeyed Achilles,* it is easy to compose equivalents:

*ὣς φάτο, Πάτροκλος δὲ θοῶς ἐπεπείθετ' Ἀχιλλεῖ

*ὣς φάτο, Πάτροκλος δὲ θοῶς ἐπεπείθετ' ἄνακτι

*ὣς φάτο, Πάτροκλος δ' ἐπεπείθετο Πηλεΐωνι

*ὣς ἔφατ', οὐδ' ἀπίθησ' Ἀχιλεῖ δῖος Πάτροκλος

*ὣς ἔφατ', οὐδ' ἀπίθησ' ἑταίρῳ δῖος Πάτροκλος

*ὣς ἔφατ', οὐδ' ἀπίθησε βοὴν ἀγαθὸς Πάτροκλος.

Any of these would repair Homer's hiatus, which does not fall at a pause.

If φίλῳ ἐπεπείθεθ' ἑταίρῳ was formulaic, it might have referred conveniently to other heroes:

*ὣς ἔφατ', Ἀτρεΐδης δὲ φίλῳ ἐπεπείθεθ' ἑταίρῳ.

Homer complicates versification with unformulaic precision:

VII 120–21

ὣς εἰπὼν παρέπεισεν ἀδελφειοῦ φρένας ἥρως
αἴσιμα παρειπών, ὁ δ' ἐπείθετο.

Confusing kith and kin would make a telling oral formulaic absurdity. In fact, no one else ever obeys a φίλῳ ἑταίρῳ but Patroclus; the line might have been especially reserved for him. But if the *Iliad* itself is to make any sense, Achilles and Patroclus must have been very *dear friends* indeed. The text, of course, bears this out:

XVII 655

εἰπεῖν ὅττι ῥά οἱ πολὺ φίλτατος ὤλεθ' ἑταῖρος

XVIII 80

ἀλλὰ τί μοι τῶν ἦδος, ἐπεὶ φίλος ὤλεθ' ἑταῖρος

XXII 390

αὐτὰρ ἐγὼ καὶ κεῖθι φίλου μεμνήσομ' ἑταίρου

XXIII 178

ᾤμωξέν τ' ἄρ' ἔπειτα, φίλον δ' ὀνόμηνεν ἑταῖρον.

The significant phrase prepares the audience for the tragedy of Achilles. A literate poet could allude to any especially significant phrase. A nonliterate bard would have to memorize it and still risk losing it to analogy and equivalence.

In the last foot-and-a-half of the verse, Homer regularly calls
Achilles Ἀχιλῆϊ. Eight instances occur. Ἀχιλῆϊ yields to another
expression signifying Achilles in only one case:

XXIII 125–26

κὰδ δ' ἄρ' ἐπ' ἀκτῆς βάλλον ἐπισχερώ, ἔνθ' ἄρ' Ἀχιλλεὺς
φράσσατο Πατρόκλῳ μέγα ἠρίον ἠδὲ <u>οἷ αὐτῷ</u>.

Homer fails to react systematically; he consults the context and
composes a prosaic unformulaic expression, οἷ αὐτῷ. Using Ἀχιλλεύς
and Ἀχιλῆϊ as subject and object would have been sufficient proof of
mechanical versification.

Although it is Homer's practice to use indirect expressions quite
freely in place of proper names, nevertheless ἥρωϊ is never substituted for Ἀχιλῆϊ at the end of a verse:

XXI 327–28

. . . . κατὰ δ' ᾕρεε Πηλεΐωνα·
Ἥρη δὲ μέγ' ἄϋσε περιδείσασ' Ἀχιλῆϊ.

The reason for this seems to be that Homer accepted the metrical
restriction that the fifth foot should if possible be trisyllabic,
especially if the fourth foot is spondaic. Dactylic rhythm is absent in
περιδείσασ' ἥρωϊ. Ἥρωϊ never has final position, whereas βασιλῆϊ
often does. To this extent at least, Homer's choice of diction is
determined by the hexameter. To this extent also, any poet's choice
of diction is determined by the meter.

After the fourth diaeresis, Achilles is called Πηλεΐωνι three times
and ποιμένι λαῶν once. Although Πηλεΐωνι is always preceded by an
epithet, Πηλεΐωνος and Πηλεΐωνα occur in the same position both
with and without an epithet. Πηλεΐωνι too could surely stand alone.
Ποιμένι λαῶν refers to various heroes and serves either as an epithetic
phrase after a name to end the verse or as a pronominal reference for
a hero named in a preceding sentence.[3] It belongs to Nestor in these
two lines:

XXIII 411

οὐ σφῶϊν κομιδὴ παρὰ Νέστορι ποιμένι λαῶν / ἔσσεται

II 85

οἱ δ' ἐπανέστησαν πείθοντό τε ποιμένι λαῶν.

Achilles' case is the following:

XVI 2

Πάτροκλος δ' Ἀχιλῆϊ παρίστατο ποιμένι λαῶν.

If ποιμένι λαῶν had served as a pronoun for Achilles rather than an epithet, the constraint of meter and traditional diction could have been blamed, since Πηλεΐωνι could not render that service. Here however Πηλεΐωνι is the usual way of naming Achilles. The function of traditional diction is to provide the bard with ready expressions, formulaic solutions to hexametric problems, because he does not have time to consider and choose alternative expressions that may be contextually more apt. Homer shows that he has time to seek an original solution to the problems of composition. Homer's line and its near equivalent

*Πάτροκλος δ' Ἀχιλῆϊ παρίστατο Πηλεΐωνι

are hyperbatic: the name and epithet are uncontiguous, although each word separately occurs in a usual position. Traditional noun-epithet formulae in normal order are easily composed:

*Πάτροκλος δὲ παρίστατ' Ἀχιλλῆϊ προλιπόρθῳ

*Πηλεΐδῃ δ' Ἀχιλῆϊ παρίστατο πιστὸς ἑταῖρος.

Homer composed his line deliberately to imply that Patroclus came to Achilles as a man comes to the shepherd of his people, a ward to a guardian, a child to a parent.[4] Achilles confirms and develops the image:

XVI 7–8

τίπτε δεδάκρυσαι, Πατρόκλεες, ἠΰτε κούρη

νηπίη, ἥ θ' ἅμα μητρὶ θέουσ' ἀνελέσθαι ἀνώγει.

After the hephthemimeral caesura, there is a unique formula of unique occurrence:

IX 164

δῶρα μὲν οὐκέτ' ὀνοστὰ διδοῖς Ἀχιλῆϊ ἄνακτι.

If Homer had had a second occasion to refer to Achilles in two-and-a-half feet, equivalence might have been established or formularity demonstrated. Such disuse of formulae, however, makes analogical formations and equivalence all the more likely to occur. If formulae were difficult to compose they would have to be systematically preserved; if analogy created them easily, there was no need for exact systems of fixed formulae.

The digamma preventing hiatus gives Ἀχιλῆϊ ἄνακτι the look of reliable antiquity. If it was a traditional noun-epithet formula, Homer regularly canceled the epithet:

XXII 36
ἑστήκει, ἄμοτον μεμαὼς Ἀχιλῆϊ μάχεσθαι

XXII 55
ἔσσεται, ἢν μὴ καὶ σὺ θάνῃς Ἀχιλῆϊ δαμασθείς

XXIV 154
ὃς ἄξει ἧός κεν ἄγων Ἀχιλῆϊ πελάσσῃ

XXIV 183
ὃς σ' ἄξει ἧός κεν ἄγων Ἀχιλῆϊ πελάσσῃ.

These lines suggest a way in which the *Iliad* and *Odyssey* might have differed from earlier epic. Homer was not unwilling to express himself with noun-epithet formulae, but he often preferred a naked name. Homer's renowned rapidity is perhaps as much the result of his terseness as of his formulae. Here is an expansion of XXII 36:

*ἑστήκει, ἄμοτον μεμαὼς Ἀχιλῆϊ ἄνακτι
ἀντίβιον μαχέσθαι ἐν αἰνῇ δηϊοτῆτι.

Homeric style often lacks this ampleness; his lines are easily expanded. But if Homer could contract and expand formulaic diction with ease, then he could distinguish between Ἀχιλῆϊ and Ἀχιλῆϊ ἄνακτι, and metrical convenience is less a poet than Homer is.

Homer let the noun-epithet formula stand only once. If he had meant (instead of διδοῖς Ἀχιλῆϊ ἄνακτι)

*δῶρα μὲν οὐκέτ' ὀνοστὰ διδοῖς Ἀχιλῆϊ φέρεσθαι

*δῶρα μὲν οὐκέτ' ὀνοστὰ διδοῖς οἶκόνδε φέρεσθαι

*δῶρα μὲν οὐκέτ' ὀνοστὰ διδοῖς ἥρωϊ ἄνακτι

*δῶρα μὲν οὐκέτ' ὀνοστὰ διδοῖς Ἀχιλῆϊ γ' ἄποινα

*δῶρα μὲν οὐκέτ' ὀνοστὰ διδοῖς, κρείων Ἀγάμεμνον

*δῶρα μὲν οὐκέτ' ὀνοστὰ διδοῖς, μεγάθυμ' Ἀγάμεμνον

δῶρα μὲν οὐκέτ' ὀνοστὰ διδοῖς ἀρέσαι γ' Ἀχιλῆϊ
δῶρα μὲν οὐκέτ' ὀνοστὰ διδοῖς ᾧ Ζεύς γε φιλήσῃ,[5]

he presumably could have said so.

In his speech of concessions (IX 115–161), Agamemnon peevishly refuses to concede name and style to *the hero that Zeus loved* (IX 117). Nestor's reply shows that he is aware of Agamemnon's rancor and Achilles' slighted name: (IX 164) *Great gifts indeed [μέν] you give to glorious Achilles* (but a greater thing is a glorious name). Nestor had called for both in his last speech:

IX 113
 δώροισίν τ' ἀγανοῖσιν ἔπεσσί τε μειλιχίοισι.

The χάρις that Achilles wants is his glorious good name, which is here signified by glorious noun-epithet formulaic names. The absence of these in Agamemnon's speech is tantamount to an insult; Nestor's Ἀχιλῆϊ ἄνακτι is therefore tantamount to a compliment (not a mere metrical complement). Epithets that help to interpret the epic are not otiose ornaments.

After the tritotrochaic caesura, ποδώκεϊ Πηλεΐωνι, and Ἀχιλλῆϊ πτολιπόρθῳ stand as unique systematic formulae. Homer has the former twice, the latter once:

XXIII 249
 ὣς ἔφατ', οἱ δ' ἐπίθοντο ποδώκεϊ Πηλεΐωνι

XXIV 458
 ἐς δ' ἄγαγε κλυτὰ δῶρα ποδώκεϊ Πηλεΐωνι

XXIV 108
 Ἕκτορος ἀμφὶ νέκυι καὶ Ἀχιλλῆϊ πτολιπόρθῳ.

In the interests of economic formular diction, the inquiry should stop here. But one might ask whether Homer had occasion elsewhere to use these noble and convenient phrases and found them unsuitable. Three times, Homeric concision cuts off the epithet from Ἀχιλλῆϊ πτολιπόρθῳ:

XVII 121
 σπεύσομεν, αἴ κε νέκυν περ Ἀχιλλῆϊ προφέρωμεν / γυμνόν

XX 376
Ἕκτορ, μηκέτι πάμπαν Ἀχιλλῆϊ προμάχιζε

XXIV 110
αὐτὰρ ἐγὼ τόδε κῦδος Ἀχιλλῆϊ προτιάπτω.

If the noun-epithet formula had any integrity, Homer would have been inclined to compose along these lines:

*σπεύσομεν, αἵ κε νέκυν περ Ἀχιλλῆϊ πτολιπόρθῳ
ἐκπροφέρωμεν γυμνόν

*Ἕκτορ, μὴ προμάχιζε ποδώκεϊ Πηλείωνι

*Ἕκτορ, μηκέτι πάμπαν Ἀχιλλῆϊ πτολιπόρθῳ
μάρναο

*αὐτὰρ ὀπάζω κῦδος Ἀχιλλῆϊ πτολιπόρθῳ

*αὐτὰρ ἐγὼ τόδε κῦδος Ἀχιλλῆϊ πτολιπόρθῳ
Πηλείδῃ παρέχω.

Inclusion and exclusion of epithets is not simply a matter of metrical need and systematic diction. Homer's own καὶ Ἀχιλλῆϊ πτολιπόρθῳ balances Ἕκτορος ἀμφὶ νέκυι[6] and appears to suggest that the city is as good as sacked now that Hector is a corpse: οἶος γὰρ ἐρύετο Ἴλιον Ἕκτωρ (VI 403).

Homer also neglects ποδώκεϊ Πηλείωνι more often than he uses it.[7] In the following lines, systematic uniformity could be taken for proof of professional, expeditious, unreflective, formulaic composition:

XI 616
ὣς φάτο, Πάτροκλος δὲ φίλῳ ἐπεπείθεθ' ἑταίρῳ
*ὣς φάτο, Πάτροκλος δὲ ποδώκεϊ Πηλείωνι/πείθετο

XVII 78
ἄλλῳ γ' ἢ Ἀχιλῆϊ, τὸν ἀθανάτη τέκε μήτηρ
*ἄλλῳ γ' ἢ Ἀχιλῆϊ ποδώκεϊ Πηλείωνι/τὸν τέκε

XI 791
ταῦτ' εἴποις Ἀχιλῆϊ δαΐφρονι, αἴ κε πίθηται
*ταῦτ' εἴποις Ἀχιλῆϊ ποδώκεϊ Πηλείωνι/αἴ κε πίθηται

XI 839–40

ἔρχομαι, ὄφρ' Ἀχιλῆϊ δαΐφρονι μῦθον ἐνίσπω
ὃν Νέστωρ ἐπέτελλε Γερήνιος, οὖρος Ἀχαιῶν

*ἔρχομαι, ὄφρ' Ἀχιλῆϊ ποδώκεϊ Πηλεΐωνι
μῦθον ἐνίσπω ὅν μ' ὁ γέρων ἐπετέλλετο Νέστωρ

XVII 654

ὄτρυνον δ' Ἀχιλῆϊ δαΐφρονι θᾶσσον ἰόντα/εἰπεῖν

*ὄτρυνον δ' Ἀχιλῆϊ ποδώκεϊ Πηλεΐωνι/εἰπεῖν.⁸

Ease and convenience of deployment do not determine the use of the noun-epithet formula ποδώκεϊ Πηλεΐωνι. In the first two examples, Homer's expression for Achilles derives from its context: Patroclus obeys his own dear companion, and ordinary mortals are compared with divinely parented Achilles. Yet each line with the formula instead of Homer's special phrase is easily composed and sung; each gets the essential ideas across without particularization.

In the other three examples, Homer seems to rely on the formula Ἀχιλῆϊ δαΐφρονι or, more likely, on the simple name Ἀχιλῆϊ extended by the generic epithet that often fills the space from tritotrochaic caesura to fourth diaeresis. This does not constitute a formulaic type, because the main caesura cuts into words the phrase that must cohere if it is to be a formula. Moreover, if ποδώκεϊ Πηλεΐωνι, is a formula, Ἀχιλῆϊ ποδώκεϊ Πηλεΐωνι would be a simple extension of it, and Ἀχιλῆϊ ποδώκεϊ would be a simple contraction of that. The commensurate generic epithet δαΐφρονι might reasonably find some use beside the distinctive ποδώκεϊ if the two differ in particular significance. In fact, Homer has 'Ἀχιλῆϊ δαΐφρονι only with ταῦτ' εἴποις, μῦθον ἐνίσπω, and εἰπεῖν ὅττι. The epithet will imply *tell Achilles,* so that he may be of *knowing mind* or *tell Achilles,* for he should *know* what to do.

Epithets, of course, are commonly just ornamental extensions of names: οὐ πρός τι ἀλλὰ κόσμον χάριν. It can hardly be denied, however, that δαΐφρων and ποδώκης are occasionally used οὐ κόσμου χάριν ἀλλὰ πρός τι:

i 48

ἀλλά μοι ἀμφ' Ὀδυσῆϊ <u>δαΐφρονι δαίεται</u> ἦτορ

XVII 614

εἰ μὴ Κοίρανος ὦκα <u>ποδώκεας</u> ἤλασεν ἵππους.

It is not so easy to feel certain that Homer found and intended us to find particular meaning in the three instances of Ἀχιλῆϊ δαΐφρονι. Nevertheless, it is certain that Homer could have composed more thriftily. Convenient systematic versification has no need of equivalent otiose epithets for Achilles.

Ποδώκεϊ Πηλεΐωνι might have been used more often, or it might never have been used at all:

XXIII 249

   ὣς ἔφατ', οἱ δ' ἐπίθοντο ποδώκεϊ Πηλεΐωνι

   *ὣς ἔφατ', οἱ δ' ἐπίθοντο κάρη κομόωντες Ἀχαιοί

XXIV 457–58

   δή ῥα τόθ' Ἑρμείας ἐριούνιος ᾧξε γέροντι,

   ἐς δ' ἄγαγε κλυτὰ δῶρα ποδώκεϊ Πηλεΐωνι

   *ἐς δ' ἄγαγε κλυτὰ δῶρα διάκτορος Ἀργειφόντης

   *ἐς δ' ἄγαγε κλυτὰ δῶρα διοτρεφέος Πριάμοιο.

In the first passage, Homer chose to say *so said he* [Achilles], *and they obeyed Achilles. So said he, and the Achaeans obeyed him* expresses essentially the same idea.[9] In this case then, ποδώκεϊ Πηλεΐωνι and κάρη κομόωντες Ἀχαιοί would be almost equivalent formulae. Metrical convenience cannot help the poet to compose the verse; he must calculate nuances and shades of emphasis. The explanation of ποδώκεϊ Πηλεΐωνι, therefore, might be that since the Achaeans here are merely ancillary supernumeraries and the scene by the pyre is all Achilles', Achilles is recalled and enlarged by an epithet. Whether the subject or the object of the sentence (or both or neither) is expanded into a noun-epithet formula is optional and therefore can express the poet's intention. Even so common and convenient a formula as κάρη κομόωντες Ἀχαιοί does not impose itself upon Homer unwilling.

In the second passage, ποδώκεϊ Πηλεΐωνι emphasizes Achilles, whereas διάκτορος Ἀργειφόντης and διοτρεφέος Πριάμοιο would suppress him. Homer could also have stopped the sentence after κλυτὰ δῶρα. Or he might have emphasized the gifts:

   *ἐς δ' ἄγαγε κλυτὰ δῶρα θεός, τά κε θυμὸν ἰήνῃ

   *ἐς δ' ἄγαγε κλυτὰ δῶρα θεός, περικαλλέα πολλά

*ἐς δ' ἄγαγε κλυτὰ δῶρ' ἐρικυδέα Πηλεΐωνι
*ἐς δ' ἄγαγε κλυτὰ δῶρ' ἐρικυδέα κάλλιμα πολλά.

Metrically equivalent epithets allow further choice. Besides ποδώκεϊ and δαΐφρονι, ἀγαπήνορι is also possible:

*ἐς δ' ἄγαγε κλυτὰ δῶρ' ἀγαπήνορι Πηλεΐωνι.

Elision aggravates the problem of equivalence. Epithets and formulae that appear metrically distinct on neat tables of traditional diction can be equivalent in practice. Words beginning with a consonant are metrically equivalent to words beginning with a vowel that are one mora longer, if elision is possible.[10] This complicates the systematic use of fixed formulae. Homer is not obliged to use even the unique formula ποδώκεϊ Πηλεΐωνι.

After the penthemimeral caesura, a datival noun-epithet formula for Achilles finds little or no use in Homer. Μεγαθύμῳ Πηλεΐωνι and *ῥηξήνορι Πηλεΐωνι are possibly traditional formulae. The former is a disputed reading in one passage:

XVII 213-14 (v. l.)
. . . . ἰνδάλλετο δέ σφισι πᾶσι
τεύχεσι λαμπόμενος μεγαθύμῳ Πηλεΐωνι.

In the shining armor [of Achilles], *Hector looked like Achilles to them all.* The mind generally boggles at three consecutive datives.[11] The last dative is most easily emended; even Homer might have been responsible for the change:

XVII 214
τεύχεσι λαμπόμενος μεγαθύμου Πηλεΐωνος.

In the shining armor of Achilles, Hector appeared to them all, [looking like Achilles]. Either way, one grammatical case is explicit and the other implicit. The previous sentence has Hector going (appearing) among his allies with a shout:

XVII 212-13
. . . . μετὰ δὲ κλειτοὺς ἐπικούρους
βῆ ῥα μέγα ἰάχων· ἰνδάλλετο δέ σφισι πᾶσι.

If Homer had wanted him now merely to appear to them all in

Achilles' armor, he might easily have adapted the adjacent line:

XVII 199

τεύχεσι Πηλεΐδαο κορυσσόμενον θείοιο,

with a simple change of tense:

*. . . . . ἰνδάλλετο δέ σφισι πᾶσι
τεύχεσι Πηλεΐδεω κεκορυθμένος θείοιο.

Easier still, he might have repeated whole-verse formulae:

XX 46

τεύχεσι λαμπόμενον, βροτολοιγῷ ἶσον Ἄρηϊ

XIX 398

τεύχεσι παμφαίνων, ὥς τ' ἠλέκτωρ Ὑπερίων.

Homer often fails to repeat himself and can easily be emended to repeat himself.

If, on the other hand, Homer had wanted Hector to resemble Achilles without reference to Achilles' shining armor, he might easily have composed a more lucid hemistich or whole verse:

. . . . ἰνδάλλετο δέ σφισι πᾶσι
*δίῳ Ἀχιλλῆϊ μεγαθύμῳ Πηλεΐωνι
*Πηλεΐδη Ἀχιλῆϊ δαΐφρονι, ποιμένι λαῶν
*ἀντιθέῳ Ἀχιλῆϊ ποδώκεϊ Πηλεΐωνι
*Ἕκτωρ Πριαμίδης μεγαθύμῳ Πηλεΐωνι
*Πηλεΐδη Ἀχιλῆϊ μέγας κορυθαίολος Ἕκτωρ
*Τρωσί τε καὶ Δαναοῖσι ποδώκεϊ Πηλεΐωνι
*Τρωσί τε καὶ Λυκίοισι ποδώκεϊ Πηλεΐωνι
*Τρωσὶ φιλοπτολέμοισι ποδώκεϊ Πηλεΐωνι.

Homer rejected much facile versification; presumably, he wished to express his own meaning. Hector both appears to them all in Achilles' armor and looks like Achilles to them all.

While μεγαθύμῳ Πηλεΐωνι can be granted one occurrence, the equivalent *ῥηξήνορι Πηλεΐωνι never occurs in Homer. It can, however, be related to Ἀχιλλῆϊ ῥηξήνορι, which is extant:

XIII 324

οὐδ' ἂν Ἀχιλλῆϊ ῥηξήνορι χωρήσειεν

XVI 575
οἱ δ᾽ ἅμ᾽ Ἀχιλλῆϊ ῥηξήνορι πέμπον ἕπεσθαι.

Three interpretations of Ἀχιλλῆϊ ῥηξήνορι suggest themselves: that it is a formula in itself; that it is rather a contraction of Ἀχιλλῆϊ ῥηξήνορι Πηλεΐωνι, which is itself an expansion of ῥηξήνορι Πηλεΐωνι; that it is not a formula, but a name followed by an adjective.

The argument for formularity holds that if Ἀχιλλῆϊ ῥηξήνορι occurred twice it might have occurred twenty times. Three points conflict with this. First, a phrase that bestrides the main caesura is not a principal type of noun-epithet formula. It would therefore be less handy to manipulate than a common hemistichal formula:

*οὐδ᾽ ἂν χωρήσειε ποδώκεϊ Πηλεΐωνι

*οἱ δ᾽ ἅμα πέμπον ἕπεσθαι Ἀχιλλῆϊ πτολιπόρθῳ.

But Homer even lacks coverage of principal types of formulae.

Secondly, Homer did not use Ἀχιλλῆϊ ῥηξήνορι hastily and habitually; otherwise whenever he had Ἀχιλλῆϊ before the caesura, ῥηξήνορι would be sure to follow:

I 283
λίσσομ᾽ Ἀχιλλῆϊ μεθέμεν χόλον, ὃς μέγα πᾶσιν

XXIV 119
δῶρα δ᾽ Ἀχιλλῆϊ φερέμεν, τά κε θυμὸν ἰήνῃ.

Homer's simplicity abridges epic fullness of diction: here, no otiose epithets remain. Would a bard, composing from left to right and from formula to formula, misprize a noun-epithet formula? Both flouting and flaunting of fixed epithets is suspect. Noun bespeaks epithet; the line proceeds:[12]

*λίσσομ᾽ Ἀχιλλῆϊ ῥηξήνορι λῆγε χόλοιο

*λίσσομ᾽ Ἀχιλλῆϊ ῥηξήνορι μῆνιν ἀφεῖναι

*λίσσομ᾽ Ἀχιλλῆϊ ῥηξήνορι ἐξ ἔριν εἶναι

*λίσσομ᾽ Ἀχιλλῆϊ ῥηξήνορι ἐκ κότον εἶναι

*λίσσομ᾽ Ἀχιλλῆϊ ῥηξήνορι χωόμενός περ
    παύε᾽, ἔα δὲ χόλον θυμαλγέα

*λίσσομ᾽ Ἀχιλλῆϊ ῥηξήνορι μηνιθμοῖο
    παύε᾽, ἔα δὲ χόλον θυμαλγέα

*λίσσομ' Ἀχιλλῆϊ ῥηξήνορι θᾶσσον ἀρέσσαι
*λίσσομ' Ἀχιλλῆϊ ῥηξήνορι Πηλεΐωνι / θυμὸν ἐᾶν
*λίσσομ' Ἀχιλλῆϊ μεγαθύμῳ θυμολέοντι / θυμὸν ἐᾶν.[13]

The bard need not first compose the end of the line to determine whether he had space for ῥηξήνορι. There is not just a single way to complete the thought of the line; formulae would not leave a bard stranded after ῥηξήνορι.

Thirdly, Ἀχιλλῆϊ ῥηξήνορι rather than Ἀχιλλῆϊ μεγαθύμῳ follows μέγας Τελαμώνιος Αἴας (XIII 321), μεγάλοισί τε χερμαδίοισιν (XIII 323), and Ἀγακλῆος μεγαθύμου (XVI 571). Moreover, ῥηξήνορι admirably suits the context as a significant adjective in the first passage. It is possible therefore that ῥηξήνορι is an unformular replacement for formulaic μεγαθύμῳ. If Homer is allowed deliberate artistry, two instances of Ἀχιλλῆϊ ῥηξήνορι seem too few to establish formularity.

The second interpretation of Ἀχιλλῆϊ ῥηξήνορι assumes a whole-verse formula with substitutions of essential words for epithets:

*δίῳ Ἀχιλλῆϊ ῥηξήνορι Πηλεΐωνι
*. . Ἀχιλλῆϊ ῥηξήνορι Πηλεΐωνι
*. . . . ῥηξήνορι Πηλεΐωνι
*. . . . . . . Πηλεΐωνι
*. . Ἀχιλλῆϊ . . . Πηλεΐωνι
*δίῳ Ἀχιλλῆϊ . . . Πηλεΐωνι
*δίῳ . . . . . Πηλεΐωνι
*δίῳ . . ῥηξήνορι Πηλεΐωνι
*δίῳ Ἀχιλλῆϊ ῥηξήνορι
*δίῳ Ἀχιλλῆϊ
. . Ἀχιλλῆϊ ῥηξήνορι
. . Ἀχιλλῆϊ.

These combinations would satisfy many demands for Achilles in the dative case. A whole-verse formula cut at the trochaic caesura also provides twelve ways of saying Achilles:

*ἀντιθέῳ Ἀχιλῆϊ ποδώκεϊ Πηλεΐωνι.

But even all these fail to exhaust and account for Homer's great variety of diction that defies systematization and convenient solutions to metrical problems. If neat and convenient systems were required for traditional bardic poetry, these whole-verse formulations would seem like computer chips compared with Parry's tables of complex circuitry.

The third interpretation of Ἀχιλλῆϊ ῥηξήνορι has Homer composing word by word. He could have said Ἀχιλλῆϊ μεγαθύμῳ. In the genitive case, μεγαθύμου and ῥηξήνορος are metrically distinct epithets falling between the main caesura and the fourth diaeresis:

iii 189

οὓς ἄγ᾽ Ἀχιλλῆος μεγαθύμου φαίδιμος υἱός

iv 5

τὴν μὲν Ἀχιλλῆος ῥηξήνορος υἱέϊ πέμπεν.

If ῥηξήνορος habitually followed Ἀχιλλῆος at the caesura, the former line would presumably have read

*οὓς ἄγ᾽ Ἀχιλλῆος ῥηξήνορος ἄλκιμος (ἀγλαὸς) υἱός.

In composing from left to right, it is not the ending of the epithet but rather the beginning of the next formula that should be variable. Writing, on the other hand, does not restrict the order of composition.[14]

Achilles is ῥηξήνορος to avoid hiatus at iv 5; ῥηξήνορα to avoid anadiplosis at VII 228 (*μεγάθυμον θυμολέοντα); ῥηξήνορι to avoid repetition at XVI 575 (with μεγαθύμου, XVI 571); ῥηξήνορι because even the *man-breaker* could not break manly Aias at XIII 324; and ῥηξήνορα for no apparent reason at XVI 146. Formulaic diction that could suit all these needs would be quite versatile indeed.

A metrical reason for the alternative genitival epithets might have been whole-verse formulae:

*δίου Ἀχιλλῆος μεγαθύμου Πηλεΐωνος

*δίου Ἀχιλλῆος ῥηξήνορος Αἰακίδαο.

There is no metrical excuse in the dative case:

*δίῳ Ἀχιλλῆϊ μεγαθύμῳ Πηλεΐωνι

*δίῳ Ἀχιλλῆϊ ῥηξήνορι Πηλεΐωνι.

But that did not prevent their declension and retention, at least in

Homer. Homer sometimes gave sound and sense to metrical equivalents.

Homer's variety of diction is astonishing:

xi 556-58

τοῖος γάρ σφιν πύργος ἀπώλεο· σεῖο δ' Ἀχαιοὶ
ἶσον Ἀχιλλῆος κεφαλῇ Πηληϊάδαο
ἀχνύμεθα φθιμένοιο διαμπερές.

A nuance of meaning evokes a circumlocution although a convenient formula is to hand:

*ἶσον Ἀχιλλῆϊ ῥηξήνορι Πηλεΐωνι.

Before the penthemimeral caesura, only two oblique references to Achilles fill the hemistich:

XVIII 457-58

τοὔνεκα νῦν τὰ σὰ γούναθ' ἱκάνομαι, αἴ κ' ἐθέλησθα
υἱεῖ ἐμῷ ὠκυμόρῳ δόμεν ἀσπίδα καὶ τρυφάλειαν

XXIV 211-13

ἀργίποδας κύνας ἆσαι ἑῶν ἀπάνευθε τοκήων
ἀνδρὶ πάρα κρατερῷ, τοῦ ἐγὼ μέσον ἧπαρ ἔχοιμι
ἐσθέμεναι προσφῦσα.

In the former, the epithet is significant, and the phrase is of restricted use—unless it can be proved to be systematic diction of all parents speaking to sons. In the latter, the phrase does not suit other prepositions nor any uses of the dative without a preposition. Neither is suitable when Achilles must be named directly. For this purpose, one might easily devise *Πηλεΐδῃ κρατερῷ or *δίῳ Ἀχιλλῆϊ.

Homer can be remarkably chary of noun-epithet phrases; a name often stands alone although it can easily be given epic fullness and formulaic style:

XIX 83

Πηλεΐδῃ μὲν ἐγὼν ἐνδείξομαι· αὐτὰρ οἱ ἄλλοι
*Πηλεΐδῃ κρατερῷ μὲν ἐγὼν ἐνδείξομαι αὐτός

XX 120-21

αὐτόθεν· ἤ τις ἔπειτα καὶ ἡμείων Ἀχιλῆϊ
παρσταίη, δοίη δὲ κράτος μέγα, μηδέ τι θυμῷ

*αὐτόθεν· ἤ τις ἔπειτα καὶ ἡμείων παρασταίη
Πηλεΐδη κρατερῷ, δοίη δὲ κράτος τε μένος τε

XXIV 110
αὐτὰρ ἐγὼ τόδε κῦδος Ἀχιλλῆϊ προτιάπτω
*αὐτὰρ ἐγὼ τόδε κῦδος ὑπέρτερον ἐγγυαλίζω
Πηλεΐδη κρατερῷ.[15]

Homer often reduces Achilles to a pronoun or common noun in spite of the convenience and the heroic-epic quality of noun-epithet formulae:

XVIII 143–44
εἶμι παρ' Ἥφαιστον κλυτοτέχνην, αἴ κ' ἐθέλησιν
<u>υἱεῖ ἐμῷ</u> δόμεναι κλυτὰ τεύχεα παμφανόωντα
*εἶμι παρ Ἥφαιστον κλυτοτέχνην, αἴ κε διδοίη
Πηλεΐδη κρατερῷ κλυτὰ τεύχεα παμφανόωντα

XVIII 147
ἤϊεν, ὄφρα <u>φίλῳ παιδὶ</u> κλυτὰ τεύχε' ἐνείκαι
*ἤϊεν, ὄφρα πόροι κλυτὰ τεύχεα παμφανόωντα
Πηλεΐδη κρατερῷ

XVIII 457–58
τοὔνεκα νῦν τὰ σὰ γούναθ' ἱκάνομαι, αἴ κ' ἐθέλησθα
<u>υἱεῖ ἐμῷ ὠκυμόρῳ</u> δόμεν ἀσπίδα καὶ τρυφάλειαν
*τοὔνεκα νῦν τὰ σὰ γούναθ' ἱκάνομαι, αἴ κ' ἐθέλησθα
υἱεῖ ἐμῷ δόμεναι κλυτὰ τεύχεα παμφανόωντα
*τοὔνεκα νῦν τὰ σὰ γούναθ' ἱκάνομαι, αἴ κε διδοίη
Πηλεΐδη κρατερῷ κλυτὰ τεύχεα παμφανόωντα

XXII 110
ἠέ κεν <u>αὐτῷ</u> ὀλέσθαι ἐϋκλειῶς πρὸ πόληος
*ἠέ κεν αὐτὸν ὀλέσθαι ἐϋκλειῶς πρὸ πόληος
Πηλεΐδη κρατερῷ

XXII 126–28
οὐ μέν πως νῦν ἔστιν ἀπὸ δρυὸς οὐδ' ἀπὸ πέτρης
<u>τῷ</u> ὀαριζέμεναι, ἅ τε παρθένος ἠΐθεός τε,
παρθένος ἠΐθεός τ' ὀαρίζετον ἀλλήλοιιν

*οὐ μέν πως νῦν ἔστιν ἀπὸ δρυὸς οὐδ' ἀπὸ πέτρης
Πηλεΐδῃ κρατερῷ ὀαριζέμεναι, ἅ τε κοῦροι,
παρθένος ἠΐθεός τ' ὀαρίζετον ἀλλήλοιιν.¹⁶

It is clear that Homer often composed without the aid of
convenient noun-epithet phrases for Achilles. This is the sort of
composition that is identified with Apollonius and Vergil. Homer
composed like Apollonius and Vergil. This is not the sort of
composition that Homer often uses: noun-epithet formulae for
Achilles. Homer composed both like and unlike Apollonius and
Vergil.

The hemistich before the tritotrochaic caesura has a paragon of a
noun-epithet formula: Πηλεΐδη Ἀχιλῆϊ. Homer has it six times with
no equivalents. It looks irresistible in a table of systematic diction.
Homer, however, does not use it systematically. Homer seems to
have as many ways to say Achilles as there are nuances of meaning
to express.

XXII 57–58
Τρῶας καὶ Τρῳάς, μηδὲ μέγα κῦδος ὀρέξῃς
Πηλεΐδη, αὐτὸς δὲ φίλης αἰῶνος ἀμέρθης
*Πηλεΐδη Ἀχιλῆϊ, φίλης δ' αἰῶνος ἀμέρθης

XXIV 39
ἀλλ' ὀλοῷ Ἀχιλῆϊ, θεοί, βούλεσθ' ἐπαρήγειν
*Πηλεΐδη Ἀχιλῆϊ, θεοί, βούλεσθ' ἐπαρήγειν

XXII 277
ἂψ δ' Ἀχιλῆϊ δίδου, λάθε δ' Ἕκτορα ποιμένα λαῶν
*Πηλεΐδη δ' Ἀχιλῆϊ δίδου, λάθε δ' Ἕκτορα δῖον

XXII 40
Πηλεΐωνι δαμείς, ἐπεὶ ἦ πολὺ φέρτερός ἐστι
*Πηλεΐδη Ἀχιλῆϊ δαμείς, ὅ τε φέρτερός ἐστι

XXIII 173
ἐννέα τῷ γε ἄνακτι τραπεζῆες κύνες ἦσαν
*Πηλεΐδη Ἀχιλῆϊ τραπεζῆες κύνες ἦσαν / ἐννέα

XI 783

Πηλεὺς μὲν ᾧ παιδὶ γέρων ἐπέτελλ' Ἀχιλῆϊ

*Πηλεΐδῃ Ἀχιλῆϊ πατὴρ ἐπετέλλετο Πηλεύς

XXI 569

ἐν δὲ ἴα ψυχή, θνητὸν δέ ἑ φασ' ἄνθρωποι

*Πηλεΐδῃ Ἀχιλῆϊ ἴα ψυχή τε καὶ αἰών,
ἀνδρὶ θνητῷ ἐόντι, πάλαι πεπρωμένῳ αἴσῃ

XXI 570

ἔμμεναι· αὐτάρ οἱ Κρονίδης Ζεὺς κῦδος ὀπάζει

*ἔμμεναι· ἀλλ' αὐτὸς Κρονίδης Ζεὺς κῦδος ὀπάζει
Πηλεΐδῃ Ἀχιλῆϊ δαΐφρονι θυμολέοντι.[17]

If these many expressions for Achilles all signify nuances of meaning that were chosen despite the convenient formula, then the use of the formula also can be significant. The ease of its replacement implies some meaning in its use:

XVII 103–5

ἄμφω κ' αὖτις ἰόντες ἐπιμνησαίμεθα χάρμης
καὶ πρὸς δαίμονά περ, εἴ πως ἐρυσαίμεθα νεκρὸν
Πηλεΐδῃ Ἀχιλῆϊ· κακῶν δέ κε φέρτατον εἴη

*γυμνὸν Πατρόκλοιο· κακῶν δέ κε φέρτατον εἴη

*δίου Πατρόκλοιο· κακῶν δέ κε φέρτατον εἴη

*νηυσὶν ἔπι γλαφυρῇσι· κακῶν δέ κε φέρτατον εἴη

*δηΐου ἐκ πολέμοιο· κακῶν δέ κε φέρτατον εἴη

*Πατρόκλοιο θανόντος· κακῶν δέ κε φέρτατον εἴη

XVII 700–701

τὸν μὲν δάκρυ χέοντα πόδες φέρον ἐκ πολέμοιο
Πηλεΐδῃ Ἀχιλῆϊ κακὸν ἔπος ἀγγελέοντα

*Νέστορος ἀγλαὸν υἷα κακὸν ἔπος ἀγγελέοντα

*νηυσὶν ἔπι γλαφυρῃσι κακὸν ἔπος ἀγγελέοντα

XX 310–12

ἐννοσίγαι', αὐτὸς σὺ μετὰ φρεσὶ σῇσι νόησον
Αἰνείαν, ἤ κέν μιν ἐρύσσεαι, ἤ κεν ἐάσῃς
Πηλεΐδῃ Ἀχιλῆϊ δαμήμεναι, ἐσθλὸν ἐόντα

*χέρσ' ὕπο Πηλεΐδαο δαμήμεναι, ἐσθλὸν ἐόντα
*τούτῳ ἐνὶ προμάχοισι δαμήμεναι, ἐσθλὸν ἐόντα

XX 321-22
αὐτίκα τῷ μὲν ἔπειτα κατ' ὀφθαλμῶν χέεν ἀχλὺν,
Πηλεΐδῃ Ἀχιλῆϊ· ὁ δὲ μελίην εὔχαλκον
*θεσπεσίην Ἀχιλῆϊ· ὁ δὲ μελίην εὔχαλκον
*θεσπεσίην· ὁ δ' ἔπειτα πελώριον ὄβριμον ἔγχος.

Systematic diction does not account for the use and disuse of
Πηλεΐδῃ Ἀχιλῆϊ. Mechanical composition of metrically convenient
formulae is sabotaged by variety. Homer has two sorts of expressions for Achilles: proper names (Ἀχιλῆϊ, Πηλεΐωνι, Πηλεΐδῃ)
and pronominal expressions (τῷ, οἱ, τούτῳ). Either of these can be
extended and emphasized with epithets and other names:

τῷ γε ἄνακτι
τῷ . . . Πηλεΐωνι
ὀλοῷ Ἀχιλῆϊ
Πηλεΐδῃ Ἀχιλῆϊ.

The simple names and pronouns are used as if in accordance with
principles of standard prose style. There is no revealing misusage: a
name where prose would have had a pronoun and conversely a
pronoun where a name must stand. If metrical convenience, however, had determined their use, epic would show a precarious pell-
mell of expressions for Achilles. Convenient ineptitudes might have
occurred in every verse. Before Homer, oral bards might have relied
more on the convenience of noun-epithet formulae and produced
formulaic pastiches. This artificiality might have convinced poets of
the need to control traditional diction and use it sensitively. Since
Homer did not use Πηλεΐδῃ Ἀχιλῆϊ promiscuously, he must not have
used it insensitively and insignificantly.

The closest to a whole-verse formula is

xi 557
ἶσον Ἀχιλλῆος κεφαλῇ Πηληϊάδαο.

One can hardly infer, however, that the entire unique traditional whole-verse noun-epithet formula for Achilles in the dative case was

*δίου Ἀχιλλῆος κεφαλῇ Πηληϊάδαο.

Homer's phrase is clearly meant for endearment, not for standard use. If the formula was

*δίῳ Ἀχιλλῆϊ μεγαθύμῳ Πηλεΐωνι,

it could have been quickly and conveniently applied to the metrical problem and the bard could have hurried on:

*ἶσον Ἀχιλλῆϊ μεγαθύμῳ Πηλεΐωνι.

Homer had time to compose a significant circumlocution.

Homer had occasion to use thirty-two different expressions for Achilles in the dative case. Only five of the expressions fall into Parry's categories called principal types. Only one phrase occurs more than twice. The idea of datival Achilles is expressed with consummate complexity.

V

Unique and Equivalent Formulae for Achilles: Accusative Case

When the accusative for Achilles was needed in the last syllable of the verse, μίν, τόν, and ἑ, which refer to Achilles elsewhere in the verse, would doubtless be serviceable. All three would then be equivalent. A multiplicity of pronominal forms, however, should serve a multiplicity of metrical needs and display the economy and extension of traditional artificial diction. Homer's *Kunstsprache* cannot be reduced to an art of facile versification.

Accusatives of two syllables that refer to Achilles are τόν γε, τοῦτον, κεῖνον, αὐτόν, υἱόν. They can occur in any foot of the verse. Although they show equivalence of meter, they are distinct in meaning.

XXIV 122–23

    ἷξεν δ᾽ ἐς κλισίην οὗ υἱέος· ἔνθ᾽ ἄρα τόν γε
    εὗρ᾽ ἁδινὰ στενάχοντα· φίλοι δ᾽ ἀμφ᾽ αὐτὸν ἑταῖροι.

Τόν γε does not mean τοῦτον or κεῖνον. Αὐτόν is the vocalic counterpart for τόν γε. Meter then decides between τόν γε and αὐτόν; the poet, between τόν γε, τοῦτον, and κεῖνον.

    Ἄνδρα is used to make phrases alluding to Achilles:

XXI 313–14

    ἵστη δὲ μέγα κῦμα, πολὺν δ᾽ ὀρυμαγδὸν ὄρινε
    φιτρῶν καὶ λάων, ἵνα παύσομεν ἄγριον ἄνδρα.

XXII 84
τῶν μνῆσαι, φίλε τέκνον, ἄμυνε δὲ δήϊον <u>ἄνδρα.</u>

Thetis has special diction for Achilles, not ἄνδρα, nor τόν γε, not even κεῖνον:

I 503–5
Ζεῦ πάτερ, εἴ ποτε δή σε μετ' ἀθανάτοισι ὄνησα
ἢ ἔπει ἢ ἔργῳ. τόδε μοι κρήηνον ἐέλδωρ·
τίμησόν μοι <u>υἱόν,</u> ὃς ὠκυμορώτατος ἄλλων.

Homer was able to let her speak as a mother would, not as systematic artificial diction might. In this, at least, Homer composes like Apollonius and Vergil.

The traditional heroic way of referring to Achilles in the last three syllables of a verse might have been ἄνακτα, ἄνακτι, ἄνακτος. The presence or absence of digamma is metrically convenient. Achilles is twice ἄνακτι in this position. Ἄνακτα could have been used in the following two examples, but Homer was more concerned with context and precise prosaic meaning:

XXI 317–19
οὔτε τὰ τεύχεα καλά, τά που μάλα νειόθι λίμνης
κείσεθ' ὑπ' ἰλύος κεκαλυμμένα· <u>κὰδ δέ μιν αὐτὸν</u>
εἰλύσω ψαμάθοισιν ἅλις χέραδος περιχεύας

XXIV 472–73
τῇ ῥ' Ἀχιλεὺς ἵζεσκε Διὶ φίλος· <u>ἐν δέ μιν αὐτὸν</u>
εὗρ', ἕταροι δ' ἀπάνευθε καθήατο· τὼ δὲ δύ' οἴω.

Not only did he withhold ἄνακτα, but he even disregarded the metrically convenient proper name: κὰδ δ' Ἀχιλῆα and ἐν δ' Ἀχιλῆα.[1] Elision often makes unequal meters equivalent and gives the poet a choice of expressions. The mere fact of elision makes systematic composition unlikely.

In the last foot-and-a-half, Achilles is regularly Ἀχιλῆα. It is natural, however, that Thetis should take the liberty to substitute φίλον υἱόν for Ἀχιλῆα here. Indeed, she avoided *τίμησον μ' Ἀχιλῆα ὅς, in favor of

I 505

τίμησόν μοι υἱόν, ὃς ὠκυμορώτατος ἄλλων,

at the cost of hiatus and neglected digamma. Not even the regularity of Ἀχιλῆα proves fixed diction. Homer's simplicity is often that of nature, rather than that of art and artificial diction.

The abundant variety available in Homer's diction is demonstrated by the eight accusative expressions for Achilles in the last two feet of the verse:

Πηλεΐωνα
ποιμένα λαῶν
δήϊον ἄνδρα
ὃν φίλον υἱόν
ὄρχαμον ἀνδρῶν
ἄγριον ἄνδρα
ἀνέρα τοῦτον
οἷος ἐκεῖνος.

The plain name occurs three times and might have been standard in thrifty verse.

I 194–97

ἕλκετο δ' ἐκ κολεοῖο μέγα ξίφος, ἦλθε δ' Ἀθήνη
οὐρανόθεν· πρὸ γὰρ ἧκε θεὰ λευκώλενος "Ηρη
ἄμφω ὁμῶς θυμῷ φιλέουσά τε κηδομένη τε
στῆ δ' ὄπιθεν, ξανθῆς δὲ κόμης ἕλε <u>Πηλεΐωνα</u>.

Any of the eight expressions would fit the meter, for paragogic *nu*, like elision, often makes unique forms equivalent. Only Πηλεΐωνα however, clearly identifies behind which of ἄμφω she stood. On the other hand, if this was a traditional scene in a traditional epic, then the audience knew as well as the bard that Athena tweaked Achilles. An unambiguous ἕλεν ἄγριον ἄνδρα would have opportunely showed the force of tradition and the foreknowledge of the audience. Homer, however, composed as if the scene had to be made clear and the audience told whom she approached, lest even a moment's confusion should ensue.

XX 364–66

ὡς φάτ᾽ ἐποτρύνων· Τρώεσσι δὲ φαίδιμος Ἕκτωρ
κέκλεθ᾽ ὁμοκλήσας, φάτο δ᾽ ἴμμεναι ἄντ᾽ Ἀχιλῆος·
Τρῶες ὑπέρθυμοι, μὴ δείδιτε Πηλεΐωνα.

Homer has Hector use the direct name—as Hector would. There is
no mincing of words when Hector harangues the troops.

XXI 324–27

ἦ, καὶ ἐπῶρτ᾽ Ἀχιλῆϊ κυκώμενος, ὑψόσε θύων,
μορμύρων ἀφρῷ τε καὶ αἵματι, καὶ νεκύεσσι.
πορφύρεον δ᾽ ἄρα κῦμα διιπετέος ποταμοῖο
ἵστατ᾽ ἀειρόμενον, κατὰ δ᾽ ᾕρεε Πηλεΐωνα

XXI 313–14

ἵστη δὲ μέγα κῦμα, πολὺν δ᾽ ὀρυμαγδὸν ὄρινε
φιτρῶν καὶ λάων, ἵνα παύσομεν ἄγριον ἄνδρα.

Πηλεΐωνα occurs in circumstantial narrative, whereas ἄγριον ἄνδρα is
exclaimed in emotional rhetoric.

Systematic diction might have been expected to have a vocalic
counterpart for Πηλεΐωνα. Not only has Homer too many expressions for Achilles to suit a systematic economical diction, but he
also has one too few. The need for such a formula arises in the
following four passages, where Homer makes shift and never repeats
himself:

VI 99–100

οὐδ᾽ Ἀχιλῆα ποθ᾽ ὧδέ γ᾽ ἐδείδιμεν ὄρχαμον ἀνδρῶν,
ὅν πέρ φασι θεᾶς ἐξ ἔμμεναι· ἀλλ᾽ ὅδε λίην

XIX 4–5

εὗρε δὲ Πατρόκλῳ περικείμενον ὃν φίλον υἱόν,
κλαίοντα λιγέως· πολέες δ᾽ ἀμφ᾽ αὐτὸν ἑταῖροι

XXII 38

Ἕκτορ, μή μοι μίμνε, φίλον τέκος, ἀνέρα τοῦτον

XI 652–54

νῦν δὲ ἔπος ἐρέων πάλιν ἄγγελος εἰμ᾽ Ἀχιλῆϊ
εὖ δὲ σὺ οἶσθα, γεραιὲ διοτρεφές, οἷος ἐκεῖνος
δεινὸς ἀνήρ· τάχα κεν καὶ ἀναίτιον αἰτιόωτο.

It is incredible that traditional diction, after half a millennium of naming Achilles, should have left the bard to his own resources. Homer is equally capable of using generic metrical filler ὄρχαμον ἀνδρῶν, vivid description ἄγριον ἄνδρα, understated demonstratives ἀνέρα τοῦτον, familial reference ὃν φίλον υἱόν, and clausal substitution οἷος ἐκεῖνος. Another poet might easily have expressed himself differently:

> *φιτρῶν καὶ λάων, ἵνα παύσομεν ἀνέρα τοῦτον
>
> *οὐδ᾽ Ἀχιλῆα ποθ᾽ ὧδέ γ᾽ ἐδείδιμεν ἄγριον ἄνδρα
>
> *εὗρε δὲ Πατρόκλῳ περικείμενον ὄρχαμον ἀνδρῶν
>
> *Ἕκτορ, μή μοι μίμνε, φίλον τέκος, ἄγριον ἄνδρα
>
> *εὖ δὲ σὺ οἶσθα, γεραιὲ διοτρεφές, ἀνέρα κεῖνον.

It might have been still easier not to express *himself* but to insert whatever happened to be the traditional systematic expression:

> *φιτρῶν καὶ λάων, ἵνα παύσομεν Αἰακίδηα
>
> *οὐδ᾽ Ἀχιλῆα ποθ᾽ ὧδέ γ᾽ ἐδείδιμεν Αἰακίδηα
>
> *εὗρε δὲ Πατρόκλῳ περικείμενον Αἰακίδηα
>
> *Ἕκτορ, μή μοι μίμνε, φίλον τέκος, Αἰακίδηα
>
> *εὖ δὲ σὺ οἶσθα, γεραιὲ διοτρεφές, Αἰακίδηα.[2]

The consonantal counterparts of ὄρχαμον ἀνδρῶν and ἄγριον ἄνδρα are ποιμένα λαῶν and δήϊον ἄνδρα:

XIX 384–86

> πειρήθη δ᾽ ἕο αὐτοῦ ἐν ἔντεσι δῖος Ἀχιλλεύς,
>
> εἰ οἷ ἐφαρμόσσειε καὶ ἐντρέχοι ἀγλαὰ γυῖα·
>
> τῷ δ᾽ εὖτε πτερὰ γίγνετ᾽, ἄειρε δὲ <u>ποιμένα λαῶν</u>

XXII 84–85

> τῶν μνῆσαι, φίλε τέκνον, ἄμυνε δὲ <u>δήϊον ἄνδρα</u>
>
> τείχεος ἐντὸς ἐών, μηδὲ πρόμος ἵστασο τούτῳ.

Ποιμένα λαῶν serves as an extended pronoun. In different metrical circumstances, τῷ might have been answered by τόν. One can hardly translate otherwise than: *to him they became as wings and lifted him.* Alternatively, like other pronouns in Homer, it might have been left unsaid, and the sentence stopped after ἄειρε δέ. On the other hand, δήϊον ἄνδρα is clearly rhetorical, like τούτῳ in the next line. The absent name is forceful. If Πηλεΐωνα had occurred in both these cases, it could be attributed or imputed to traditional formulaic diction, and the *Iliad* would be the poorer. If Homer's diction is to be fully systematic, triple tables should be established throughout for the three distinct functions of Πηλεΐωνα, ποιμένα λαῶν and δήϊον ἄνδρα.

If superfluity in systematic traditional diction is suspect, so is deficiency. Homer has no full noun-epithet formula for accusatival Achilles after the hephthemimeral caesura. Even vestiges of the antique style are meager: a prepositional phrase and a name deprived of its epithet.

XVIII 68–69

ἀκτὴν εἰσανέβαινον ἐπισχερώ, ἔνθα θαμειαὶ
Μυρμιδόνων εἴρυντο νέες <u>ταχὺν ἀμφ' Ἀχιλῆα</u>

XXIV 433–34

πειρᾷ ἐμεῖο, γεραιέ, νεωτέρου, οὐδέ με πείσεις,
ὅς με κέλεαι σέο δῶρα παρὲξ <u>Ἀχιλῆα</u> δέχεσθαι.

If even these, however, should be referred to heroic prepositional phrases filling the second hemistich of the verse, namely πόδας ταχὺν ἀμφ' Ἀχιλῆα (XVIII 354) and *παρὲξ Ἀχιλῆα ἄνακτα, then nothing at all remains for the hephthemimeral caesura.

Analogy makes noun-epithet phrases easy to formulate:

*Ἀχιλῆα ἄνακτα
*ἥρω' Ἀχιλῆα
*βασιλῆ' Ἀχιλῆα
*κρείοντ' Ἀχιλῆα.[3]

They are as easy to use as they are to make:

IX 224

πλησάμενος δ' οἴνοιο δέπας δείδεκτ' <u>Ἀχιλῆα</u>
*πλησάμενος δ' οἴνοιο δέπας βασιλῆ' Ἀχιλῆα
χρυσείῳ δέπαϊ δειδίσκετο φώνησέν τε[4]

XI 805

βῆ δὲ θέειν παρὰ νῆας ἐπ' <u>Αἰακίδην Ἀχιλῆα</u>
*βῆ δὲ θέειν παρὰ νῆας ἐπὶ κρείοντ' Ἀχιλῆα

XXIV 629

ἤτοι Δαρδανίδης Πρίαμος θαύμαζ' Ἀχιλῆα
*ἤτοι Δαρδανίδης θαύμαζ' ἥρω' Ἀχιλῆα
*ἤτοι Δαρδανίδης θαύμαζ' Ἀχιλῆα ἄνακτα.

Homer apparently found it as easy to compose without such formulae.

While the preceding principal type of noun-epithet formula is lacking in Homer, the despised three-footer appears in three forms:

XI 805

βῆ δὲ θέειν παρὰ νῆας ἐπ' Αἰακίδην Ἀχιλῆα

XXIV 337–38

ὣς ἄγαγ', ὣς μήτ' ἄρ τις ἴδῃ μήτ' ἄρ τε νοήσῃ
τῶν ἄλλων Δαναῶν, πρὶν Πηλεΐωνάδ' ἱκέσθαι

XIII 347–50

Ζεὺς μέν ῥα Τρώεσσι καὶ Ἕκτορι βούλετο νίκην
κυδαίνων Ἀχιλῆα πόδας ταχύν· οὐδέ τι πάμπαν
ἤθελε λαὸν ὀλέσθαι Ἀχαϊκὸν Ἰλιόθι πρό,
ἀλλὰ Θέτιν κύδαινε καὶ υἱέα καρτερόθυμον.

The second passage indicates that there was probably a consonantal counterpart of Αἰακίδην Ἀχιλῆα: perhaps *Πηλεΐωνα ἄνακτα or *Πηλεΐων' Ἀχιλῆα or more likely *Πηλεΐδην Ἀχιλῆα. Homer might have sung in full style

*τῶν ἄλλων Δαναῶν, πρὶν Πηλεΐδην Ἀχιλῆα
ἴκειν ἄνδρα φέριστον ὃν ἀθάνατοί περ ἔτεισαν.

He could doubtless express the idea in few or many feet, with or without embellishments and associations, succinctly or amply.

The third passage contributes to the problem and to the solution of equivalence. Υἱέα καρτερόθυμον can represent Achilles only in a context of this sort. Αἰακίδην Ἀχιλῆα can represent Achilles regardless of context, and it would have been, for traditional poetry, the unique systematic noun-epithet formula for accusatival Achilles in the last three feet of the verse. Nevertheless, Homer was capable of regarding as frigid or inexpressive the line

*ἀλλὰ Θέτιν κύδαινε καὶ Αἰακίδην Ἀχιλῆα.

For him at least, it was not sufficient to drone the formula for Achilles and sing on. For a bard oblivious to the vernacular meanings of formulaic words, *Αἰακίδην Ἀχιλῆα* would have been satisfactory here. Homer required various ways of referring to Achilles in a given meter. Distinguishing the appropriateness of a variety of phrases is associated with deliberate literate composition. Homer shows semantic sensitivity rather than deterministic convenience. *Αἰακίδην Ἀχιλῆα* and *υἱέα καρτερόθυμον* are equivalent only if each does nothing more than identify Achilles.

After the tritotrochaic caesura, systematic simplicity requires *ἀμύμονα Πηλεΐωνα* and *ποδώκεα Πηλεΐωνα* and nothing more. Since Homer has each of these ten times, it might be imagined that he uses them habitually and heedlessly. The many violations of thrifty simplicity, however, show this to be untrue.

If *ἀμύμονα Πηλεΐωνα* had occurred in the following six passages, one might have more confidence in the forceful influence of the tradition and the hexameter and in the feeble influence of simple-minded bards.

VIII 370–72

> νῦν δ᾽ ἐμὲ μὲν στυγέει, Θέτιδος δ᾽ ἐξήνυσε βουλάς,
> ἥ οἱ γούνατ᾽ ἔκυσσε καὶ ἔλλαβε χειρὶ γενείου,
> λισσομένη τιμῆσαι Ἀχιλῆα πτολίπορθον

XV 76–77

> ἤματι τῷ ὅτ᾽ ἐμεῖο θεὰ Θέτις ἥψατο γούνων,
> λισσομένη τιμῆσαι Ἀχιλῆα πτολίπορθον.

In these two passages, the presence of a goddess-mother eclipses the blameless patronymical formula, *ἀμύμονα Πηλεΐωνα*. Peleides is often just another name for Achilles; in this context, however, it would evidently bear an unwanted connotation: Peleus' son. Here is a notable proof that words enshrined in formulae do not cease to be ordinary words capable of ordinary meanings, at least in Homer. Bards and their audiences are supposed to be indifferent to such fastidiousness. Penelope's *heavy hand* wants comparison with Thetis' *Peleides*. In this case, *ἀμύμονα Πηλεΐωνα* is unequal to its equivalent *Ἀχιλῆα πτολίπορθον*.

It is probably reasonable to assume that Homer, as is the wont of human beings, was sometimes sensitive and sometimes insensitive.

The same applies to Homer's audience, both then and now: Homerists are both sensitive and insensitive. Parry considers the audience singular: one ear, one mind. This is certainly not the case now; nor is it likely to have been the case then. We often misunderstand the ambiguities of art. Unclarity is a fact of life. The classical Hellenic penchant for clarity is a response to (and so a proof of) a state of unclarity. Parry's thinking his way back into the minds of Homer's audience is *not* a guarantee of a clear, unambiguous picture of Homer. Both ambiguity and clarity are essential in art and in the audience's appreciation of art.

XXI 544–50

> ἔνθα κεν ὑψίπυλον <u>Τροίην</u> ἕλον υἷες Ἀχαιῶν,
> εἰ μὴ Ἀπόλλων Φοῖβος Ἀγήνορα δῖον ἀνῆκε
>
> ·
>
> αὐτὰρ ὅ γ' ὡς ἐνόησεν Ἀχιλλῆα πτολίπορθον, / ἔστη.

This passage shows πτολίπορθον as a significant epithet: the Achaeans and *city-sacking Achilles* nearly sacked Troy. Homer had his choice of three metrically equivalent formulae. Neither *ἐνόησεν ἀμύμονα Πηλεΐωνα nor *ἐνόησε ποδώκεα Πηλεΐωνα suited the context and the poet as well as did ἐνόησεν Ἀχιλλῆα πτολίπορθον. This could more credibly be regarded as a fortuitous analogical formation if it were not so apt.

IX 109–11

> · · · · · · · σὺ δὲ σῷ μεγαλήτορι θυμῷ
> εἴξας ἄνδρα φέριστον, ὃν ἀθάνατοί περ ἔτεισαν,
> ἠτίμησας· ἑλὼν γὰρ ἔχεις γέρας· ἀλλ' ἔτι καὶ νῦν

XVIII 54–56

> ὤ μοι ἐγὼ δειλή, ὤ μοι δυσαριστοτόκεια,
> ἥ τ' ἐπεὶ ἄρ τέκον υἱὸν <u>ἀμύμονά τε κρατερόν τε</u>
> ἔξοχον ἡρώων· ὁ δ' ἀνέδραμεν ἔρνεϊ ἶσος

XXII 418

> λίσσωμ' ἀνέρα τοῦτον ἀτάσθαλον ὀβριμοεργόν.[5]

In these three examples, three pertinent phrases preempt the proprietary place of simple-minded ἀμύμονα Πηλεΐωνα. Homer has doubtless gone to some trouble with extraordinary phrases, although the formulaic tradition must have condoned, or rather commended, the bard who parroted familiar parlance:

Nestor's

*ἄνδρα φέριστον, ἀμύμονα Πηλεΐωνα / ἠτίμησας,

Thetis'

*ἐπεὶ ἄρ τέκον υἱόν, ἀμύμονα Πηλεΐωνα,

and Priam's

*λίσσωμ' ἀνέρα τοῦτον, ἀμύμονα Πηλεΐωνα.

Familiar formulae facilitate oral composition-performance; Homer's disuse of them is a sign of leisurely literacy.

When, instead of a vowel, a consonant is needed after the caesura, ποδώκεα Πηλεΐωνα is used and disused.

XVIII 63
ἀλλ' εἶμ', ὄφρα ἴδωμι φίλον τέκος, ἠδ' ἐπακούσω.

Thetis has special unartificial diction for Achilles. This complicates composition, for the same idea in another context would have to be expressed differently:

*ἀλλ' εἶμ', ὄφρα ἴδωμι ποδώκεα Πηλεΐωνα.

Homer resists the impulse to use the formula that would seem uncouth or incongruous in context.

II 239–40
ὃς καὶ νῦν Ἀχιλῆα, ἕο μέγ' ἀμείνονα φῶτα
ἠτίμησεν· ἑλὼν γὰρ ἔχει γέρας, αὐτὸς ἀπούρας

IX 110–11
εἴξας ἄνδρα φέριστον, ὃν ἀθάνατοί περ ἔτεισαν,
ἠτίμησας· ἑλὼν γὰρ ἔχεις γέρας· ἀλλ' ἔτι καὶ νῦν.

Homer is both imitative and unimitative. Nestor's and Thersites' ἠτίμησεν· ἑλὼν γὰρ ἔχει γέρας are alike. But Nestor's ὃν ἀθάνατοί περ ἔτεισαν is unlike taunting Thersites, and Thersites' ἕο μέγ' ἀμείνονα φῶτα is unlike tactful Nestor. Convenient formulae are like and unlike Homer:

*ὃς καὶ νῦν Ἀχιλῆα, ποδώκεα Πηλεΐωνα

*εἴξας ἄνδρα φέριστον, ἀμύμονα Πηλεΐωνα.

XI 771–72

ἔνθα δ᾽ ἔπειθ᾽ ἥρωα Μενοίτιον εὕρομεν ἔνδον
ἠδὲ σέ, πὰρ δ᾽ Ἀχιλῆα· γέρων δ᾽ ἱππηλάτα Πηλεύς.

Instead of grand heroic style and ample formulaic diction, for example,

*ἠδὲ σέ, πὰρ δ᾽ Ἀχιλῆα ποδώκεα Πηλεΐωνα· / Πηλεύς,

the careless juxtaposition of Πηλεΐωνα and Πηλεύς, which might indicate formulaic poetry, is avoided. Indeed, the grand formula never occurs in Homer. Of the fifteen times that Ἀχιλῆα stands before the caesura, nine times no epithet follows it. Six times an epithet follows: three times πόδας ταχύν, twice πελώριον, and once δαΐφρονα. Ἀχιλῆα ποδώκεα Πηλεΐωνα would have conveniently filled the line, making the verse the unit of thought.

XIII 348

    κυδαίνων Ἀχιλῆα πόδας ταχύν· οὐδέ τι πάμπαν

*κυδαίνων Ἀχιλῆα ποδώκεα Πηλεΐωνα·
οὐδέ τι πάμπαν

XVIII 30

    ἔδραμον ἀμφ᾽ Ἀχιλῆα δαΐφρονα, χερσὶ δὲ πᾶσαι

*ἔδραμον ἀμφ᾽ Ἀχιλῆα ποδώκεα Πηλεΐωνα·
χερσὶ δὲ πᾶσαι

XXI 527

    ἐς δ᾽ ἐνόησ᾽ Ἀχιλῆα πελώριον· αὐτὰρ ὑπ᾽ αὐτοῦ

*ἐς δ᾽ ἐνόησ᾽ Ἀχιλῆα ποδώκεα Πηλεΐωνα·
αὐτὰρ ὑπ᾽ αὐτοῦ.

Instead of the convenience of a line-ending formula, Homer prefers to stop his sentence after the fourth foot. The final epithet, however, still cannot be sung before the composition of the last two feet determines whether the inevitable fixed epithet was one ending in a vowel—δαΐφρονα—or one ending in a consonant—πόδας ταχύς, πελώριον. And then, moreover, Homer must still have had time to decide between ornamental πόδας ταχύν and significant πελώριον. Homer's composition must have been dilatory. Rapidity might be served by dropping the epithet after Ἀχιλῆα:

XIX 151

 ὥς κέ τις αὖτ' Ἀχιλῆα μετὰ πρώτοισιν ἴδηται

 *ὥς κέ τις αὖτ' Ἀχιλῆα ποδώκεα Πηλεΐωνα

 ἐν πρώτοισι ἴδηται.

Then, the composition of the second hemistich determines whether the inevitable fixed epithet was needed or not. But a noun without an epithet is not a full formula nor ample heroic style. Noun-epithet formulae are optionally used, half-used, and disused.

Formulaic poetry should show neither excessive wealth of diction after the tritotrochaic caesura nor abject poverty of diction after the penthemimeral caesura. Homeric diction is without a noun-epithet formula for accusatival Achilles filling the meter between the penthemimeral caesura and the end of the verse. Homer forgoes the convenience of the obvious phrase *ῥηξήνορα Πηλεΐωνα.

VII 228

 καὶ μετ' Ἀχιλλῆα ῥηξήνορα θυμολέοντα

XVI 146

 τὸν μετ' Ἀχιλλῆα ῥηξήνορα τῖε μάλιστα

XXI 138, 250

 δῖον Ἀχιλλῆα, Τρώεσσι δὲ λοιγὸν ἀλάλκοι

XVI 271

 ὡς ἂν Πηλεΐδην τιμήσομεν, ὃς μέγ' ἄριστος

IX 191

 δέγμενος Αἰακίδην, ὁπότε λήξειεν ἀείδων.

If ῥηξήνορα θυμολέοντα was a regular formula for Achilles, it would regularly follow Ἀχιλλῆα and even Πηλεΐδην and Αἰακίδην. Homer uses all, part, or none of the phrase. Integrity should be characteristic of formulae, or they must remain words that can be strung together.

Even heroic ῥηξήνορα θυμολέοντα does not escape equivalence:

XX 45–46
δειδιότας, ὅθ᾽ ὁρῶντο ποδώκεα Πηλεΐωνα
τεύχεσι λαμπόμενον, <u>βροτολοιγῷ ἶσον Ἄρηϊ</u>.

Another poet might have interchanged the two phrases. They are so similar that both would not be necessary in thrifty composition. In Homer, however, it can happen that neither phrase is suitable, and another epithet is used instead:

XXIV 540
ἀλλ᾽ ἕνα παῖδα τέκεν <u>παναώριον·</u> οὐδέ νυ τόν γε.

In a different context, meaning or convenience might cause Homer to use full formulae:

*ἀλλ᾽ ἕνα παῖδα τέκε ῥηξήνορα θυμολέοντα
*ἀλλ᾽ ἕνα παῖδα τέκε βροτολοιγῷ ἶσον Ἄρηϊ.

Finally, Homer's meager circumlocution for Achilles,

XXI 308–10
φίλε κασίγνητε, <u>σθένος ἀνέρος</u> ἀμφότεροί περ
σχῶμεν, ἐπεὶ τάχα ἄστυ μέγα Πριάμοιο ἄνακτος | ἐκπέρσει,[6]

can easily be given convenient, heroic, noun-epithet style:

*φίλε κασίγνητε, ῥηξήνορα Πηλεΐωνα
σχῶμεν, ἐπεὶ τάχα ἄστυ μέγα Πριάμοιο ἄνακτος | ἐκπέρσει.

Homer provides considerable evidence against economy and extension of formulaic diction.

Before the penthemimeral caesura, there is the rare occurrence of a unique noun-epithet formula in Homer. Δῖον Ἀχιλλῆα recurs in a repeated line:

XXI 138, 250
δῖον Ἀχιλλῆα, Τρώεσσι δὲ λοιγὸν ἀλάλκοι.

Nethertheless, the improvising bard, who must compose the first hemistich before the second, will be obliged to look for a word with an initial double consonant to begin the second hemistich; whereas a literate poet, who can compose in any order he pleases, might first have conceived Τρώεσσι and then filled in the convenient formula for

Achilles. Something like *δῖον Πηλεΐδην or *ἄλκιμον Αἰακίδην must have been the generally convenient noun-epithet formula in traditional formulaic composition.

Δῖον Ἀχιλλῆα might reasonably be regarded as traditional if it was the curtailment of a whole-verse formula:

*δῖον Ἀχιλλῆα ῥηξήνορα Πηλείωνα.

Neither this, however, nor *δῖον Πηλεΐδην is allowed to be a simply convenient, unpoignant formula when Thetis speaks of Achilles:

XVIII 55–56
> ἥ τ' ἐπεὶ ἂρ τέκον υἱὸν ἀμύμονά τε κρατερόν τε,
> ἔξοχον ἡρώων· ὁ δ' ἀνέδραμεν ἔρνεϊ ἶσος

XVIII 436–37
> υἱὸν ἐπεί μοι δῶκε γενέσθαι τε τραφέμεν τε,
> ἔξοχον ἡρώων· ὁ δ' ἀνέδραμεν ἔρνεϊ ἶσος.

A systematic bard might have reproduced the traditional noun-epithet formula for Achilles:

*δῖον Πηλεΐδην· ὁ δ' ἀνέδραμεν ἔρνεϊ ἶσος

or δῖον Ἀχιλλῆα and a metrical problem to begin the second hemistich. Homer's ἔξοχον ἡρώων can serve only in special circumstances: pronominal allusion or epithetic extension. Unlike performer-composers, Homer was willing and able to spend time determining the suitable phrase for the context.

I 509–10
> τόφρα δ' ἐπὶ Τρώεσσι τίθει κράτος, ὄφρ' ἂν Ἀχαιοὶ
> υἱὸν ἐμὸν τείσωσιν ὀφέλλωσίν τέ ἑ τιμῇ
> *δῖον Πηλεΐδην τείσωσί τε δῶσί τε τιμήν

displays the same careful choice of good form and rejection of bad formula as is characteristic of Homer. Compare also

I 505
> τίμησόν μοι υἱόν, ὃς ὠκυμορώτατος ἄλλων
> *δῖον Πηλεΐδην τίμησον, ποιμένα λαῶν

XXIV 492

ὄψεσθαι φίλον υἱὸν ἀπὸ Τροίηθεν ἰόντα

*δῖον Πηλεΐδην ὄψεσθαι δήϊον ἄνδρα.

Before the tritotrochaic caesura also, there is a unique noun-epithet formula, and this one might have been of general use: *Πηλεΐδην Ἀχιλῆα*. Nevertheless, Homer generally does not use it; for it occurs only once:

XXIII 541–42

εἰ μὴ ἄρ' Ἀντίλοχος μεγαθύμου Νέστορος υἱὸς

Πηλεΐδην Ἀχιλῆα δίκῃ ἠμείψατ' ἀναστάς.

Nor is it certain that it would have occurred even here if the epithets of Antilochus and Nestor did not call for a balancing epithet of Achilles. Imbalance alters the emphasis:

εἰ μὴ ἄρ' Ἀντίλοχος μεγαθύμου Νέστορος υἱὸς

*Νεστορίδης Ἀχιλῆα δίκῃ ἠμείψατ' ἀναστάς

*τοῦ Νηληϊάδαο δίκῃ ἠμείψατ' ἄνακτα

*τοῦ Νηληϊάδαο δίκῃ ἠμείψατ' ἀναστάς.

Πηλεΐδην Ἀχιλῆα was not a cohesive unit:

XXIII 40–41

ἀμφὶ πυρὶ στῆσαν τρίποδα μέγαν, εἰ πεπίθοιεν

Πηλεΐδην λούσασθαι ἄπο βρότον αἱματόεντα

*Πηλεΐδην Ἀχιλῆα λοέσσαι ὕδατι λευκῷ

*Πηλεΐδην Ἀχιλῆα λοέσσαι τε χρῖσαί τε.

An integral formula defends its own space in the verse.

A comparison of the great variety of ways in which Homer expresses the idea *Achilles* before the caesura with the single use of a noun-epithet formula shows the relative unimportance of the latter device in Homeric composition:

Πηλεΐδην Ἀχιλῆα

– ∪ ∪ τόν γε ἄνακτα

– ∪ ∪ ἄνδρα φέριστον

– ∪ ∪ ἀνέρα τοῦτον

– ∪ σέ, Πηλέος υἱέ

$- \cup \cup - \phi\acute{\iota}\lambda o\nu\ \upsilon\acute{\iota}\acute{o}\nu$

$- \cup \cup - \mathring{A}\chi\iota\lambda\mathring{\eta}\alpha$

$- \cup \cup - \cup\ \mathring{\alpha}\rho\iota\sigma\tau o\nu$

$- \cup \cup - (\mu o\iota)\ \upsilon\acute{\iota}\acute{o}\nu$

$- \cup \cup - \cup \cup\ \kappa\epsilon\mathring{\iota}\nu o\nu$

$\upsilon\mathring{\iota}\grave{o}\nu\ \mathring{\epsilon}\mu\acute{o}\nu\ \cup \cup - \cup$

$- \mathring{A}\chi\iota\lambda\mathring{\eta}\alpha\ \cup - \cup$

$\tau o\mathring{\upsilon}\tau o\nu\ \cup - \cup \cup - \cup$

$\alpha\mathring{\upsilon}\tau\acute{o}\nu\ \cup - \cup \cup - \cup.$

These expressions seem rather like particular significant words than generalized formulae.

XX 2

> $\mathring{\alpha}\mu\phi\grave{\iota}\ \sigma\acute{\epsilon},\ \Pi\eta\lambda\acute{\epsilon}os\ \upsilon\acute{\iota}\acute{\epsilon},\ \mu\acute{\alpha}\chi\eta s\ \mathring{\alpha}\kappa\acute{o}\rho\eta\tau o\nu\ \mathring{A}\chi\alpha\iota o\acute{\iota}$
>
> *$\mathring{\alpha}\mu\phi$' $\mathring{A}\chi\iota\lambda\mathring{\eta}\alpha\ \mathring{\alpha}\nu\alpha\kappa\tau\alpha\ \mu\acute{\alpha}\chi\eta s\ \mathring{\alpha}\kappa\acute{o}\rho\eta\tau o\nu\ \mathring{A}\chi\alpha\iota o\acute{\iota}.$

If there was a traditional prepositional formula, it probably would not have been Homer's. His apostrophe is not required by the metre.[7]

IX 110

> $\epsilon\mathring{\iota}\xi\alpha s\ \underline{\mathring{\alpha}\nu\delta\rho\alpha\ \phi\acute{\epsilon}\rho\iota\sigma\tau o\nu},\ \mathring{o}\nu\ \mathring{\alpha}\theta\acute{\alpha}\nu\alpha\tau o\acute{\iota}\ \pi\epsilon\rho\ \mathring{\epsilon}\tau\epsilon\iota\sigma\alpha\nu$
>
> *$\epsilon\mathring{\iota}\xi\alpha s\ \Pi\eta\lambda\acute{\epsilon}os\ \upsilon\acute{\iota}\acute{o}\nu,\ \mathring{o}\nu\ \mathring{\alpha}\theta\acute{\alpha}\nu\alpha\tau o\acute{\iota}\ \pi\epsilon\rho\ \mathring{\epsilon}\tau\epsilon\iota\sigma\alpha\nu.$

Here Homer prefers an allusive expression.

XXIII 35

> $\alpha\mathring{\upsilon}\tau\grave{\alpha}\rho\ \underline{\tau\acute{o}\nu\ \gamma\epsilon\ \mathring{\alpha}\nu\alpha\kappa\tau\alpha\ \pi o\delta\acute{\omega}\kappa\epsilon\alpha\ \Pi\eta\lambda\epsilon\mathring{\iota}\omega\nu\alpha}$
>
> *$\alpha\mathring{\upsilon}\tau\grave{\alpha}\rho\ \mathring{A}\chi\iota\lambda\lambda\mathring{\eta}\alpha\ \mathring{\rho}\eta\xi\acute{\eta}\nu o\rho\alpha\ \theta\upsilon\mu o\lambda\acute{\epsilon}o\nu\tau\alpha.$

The two long expressions for Achilles are metrically equivalent although the latter is longer by a mora. The latter, which does occur at VII 228, was not repeated here, apparently because the present context of conciliation makes the epithets $\mathring{\rho}\eta\xi\acute{\eta}\nu o\rho\alpha\ \theta\upsilon\mu o\lambda\acute{\epsilon}o\nu\tau\alpha$ unapt. Another poet might have appreciated the implied contrast; a third might have cared only to fill the meter.

Homeric diction consists *partially* of repeated phrases that can easily be registered in tables and given the appearance of a system. This much can be established by perusing the concordances. For the other part, one must read the texts. Here are found numerous cases in which Homer did not repeat systematic formulaic diction. For example, with twenty-one occurrences of

αὐτὰρ ἐπεὶ πόσιος καὶ ἐδητύος ἐξ ἔρον ἕντο,

Homer really should not have bothered to compose

vi 99
αὐτὰρ ἐπεὶ σίτου τάρφθεν δμῳαί τε καὶ αὐτή.

Sacrificing a familiar formula for this trivial circumstantial rendering is precisely what distinguishes unformulaic from formulaic poetry. In the same way, useful heroic formulae for Achilles are disregarded and a variety of expressions take their places.

VI

Unique and Equivalent Formulae for Achilles: Vocative Case

The vocative Ἀχιλλεῦ without an epithet occurs in Homer eight times. One passage demonstrates composition both with and without an epithet:

xxiv 72–76

> ἠῶθεν δή τοι λέγομεν λεύκ' ὀστέ', <u>Ἀχιλλεῦ</u>
>
> . . . .
>
> ἐν τῷ τοι κεῖται λεύκ' ὀστέα, <u>φαίδιμ' Ἀχιλλεῦ.</u>

Repetition of formulae implies systematic composition:

> *ἠῶθεν λέγομεν λεύκ' ὀστέα, φαίδιμ' Ἀχιλλεῦ.

Schmidt's *Parallel-Homer* might easily have been a fatter tome. In Homer's verse, composition seems to proceed word by word with an occasional familiar phrase, rather than by a series of forced formulae in standard hexametric positions.

In the same way, Homer can compose a dispensable verb and dispense with a noun-epithet formula:

XVI 29

> ἕλκε' ἀκειόμενοι· σὺ δ' ἀμήχανος ἔπλευ, <u>Ἀχιλλεῦ</u>
>
> *ἕλκε' ἀκειόμενοι· σὺ δ' ἀμήχανος, ὄβριμ' Ἀχιλλεῦ.

Homer avoids an awkward succession of nominative and vocative cases that would have convicted him of unpremeditated formulaic composition.

109

Φαίδιμ᾽ Ἀχιλλεῦ and ὄβριμ᾽ Ἀχιλλεῦ are an obvious pair of systematic noun-epithet formulae that were meant to facilitate versification. Homer again fails the test of thrifty composition:

XXI 221
ἀλλ᾽ ἄγε δὴ καὶ ἔασον· ἄγη μ᾽ ἔχει, ὄρχαμε λαῶν.

Inadvertent use of a generic vocative formula by analogy, instead of exculpating the formulary bard, might show that he has no full command of the systematic names for Achilles. Intentional disuse of ὄβριμ᾽ Ἀχιλλεῦ to avoid a jingle with ἄγη μ᾽ ἔχει is rather within the special competence of premeditative poets. Verses composed of formulae juxtaposed only for their essential ideas might often have been a jangling affair.

Homer's use of this vocative can cause enjambement of an essential phrase that might otherwise easily have been incorporated into a whole-line formula, which is the fundamental form in traditional versification:

IX 434
εἰ μὲν δὴ νόστον γε μετὰ φρεσὶ, φαίδιμ᾽ Ἀχιλλεῦ,
βάλλεαι

*εἰ μὲν δὴ νόστον γε μετὰ φρεσὶ σῇσι μενοινᾷς.[1]

In fact, Homer probably chose φαίδιμ᾽ Ἀχιλλεῦ here for the meaning of the epithet. A disaffected speaker might have been made to say less courteously

*εἰ μὲν δὴ νόστον γε μετὰ φρεσὶ σῇσι, Ἀχιλλεῦ,
βάλλεαι.

Asteropaeus begins and ends his speech with vocative formulae:

XXI 153-60
Πηλεΐδη μεγάθυμε, τίη γενεὴν ἐρεείνεις;
. . . .
γείνασθαι· νῦν αὖτε μαχώμεθα, φαίδιμ᾽ Ἀχιλλεῦ.

Without the printed page or premeditation, he might have said

*γείνασθαι· νῦν αὖτε μαχώμεθα νηλέϊ χαλκῷ.

Homer can also show the meaning of formulae by their absence:

I 173

φεῦγε μάλ’, εἴ τοι θυμὸς ἐπέσσυται, οὐδέ σ’ ἔγωγε

*φεῦγε μάλ’. εἴ τοι θυμὸς ἐπέσσυται, ὄβριμ’ Ἀχιλλεῦ.

Respect and respectful formulae are here withheld.

Whereas vocatival Achilles after the bucolic diaeresis demonstrates deliberate artistry rather than systematic composition, the single expression that follows the hephthemimeral caesura counters the idea of formulaic systems in another way. As formulae are supposed to solve metrical problems, three are required: initial vowel, initial consonant, initial double consonant. Homer displays the problem rather than the solution:

I 131, XIX 155

μὴ δὴ οὕτως, ἀγαθός περ ἐών, <u>θεοείκελ’ Ἀχιλλεῦ.</u>

Traditional diction has failed to provide an expression beginning with a vowel, or Homer was not a traditional poet:

*μὴ δὴ οὕτως, ἀγαθός περ ἐών, Ἀχιλεῦ μεγάθυμε

would have avoided overlengthening.

Μέγα φέρτατ’ Ἀχαιῶν, although metrically equivalent to θεοείκελ’ Ἀχιλλεῦ, occurs only in a whole-verse formula repeated three times:

XVI 21, XIX 216, xi 478

ὦ Ἀχιλεῦ, Πηλῆος υἱέ, <u>μέγα φέρτατ’ Ἀχαιῶν.</u>[2]

If μέγα φέρτατ’ Ἀχαιῶν was sufficient in itself to represent Achilles, another equivalency would be the result. Since μέγα φέρτατ’ Ἀχαιῶν is insufficient in itself to represent Achilles, he must not have been formulaically and traditionally *the very best of the Achaeans.*

The vocatives for Achilles that follow the tritotrochaic caesura show that Homer does not see formulae blindly. Θεοῖς ἐπιείκελ’ Ἀχιλλεῦ, which occurs six times, evidently qualifies as the traditional systematic noun-epithet formula used "without second thought as the natural means of getting his idea into verse." The essential idea is Ἀχιλλεῦ, whereas θεοῖς ἐπιείκελ’ "is purely for the sake of style."[3]

XXII 214-16

Πηλεΐωνα δ' ἵκανε θεὰ γλαυκῶπις Ἀθήνη
ἀγχοῦ δ' ἱσταμένη ἔπεα πτερόντα προσηύδα·
νῦν δὴ νῶι ἔολπα, Διὶ φίλε φαίδιμ' Ἀχιλλεῦ.

Godlike Achilles does not trip off the tongue of goddess Athena. Under the circumstances Achilles is more aptly *dear to Zeus*. The epithet implies that Achilles will win the duel with Hector, who until now has been signally *dear to Zeus*.[4] If θεοῖς ἐπιείκελ' provides the unwanted meaning, it is therefore not meaningless.

The formula θεοῖς ἐπιείκελ' Ἀχιλλεῦ yields not only to a significant noun-epithet phrase but also to other expressions for Achilles that begin at the caesura.

IX 437

πῶς ἂν ἔπειτ' ἀπὸ σεῖο, φίλον τέκος, αὖθι λιποίμην

IX 444

ὡς ἂν ἔπειτ' ἀπὸ σεῖο, φίλον τέκος, οὐκ ἐθέλοιμι / λείπεσθ'

IX 601

ἐνταῦθα τρέψειε, φίλος· κάκιον δέ κεν εἴη.

In the first two examples, Phoenix refers to Achilles as his *own dear son* whom he raised from the time he was a boy:

IX 440-41

νήπιον, οὔ πω εἰδόθ' ὁμοιΐου πολέμοιο
οὐδ' ἀγορέων, ἵνα τ' ἄνδρες ἀριπρεπέες τελέθουσι.

How could I leave *my boy?* is apt in this context. How could I leave *godlike Achilles?* better suits a passage in which godliness is germane: How could I leave my *godlike defender?* Such a passage occurs later in Phoenix' speech:

IX 485

καί σε τοσοῦτον ἔθηκα, θεοῖς ἐπιείκελ' Ἀχιλλεῦ

IX 493-95

τὰ φρονέων, ὅ μοι οὔ τι θεοὶ γόνον ἐξετέλειον
ἐξ ἐμεῦ· ἀλλὰ σὲ παῖδα, θεοῖς ἐπιείκελ' Ἀχιλλεῦ
ποιεύμην, ἵνα μοί ποτ' ἀεικέα λοιγὸν ἀμύνῃς.

Τοσοῦτον is explained by the significant formulaic epithet in epexegesis. Phoenix made Achilles *godlike* in order to have a godlike defender. At the end of the same speech, there might have been a clash of gods if Homer had not avoided θεοῖς ἐπιείκελ' Ἀχιλλεῦ:

IX 600–601

   ἀλλὰ σὺ μή μοι ταῦτα νόει φρεσί, μηδέ σε <u>δαίμων</u>
   ἐνταῦθα τρέψειε, <u>φίλος</u>· κάκιον δέ κεν εἴη
  *ἐνταῦθα τρέψειε, θεοῖς ἐπιείκελ' Ἀχιλλεῦ.

In these three instances, the formulary bard could have demonstrated the habitual repetition of a unique formula for Achilles and proved himself careless of context. Homer has done the contrary; avoidance of formulae is common practice.

XXIII 626–27

   ναὶ δὴ ταῦτά γε πάντα, <u>τέκος</u>, κατὰ μοῖραν ἔειπες·
   οὐ γὰρ ἔτ' ἔμπεδα γυῖα, <u>φίλος</u>, πόδες, οὐδέ τι χεῖρες.

Nestor's use of τέκος and φίλος sets a tone of informal familiarity that suits the context. Compare the different tone of

  *ναὶ δὴ ταῦτά γε πάντα, θεοῖς ἐπιείκελ' Ἀχιλλεῦ,
   οὐ γὰρ ἔτ' ἔμπεδα γυῖα, θεοῖς ἐπιείκελ' Ἀχιλλεῦ.

XXI 74–75

   γουνοῦμαί σ', Ἀχιλεῦ· σὺ δέ μ' αἴδεο καί μ' ἐλέησον·
   ἀντί τοί εἰμ' ἱκέταο, <u>διοτρεφές</u>, αἰδοίοιο.

Διοτρεφές is preferred to a repeated Ἀχιλλεῦ, which would have facilitated versification:

  *ἀντί τοί εἰμ' ἱκέταο, θεοῖς ἐπιείκελ' Ἀχιλλεῦ.

Priam's first speech to Achilles begins with the full formality of a long vocative formula:

XXIV 486

   μνῆσαι πατρὸς σοῖο, <u>θεοῖς ἐπιείκελ' Ἀχιλλεῦ</u>.

In his succeeding speeches to Achilles, the generic διοτρεφές marks the second stage of conversation and acquaintance:

XXIV 553

   μή πώ μ' ἐς θρόνον ἷζε, <u>διοτρεφές</u>, ὄφρα κεν Ἕκτωρ

XXIV 635

λέξον νῦν με τάχιστα, <u>διοτρεφές</u>, ὄφρα καὶ ἤδη.

The last stage is plain unepitheted *Ἀχιλεῦ:*

XXIV 661

ὧδέ κέ μοι ῥέζων, Ἀχιλεῦ, κεχαρισμένα θείης.

It would doubtless have been more convenient to express the essential idea *Achilles* with a unique formula rather than with Homer's variety of names.

It is not clear from Homer what might have been the unique traditional noun-epithet formula for vocatival Achilles after the penthemimeral caesura. Πάντων ἐκπαγλότατ' ἀνδρῶν might conceivably have referred uniquely to Achilles. Homer has it twice as an epithetic phrase after Πηλεΐδη:

I 146

ἠὲ σύ, Πηλεΐδη, πάντων ἐκπαγλότατ' ἀνδρῶν

XVIII 170

ὄρσεο, Πηλεΐδη, πάντων ἐκπαγλότατ' ἀνδρῶν.[5]

If this is a distinctive formula for Achilles, he applied it with particular effect to a slain foe:

XX 389

κεῖσαι, 'Οτρυντεΐδη, πάντων ἐκπαγλότατ' ἀνδρῶν.

You are down, son of Otrynteus. Did you take yourself for Achilles? It is unlikely that the phrase was only convenient. There remains the literal meanings of the words and contextual relevance. In the first line, Agamemnon is being peevish, as is often his way. In the second, Iris bids the *most terrifying of all men* to terrify the Trojans. In the third, Achilles mocks ironically: Otrynteides was really not *very frightening,* after all. The phrase would have been merely metrically convenient and so does *not* occur in the following lines of Patroclus and Lycaon:

XI 606

τίπτέ με κικλήσκεις <u>Ἀχιλεῦ</u>; τί δέ σε χρεὼ ἐμεῖο;

*τίπτέ με κικλήσκεις, πάντων ἐκπαγλότατ' ἀνδρῶν;

XXI 74

γουνοῦμαί σ’, Ἀχιλεῦ· σὺ δέ μ’ αἴδεο καί μ’ ἐλέησον

*γουνοῦμαί σ’, Ἀχιλεῦ πάντων ἐκπαγλότατ’ ἀνδρῶν.

Homer, therefore, transmitted no systematic noun-epithet formula for Achilles in this position. If Achilles was *the best of the Achaeans,* the formula might have been *Ἀχιλεῦ μέγα φέρτατ’ Ἀχαιῶν; Homer preferred plain Ἀχιλεῦ:

XXIV 503

ἀλλ’ αἰδεῖο θεούς, Ἀχιλεῦ, αὐτόν τ’ ἐλέησον

*ἀλλ’ αἰδεῖο θεούς, Ἀχιλεῦ μέγα φέρτατ’ Ἀχαιῶν

XXIV 661

ὧδέ κέ μοι ῥέζων, Ἀχιλεῦ, κεχαρισμένα θείης

*ὧδέ κέ μοι ῥέζων, Ἀχιλεῦ μέγα φέρτατ’ Ἀχαιῶν

XI 606

τίπτέ με κικλήσκεις, Ἀχιλεῦ; τί δέ σε χρεὼ ἐμεῖο;

*τίπτέ με κικλήσκεις, Ἀχιλεῦ μέγα φέρτατ’ Ἀχαιῶν.

Thetis, of course, cannot be made to use a convenient formula for naming Achilles:

XVIII 95

ὠκύμορος δή μοι, τέκος, ἔσσεαι, οἵ’ ἀγορεύεις

*ὠκύμορος δή μοι, πάντων ἐκπαγλότατ’ ἀνδρῶν

*ὠκύμορος, Πηλῆος υἱέ, μέγα φέρτατ’ Ἀχαιῶν.

Homer's failure to use formulae is indicative of his art. Homer avoids illogical uses of formulae. If illogical usage went unrecognized in systematic traditional composition, it would probably have been frequent.

Before the penthemimeral caesura, a formulaic poet might be expected to avail himself of a *φαίδιμε Πηλεΐδη or a *Πηλεΐδη Ἀχιλεῦ. These apparent examples of formulaic convenience and ornament are unexampled in Homer. Homeric diction is simply prosaic in comparison:

– ∪ ∪ Πηλεΐδη

Πηλεΐδη ∪ ∪ –

$- \cup \cup - Ἀχιλεῦ$

$- Ἀχιλεῦ \cup \cup -.$

Homer's lines can easily be recomposed with heroic noun-epithet phrases:

XXI 288

   Πηλεΐδη, μήτ' ἄρ τι λίην τρέε μήτε τι τάρβει

   *Πηλεΐδη Ἀχιλεῦ, μήτε τρέε μήτε τι τάρβει

I 74

   ὦ Ἀχιλεῦ, κέλεαί με, Διὶ φίλε, μυθήσασθαι

   *φαίδιμε Πηλεΐδη, κέλεαί νύ με μυθήσασθαι.

Homer presumably could have composed the alternative lines, but he preferred his own, either for sound or for sense but hardly for formulaic convenience. If noun-epithet formulae are not required to facilitate composition, then they are free to be used significantly or to be significantly absent. In order to determine under what conditions Homer uses a noun-epithet formula for vocatival Achilles in the first hemistich, at least one instance of it must be found.

There are three phrases that fill the first hemistich ending at the tritotrochaic caesura. Each occurs only once:

XXI 153

   Πηλεΐδη μεγάθυμε, τίη γενεὴν ἐρεείνεις;

XVI 203

   σχέτλιε Πηλέος υἱέ, χόλῳ ἄρα σ' ἔτρεφε μήτηρ, / νηλεές

xxiv 36

   ὄλβιε Πηλέος υἱέ, θεοῖς ἐπιείκελ' Ἀχιλλεῦ.

The last two are particularly pertinent to their immediate contexts and do not therefore merely facilitate versification. The first line has a close parallel:

VI 145

   Τυδεΐδη μεγάθυμε, τίη γενεὴν ἐρεείνεις;

Neither μεγάθυμε nor τίη γενεὴν ἐρεείνεις occurs a third time. Πηλεΐδη occurs three times without a following μεγάθυμε. A formulaic bard should not be expected to compose the line backwards in order to discover how much of a vocative he is permitted to sing. A formulaic Πηλείδη μεγάθυμε should have precedence. It often seems that Homer must have composed the rest of the line first and added convenient or significant epithets thereafter.

Bards composing in systematic traditional diction might have found it quite convenient to begin lines with either Πηλείδη μεγάθυμε or Πηλείδη Ἀχιλεῦ. Homer avoids such automatic openers, and rather puts himself to the trouble of composing a vocative for Achilles that suits the line literally. The meaning of ὄλβιε Πηλέος υἱέ or σχέτλιος Πηλέος υἱέ contrasts with the rapidity and familiarity of the systematic formula. Homer's own rapidity and familiarity often consist in unepitheted names or truncated formulae that make it difficult to distinguish Homeric style from that of later poets.

XVIII 18

ὤ μοι, Πηλέος υἱὲ δαΐφρονος, ἦ μάλα λυγρῆς

shows the groan ὤ μοι to be more important than a convenient formula:

*Πηλείδη μεγάθυμε διοτρεφές, ἦ μάλα λυγρῆς.

XX 1–2

ὣς οἱ μὲν παρὰ νηυσὶ κορωνίσι θωρήσσοντο
ἀμφὶ σέ, Πηλέος υἱέ, μάχης ἀκόρητον Ἀχαιοί.

The prepositional phrase might have been assumed, not stated:

*ὣς οἱ μὲν παρὰ νηυσὶ κορωνίσι θωρήσσοντο,
Πηλείδη μεγάθυμε, κάρη κομόωντες Ἀχαιοί.

XXII 8

τίπτέ με, Πηλέος υἱέ, ποσὶν ταχέεσσι διώκεις.

Emphasis on τίπτε disrupts convenient regularity:

*Πηλείδη μεγάθυμε, τίη μέλεόν με διώκεις;

I 414

ὤ μοι, τέκνον ἐμόν, τί νύ σ' ἔτρεφον αἰνὰ τεκοῦσα;

can easily be rendered lifeless with convenient regularity:

*Πηλείδη μεγάθυμε, τί σ' ἔτρεφον αἰνὰ τεκοῦσα;
*Πηλείδη Ἀχιλεῦ, τί νύ σ' ἔτρεφον αἰνὰ τεκοῦσα;

Homer's natural informal vocatives in

IX 252–54

ὦ πέπον, ἦ μέν σοί γε πατὴρ ἐπετέλλετο Πηλεὺς
ἤματι τῷ ὅτε σ' ἐκ Φθίης Ἀγαμέμνονι πέμπε·
τέκνον ἐμόν, κάρτος μὲν Ἀθηναίη τε καὶ "Ηρη / δώσουσ'

contrast with diction of artificial convenience and heroic fullness:

*Πηλεΐδη μεγάθυμε, πατὴρ ἐπετέλλετο Πηλεὺς
ἤματι τῷ ὅτε σ' ἐκ Φθίης Ἀγαμέμνονι πέμπε·
Πηλεΐδη μεγάθυμε Διὶ φίλε, κάρτος τε βίη τε
"Ηρη τ' Ἀργείη καὶ Ἀλαλκομενηῒς Ἀθήνη
δώσουσ'.

Parry's theories are well suited for forgiving Homer faults that he does not often commit.

Artificiality can be compared with colloquialism:

XVIII 128

ναὶ δὴ ταῦτά γε, τέκνον, ἐτήτυμον οὐ κακόν ἐστι

*Πηλεΐδη μεγάθυμος, ἐτήτυμον οὐ κακόν ἐστι.[6]

Any irregularity could be attributed to regular formulaic diction:

XIX 8

τέκνον ἐμόν, τοῦτον μὲν ἐάσομεν ἀχνύμενοί περ / κεῖσθαι

*Πηλεΐδη μεγάθυμε, (Ϝ') ἐάσομεν ἀχνύμενοί περ / κεῖσθαι.

Homer's lines are better than they might have been with a regular formulaic vocative:

XXIV 128–29

τέκνον ἐμόν, τέο μέχρις ὀδυρόμενος καὶ ἀχεύων
σὴν ἔδεαι καρδίην, μεμνημένος οὔτε τι σίτου / οὔτ' εὐνῆς

*Πηλεΐδη μεγάθυμος, ὀδυρόμενος καὶ ἀχεύων
σὴν ἔδεαι καρδίην, μεμνημένος οὔτε τι σίτου / οὔτ' εὐνῆς.

Homer could have guaranteed the hypothesis of formulaic composition by consistent use of Πηλεΐδη μεγάθυμε, especially in passages in which an unformulaic poet would have avoided it.

Πηλεΐδη and ὦ Ἀχιλεῦ, when they begin the verse, appear to be distinguishable in Homer, although they would probably have been equivalent in formulaic poetry. Another word often replaces the particle in polite speeches:

IX 225

χαῖρ᾽, Ἀχιλεῦ· δαιτὸς μὲν ἐΐσης οὐκ ἐπιδευεῖς

IX 513

ἀλλ᾽ Ἀχιλεῦ, πόρε καὶ σὺ Διὸς κούρῃσιν ἕπεσθαι / τιμήν.

In flexible formulaic poetry, ὦ would have acted like an epithet for metrical convenience, rather than to set the mood of the vocative. Although Πηλεΐδη and ὦ Ἀχιλεῦ are metrically distinct within the line, in first position they could be used randomly. Homer apparently has initial Πηλεΐδη as an abrupt vocative and initial *(ὦ) Ἀχιλεῦ* for courtesy or coaxing. Achilles' enemies—Aeneas, Hector, and Asteropaeus—use the impatient form, and so does Poseidon when he rushes to reassure Achilles:

XX 200

Πηλεΐδη, μὴ δὴ ἐπέεσσί με νηπύτιον ὣς

XX 431

Πηλεΐδη, μὴ δὴ ἐπέεσσί γε νηπύτιον ὣς

XXI 153

Πηλεΐδη μεγάθυμε, τίη γενεὴν ἐρεείνεις;

XXI 288

Πηλεΐδη, μήτ᾽ ἄρ τι λίην τρέε μήτε τι τάρβει.

Achilles' friends use the courteous form:

I 74

ὦ Ἀχιλεῦ, κέλεαί με, Διὶ φίλε, μυθήσασθαι

XVI 21, XIX 216, xi 478

ὦ Ἀχιλεῦ Πηλῆος υἱέ, μέγα φέρτατ᾽ Ἀχαιῶν[7]

XXIII 543

ὦ Ἀχιλεῦ, μάλα τοι κεχολώσομαι, αἴ κε τελέσσῃς.

Scamander too uses it when he first tries to coax Achilles out of his streams:

XXI 214–21

ὦ Ἀχιλεῦ, περὶ μὲν κρατέεις, περὶ δ'αἴσυλα ῥέζεις

. . . .

ἀλλ' ἄγε δὴ καὶ ἔασον· ἄγη μ' ἔχει, ὄρχαμε λαῶν.

Although it would not be impossible for a formulaic bard to distinguish the two expressions, it would be one more nuance to slow his composition. The distinction is, however, improbable.

A third alternative expression is also present in Homer. A systematic formulary bard might have been content to make Peleus and Thetis use the formulae ὦ Ἀχιλεῦ and Πηλεΐδη; Homer provides them with a special phrase of the same meter:

IX 254

<u>τέκνον ἐμόν</u>, κάρτος μὲν Ἀθηναίη τε καὶ Ἥρη

XXIV 128

<u>τέκνον ἐμόν</u>, τέο μέχρις ὀδυρόμενος καὶ ἀχεύων.

Achilles has a whole-verse vocatival formula that might have sufficed anywhere in formulaic poetry:

ὦ Ἀχιλεῦ, Πηλῆος υἱέ, μέγα φέρτατ' Ἀχαιῶν.

It occurs three times in the *Iliad* and *Odyssey*. Homer's disuse of it, however, might demonstrate his independence of expression. Homer replaced it by three kinds of alternative expressions.

xxiv 36

ὄλβιε Πηλέος υἱέ, θεοῖς ἐπιείκελ' Ἀχιλλεῦ.

Here another whole-verse vocative is substituted, despite convenience. Instead of expressing the essential idea of ὄλβος by its own traditional formula after the standard introductory vocative for Achilles:

*ὦ Ἀχιλεῦ Πηλῆος υἱέ, μέγα φέρτατ' Ἀχαιῶν
ὄλβῳ τε πλούτῳ τε ἀνάσσεις Μυρμιδόνεσσι,[8]

Homer adopts the technique of composing with a pointed epithet, ὄλβιε.

XXI 588–89

Ἴλιον εἰρυόμεσθα· σὺ δ' ἐνθάδε πότμον ἐρέψεις,
ὧδ' ἔκπαγλος ἐὼν καὶ θαρσαλέος πολεμιστής.

Here the lordly vocatival formula is exchanged for a line of descriptive nominatives that serve this context precisely.

I 74

ὦ Ἀχιλεῦ, κέλεαί με, Διὶ φίλε, μυθήσασθαι

XXI 214

ὦ Ἀχιλεῦ, περὶ μὲν κρατέεις, περὶ δ' αἴσυλα ῥέζεις

XXIII 543

ὦ Ἀχιλεῦ, μάλα τοι κεχολώσομαι, αἴ κε τελέσσῃς.

Here Homer begins and abandons the whole-verse formula, as if it had no integrity and the metrical need of the following thought determined the metrical need of the foregoing thought. The formulaic bard could have expressed the idea that follows ὦ Ἀχιλεῦ in a whole verse after the traditional whole-verse vocative:

*ὦ Ἀχιλεῦ Πηλῆος υἱέ, μέγα φέρτατ' Ἀχαιῶν,
αὐτὰρ ἐπεὶ μάλ' ἄνωγας ἀληθέα μυθήσασθαι[9]

*ὦ Ἀχιλεῦ Πηλῆος υἱέ, μέγα φέρτατ' Ἀχαιῶν,
ἀμφότερον, περὶ μὲν κρατέεις, περὶ δ' αἴσυλα ῥέζεις

*ὦ Ἀχιλεῦ Πηλῆος υἱέ, μέγα φέρτατ' Ἀχαιῶν,
ἀνθρώπων, περὶ μὲν κρατέεις, περὶ δ' αἴσυλα ῥέζεις

*ὦ Ἀχιλεῦ Πηλῆος υἱέ, μέγα φέρτατ' Ἀχαιῶν,
ἦ μάλα πολλά νύ τοι κεχολώσομαι, αἴ κε τελέσσῃς.

Homer appears to choose the vocative that best suits the context. In the first case, the line seems adapted to the significant epithet Διὶ φίλε.[10] In the second case, μέγα φέρτατ' Ἀχαιῶν is expressed in the form περὶ μὲν κρατέεις for the sake of the antithesis. In the third case, Πηλεΐδην Ἀχιλῆα occurs in the preceding line, and the context is friendly and informal.

On the other hand, the whole-verse formula can be turned to advantage. Odysseus sees the point of an epithet that might have been consigned to indifference:

XIX 216–17

ὦ Ἀχιλεῦ, Πηλῆος υἱέ, μέγα φέρτατ' Ἀχαιῶν,
κρείσσων εἰς ἐμέθεν καὶ φέρτερος οὐκ ὀλίγον περ / ἔγχει.

But generally, the whole-verse formula conveys some pomp and dignity, as when Patroclus and Odysseus deal carefully with Achilles

(XVI 21, xi 478). Homer's composition seems to owe more to contextual sensitivity than to casual analogies, which might easily have produced alternative lines like

*Πηλεΐδη μεγάθυμε, θεοῖς ἐπιείκελ' Ἀχιλλεῦ

*Πηλεΐδη Ἀχιλεῦ, πάντων ἐκπαγλότατ' ἀνδρῶν.

VII

The Formula:
Parry and His Successors

A large proportion of Homeric criticism in English in the past fifty years has been based on the assumption that certain of Parry's demonstrations are unassailable.

Parry's researches into them [formulae] are final.[1]

I trust that at this point in the history of Homeric studies I do not need to dilate on the nature of Milman Parry's great discovery, or its momentous consequences. It is beyond doubt one of the most important contributions this country has ever made to classical scholarship. Parry himself only lived long enough to make a beginning, but a beginning *sans pareil*. His proof of Homer's use of formulae, and of the "scope" and "economy" of the system, is a classic of scientific demonstration.[2]

His reasoning in favour of the oral Homer, which has been dismissed but not challenged by argument, is that the Homeric diction is different in kind, and not merely in degree, from that of studied poetry. ... the diction is organized in a special way characteristic of Homer and only of Homer and certain other epics of early Greek literature. This organization is explicable only in terms of a prolonged and oral tradition. I refer to the familiar qualities of *extension* and *economy*. The objectivity and rigour of this argumentation have always been admired.[3]

The formula technique in the Homeric poems is, indeed, so perfect, the system of formulas, as Parry showed, is so "thrifty," so lacking in identical alternative expressions, that one marvels that this perfection could be reached without the aid of writing.[4]

Not every point in the long *thèse* commands unquestioning assent, and
some have argued that the total picture of Homeric poetry which it
suggests is wrongly coloured; but the principal arguments themselves
have never effectively been challenged. It is hard to imagine that they
will ever be, since there are several of them, all crossing and reinforcing
each other, each carefully worked out with accuracy and logic. The
cumulative weight of all of them is overwhelming. They show that
beyond a doubt the operative principle of Homeric style, at least in
regard to the recurrent epithet, was a traditional pattern of metrical
convenience rather than any sense of choosing the adjective appropriate to the immediate context.[5]

Surely the diction of Homeric poetry reveals a formulaic system
characteristic of oral poetry, and Parry's own investigation of the
subject remains our difinitive guide. To me one of the most decisive
factors in this regard is the principle of economy that we find operating
in Homeric diction.[6]

Hardly any scholar remains a rigid Parryist today; even so, those of us
who came to Homer after Parry are Parryists of one shape or another,
uneasy with the rigidity of Parry's conclusions yet unable to escape the
implications of the overwhelming evidence of the formulaic system.[7]

Parry is the Gordian knot tying up oral poetry and Homeric studies.
His intricacy is such that if anyone will pass this way he must either
undo it quite or be undone with admiration.

F. M. Combellack (characteristically) unravelled a strand, only
the better to retie the desperate knot.

What we need, if our case for novelty in the use of formulas is to be
anything but a guess, are passages in which Homer employs an
unusual phrase in a context where the normal formula would
otherwise fit but where it might seem for one reason or another less
suitable. ... But whatever the explanation may be, these two passages
[στεροπηγερέτα Ζεύς and μεγάθυμος Ἀχιλλεύς] represent, I think, the
kind of innovation which must be sought out by anyone who hopes to
show that Homer was a conscious innovator in this aspect of style.[8]

It seems incredible that such an investigation was not undertaken
fifty years ago.

Parry's principle of economy holds that there should be one and
only one expression—a unique formula—for any given essential
idea in any given metrical shape:

If we take all the noun-epithet formulae for Achilles, in all five grammatical cases, we shall find 45 different formulae of which not a single one is of the same metrical value in the same case as any other.[9]

Parry could not glean directly from the texts every expression for all the principal gods and heroes; he compiled his tables of formulaic diction from the lexica and concordances. Consequently, although he found the chief recurrent phrases containing personal names, he overlooked many expressions that can take the places of these formulae.

Indeed, he got all the phrases showing forms of Ἀχιλ(λ)εύς in all grammatical cases, including

μεγάθυμος Ἀχιλλεύς	πόδας ὠκὺς Ἀχιλλεύς
Διὶ φίλε φαίδιμ' Ἀχιλλεῦ	θεοῖς ἐπιείκελ' Ἀχιλλεῦ
ποδώκης – ∪ Ἀχιλλεύς	ποδάρκης δῖος Ἀχιλλεύς,

which already fairly contradict his statement just quoted.[10] But he deftly or daftly missed the patronymical expressions:[11]

. . . .   Θέτιδος πάϊς ἠϋκόμοιο

Πηλέος υἱός . . . .

. . . .   Αἰακίδαο

. . . .   Πηλείωνος

. . . .   Πηλείδαο

. . . .   Πηληϊάδαο

. . . .   ποδώκεος Αἰακίδαο

. . . .   ἀμύμονος Αἰακίδαο

. . . .   μεγαθύμου Πηλείωνος

. . . .   Πηλείωνι

. . . .   ποδώκεϊ Πηλείωνι

. . . .   μεγαθύμῳ Πηλείωνι

. . . .   Πηλείωνα

. . . .   ἀμύμονα Πηλείωνα

. . . .   ποδώκεα Πηλείωνα

Πηλείδη μεγάθυμε . . . .

ὄλβιε Πηλέος υἱέ . . . .

σχέτλιε Πηλέος υἱέ . . . .

Πηλείδη . . . .

Some of these increase the number of equivalencies in Homer:

ἀμύμονος Αἰακίδαο	Ἀχιλλῆος θείοιο
μεγαθύμου Πηλεΐωνος	Πηληϊάδεω Ἀχιλῆος
ἀμύμονα Πηλεΐωνα	Ἀχιλλῆα πτολίπορθον
Πηλεΐδη	ὦ Ἀχιλεῦ.

Moreover, since there are so many equivalencies employed by Homer, it is not unreasonable to suppose that there might have been more equivalencies employable by Homer:

Θέτιδος πάϊς ἠϋκόμοιο   *δουρικλυτὸς ὠκὺς Ἀχιλλεύς,

to mention only one of the many suggested in the preceding chapters.

Parry also missed the descriptive and pronominal phrases that often take the places of proper-name formulae when the latter are stylistically less suitable in the particular circumstances of the given context:

```
. . . . . . . . . . . ὅ γ' ἥρως
. . . . . . . . . . . δαίμονι ἶσος
. . . . . . . . . ἀνὴρ ἆτος πολέμοιο
οὗτος ἀνήρ . . . . . . . . . .
ὁ διογενής . . . . . . . . . .
. . . . . . . . . παιδὸς ἑοῖο (ἑῆος)
. . . . . . . . . υἱὸς ἑοῖο (ἑῆος)
. . . . . . . . . . τοῖο ἄνακτος
. . . . . . . . . . ἀνδρὸς ἑῆος
ἀνδρὸς ἀριστῆος . . . . . . . .
. . . . . . . . . . . ἄνακτι
. . . . . . . . . . . ἑταίρῳ
. . . . . . . . . . ποιμένι λαῶν
. . . . . . . . . τῷ γε ἄνακτι
υἱέι ἐμῷ ὠκυμόρῳ . . . . . . .
. . . . . . Ἀχιλλῆος κεφαλῇ Πηληϊάδαο
. . . . . . . . . . φίλον υἱόν
. . . . . . . . . . ποιμένα λαῶν
```

. . . . δήϊον ἄνδρα

. . . . ὃν φίλον υἱόν

. . . . ὄρχαμον ἀνδρῶν

. . . . ἄγριον ἄνδρα

. . . . ἀνέρα τοῦτον

. . . . υἱέα καρτερόθυμον

. . . . ἄνδρα φέριστον ὃν ἀθάνατοί περ ἔτεισαν

. . . . υἱὸν ἀμύμονα τε κρατερόν τε

. . . . . ἀνέρα τοῦτον ἀτάσθαλον ὀβριμοεργόν

. . . . παντῶν ἐκπαγλότατ᾽ ἀνδρῶν.

Some of these increase the number of equivalencies in Homer. These expressions do not seem to have much to do with Parry's systematic diction and facile versification. Metrical convenience often does not determine how Homer will name Achilles. Homer's diction is not only unlike but it is also like that of Apollonius and Vergil.

It is not that Parry was unaware of patronymical and descriptive formulae for heroes; he included a few of them in his tables of systematic diction, but in brackets that exclude them from consideration:

> The expressions given in square brackets are those which do not actually contain the name of the god or hero, but can take its place; for example, πατὴρ ἀνδρῶν τε θεῶν τε for Zeus and Τυδέος υἱός for Diomedes.[12]

Parry did not investigate these sorts of expressions, although they are of crucial importance for defining and evaluating the fundamental principles of economy and extension in systematic epic diction.

In failing to tabulate all the expressions for gods and heroes, rather than just those containing personal names, Parry enhanced economy but restricted extension. He might have been willing to include tables of formulae for dative, accusative, and vocative cases along with his tables of nominative and genitive formulae—which would also have been more extensively supplied—if he had seen them filling up with patronymical and descriptive as well as personal names. As it is, even Parry's genitive formulae are rather too sparse to confirm the principle of extension convincingly. The asterisks on

the tables are meant to excuse the lack of extension: "an asterisk *
indicates that the metre of a name makes a noun-epithet formula
impossible."[13] It should have occurred to Parry to inquire whether
epic diction expressly devised patronymics of different metrical
shapes from those of their corresponding personal names in order to
create formulae to fill such tables of systematic diction so that a bard
should never be at a loss for a metrically convenient formula.

Moreover, with this increase in the numbers of formulae, Parry's
tables might easily have been expanded to include more than a few
supposedly principal types of formulae. Indeed, the genitival formula for Achilles before the penthemimeral caesura is lacking,
although it is a principal type, whereas the genitival formula for
Achilles before the tritotrochaic caesura is represented by three
occurrences of Πηλεΐδεω Ἀχιλῆος, although it is not a principal type.
Ἀχιλῆος ἀγαυοῦ, Πηληϊάδαο, and κρατεροῦ Ἀχιλῆος would fully furnish
the post-hephthemimeral category that does not figure in Parry's
table. The classification is factitious and fallacious.

Furthermore, Πηληϊάδαο corresponds metrically with πόδας ὠκὺς
Ἀχιλλεύς, as Πηλεΐωνος and Αἰακίδαο correspond metrically with δῖος
Ἀχιλλεύς and ὠκὺς Ἀχιλλεύς. The unepitheted patronymics can
hardly be denied formulaic status; their convenient metrical shapes
nicely allow them to dispense with epithets that often only serve to
lengthen a short name anyway. Parry's tables do not fairly represent
Homeric diction. They conceal vacancies that patronymical and
descriptive formulae can fill. These allusive formulae benefit extension perhaps as much as they detract from economy.

Neither did Parry take into account the effect of elision on
extension and economy. In effect, words and formulae of different
metrical shapes can be metrically equivalent where elision is
possible:

XXIV 472

   τῇ ῥ' Ἀχιλεὺς ἴζεσκε Διὶ φίλος· ἐν δέ μιν αὐτὸν

   *τῇ ῥ' Ἀχιλεὺς ἴζεσκε Διὶ φίλος· ἐν δ' Ἀχιλῆα

XXIV 629

   ἤτοι Δαρδανίδης Πρίαμος θαύμαζ' Ἀχιλῆα

   *ἤτοι Δαρδανίδης Πρίαμος θαύμαζε ἄνακτα.

Nor did Parry take into account the similar effect of correption:

XXIII 491

εἰ μὴ Ἀχιλλεὺς αὐτὸς ἀνίστατο καὶ φάτο μῦθον

*εἰ μὴ Πηλέος υἱὸς ἀνίστατο καὶ φάτο μῦθον.

Nor did Parry take into account that paragogic *nu* and permissible overlengthening also create equivalent formulae:

XXII 193

ὡς Ἕκτωρ οὐ λῆθε ποδώκεα Πηλεΐωνα

*ὡς Ἕκτωρ οὐ λῆθεν ἀμύμονα Πηλεΐωνα

XXII 278

Ἕκτωρ δὲ προσέειπεν ἀμύμονα Πηλεΐωνα

*Ἕκτωρ δὲ προσέειπε ποδώκεα Πηλεΐωνα

XIX 40

αὐτὰρ ὁ βῆ παρὰ θῖνα θαλάσσης δῖος Ἀχιλλεύς

*αὐτὰρ ὁ βῆ παρὰ θῖνα θαλάσσης ὠκὺς Ἀχιλλεύς

XVII 271

ὄφρα ζωὸς ἐὼν θεράπων ἦν Αἰακίδαο

*ὄφρα ζωὸς ἐὼν θεράπων ἦν Πηλεΐωνος.

The accumulated evidence shows that there is less economy and more equivalence than Parry admitted.[14] Nevertheless, there remains a real sense in which thrifty diction is still a relevant factor in Homeric composition. All the recurrent diction is a sufficient demonstration of Homer's reliance on ready formulae whose metrical convenience is always apparent but whose contextual semantic relevance is not.[15] Δῖος / ὠκὺς Ἀχιλλεύς represents Parry's case at its strongest. In general, however, unique formulae are the exception, not the rule, in Homeric diction for Achilles. And even the categorical use of δῖος / ὠκὺς Ἀχιλλεύς is disputable. Homeric composition must be defined in terms of both economical and uneconomical expression.

Economical expressions cannot universally be denied particular semantic significance; and uneconomical expressions cannot adequately be explained by mechanical operation of analogy. Parry was wrong in thinking that an epithet could not be sometimes ornamental and sometimes particularized, both convenient and meaningful. In the examples cited above, it is quite possible that Achilles is

not ὠκύς at XIX 40 because he is not running, and that he is ποδώκεα
at XXII 193 because he is running. It is the underestimated factor of
equivalence that allows the poet to choose the phrase whose
meaning is more suitable in the particular context. And Parry was
wrong in thinking that analogy could solve the problem of equivalence. The operation of analogy shows that ready traditional diction
is inoperative. It is entirely improbable that an obscure analogy
should have accidentally displaced the memorable πόδας ὠκὺς
Ἀχιλλεύς in traditional formulaic poetry. If even formulae that are
indeed "holy and sweet and wondrous" can be lost to undeliberate
analogy, then analogy must have been operative almost everywhere
and always, as in deliberate literate composition.

F. A. Wolf set the Homeric Problem by making Homer a nonliterate bard and therefore incapable of composing and performing
very long epic poems. Parry solved the problem by showing precisely
how *only* nonliterate bards could have composed and performed
such heroic epics as the *Iliad* and *Odyssey*. Parry's great discovery
was *systematic traditional formulaic diction in improvised oral epic;*
and a proof of its veracity was that it accounted for Homer's
peculiarities and inconsistencies. The key to its operation is *economy*
and *extension*—unique formulae for every regular metrical need.
The result was *facile versification,* which overcame the need for
deliberation and written composition or memorization.

Rigid systematic formulae were necessary in Parry's first model of
Homeric composition. Phrases were stripped to bare *essential ideas:*
all forty-five noun-epithet formulae for Achilles were indistinguishable from each other except metrically. Achilles qua Peleides,
Achilles qua Thetis' son, Achilles qua great warrior, Achilles qua
formidable opponent, and Achilles qua whatever suits the particular
context would have made systematic diction impossibly complex
and unwieldy. The essential idea *Achilles* reduces multiplicity to
simplicity. Since each essential idea has a unique formula for any
given metrical need, anyone who has conned his tables of hard
formulae can compose and perform heroic epic.

Meillet and Parry had counted on Homer showing omniprevalent
formulae. When not enough hard formulae (repeated diction) could
be found in the *Iliad* and *Odyssey* and the other remnants of a
supposedly prolific epic tradition, then soft formulae (repeatable
diction) had to be included to make up the difference. Moreover,

unsystematic diction is created by the facile application of analogy upon systematic diction. Analogy is conditioned by constant practice in extempore oral composition. Numerous epics and frequent performances in the Dark Ages are *assumed.* Without constant professional practice, the operation of analogy would be slow: and slowness suggests premeditation and memorization.

When Parry demonstrated how systematic formulae would be convenient in oral improvisation, the inverse also seemed valid: unsystematic diction would be inconvenient because the operation of analogy cannot be so rapid as habitual formulaic reactions. In Parry's revision, analogical soft formulae had to be considered as convenient as hard formulae for extempore composition. The making of noun-epithet phrases is easier than Parry thought when he showed

> in the most conclusive manner that it is impossible for a poet by himself to create more than an insignificant number of noun-epithet formulae.[16]

A Homerist can easily create many. Analogical formulations, however, are more easily produced in thoughtful writing than extempore. Although composition with hard formulae could be shown to differ from literate style, composition with soft formulae and facile analogy makes the differentiation dubious or insignificant.

Parry plumped for a tradition of anonymous bards against the originality and individuality of Homer. What have become his last words and final verdict were written for an undelivered lecture:

> But then at the end of the lecture, as if he were afraid that the conception of unity would detract from the importance he wished to assign to the Tradition, he says, "I have spoken of a unity of conception of the story of the *Iliad,* but it would be wrong to suppose that this conception came to being in the mind of an individual poet. I do not think we shall ever know just how much of the *Iliad* was the work of Homer and just how much of his master and of the Singers who were his predecessors," and concludes by reverting to the traditional nature of the *style:* "... One who studies the traditional style ... comes to see that it is a device for expressing ideas such as could never have been brought into being by a single poet. One's admiration of the poems increases as one realizes that we have here the best thought of many poets."[17]

Since Parry, Homer has slowly been gaining support at the expense of the tradition.

Parry's closest exponents, A. B. Lord and J. A. Notopoulos, try, at the risk of contradiction, to have it both ways:

> The oral poet does not fashion fresh phrases, as the literary poet does, because he does not have the time in the midst of improvisation. Therefore he must spontaneously use the formula, a group of words already fashioned by the oral tradition, to express any and every idea or action possible in the poem. Parry's proof of this was overwhelming. ... Yugoslavic oral poetry shows that the singer of tales, even when working with a formulaic tradition, has room for individuality both in creating new formulae and sound patterns, in shaping poems which have a marked stamp of individuality, in shaping the architecture of his poems.[18]

If the oral poet must spontaneously use ready-made formulae, how can there be any room for the creation of un-ready-made formulae? The answer must be casual analogy:

> Per Parry, la formula e la cose fondamentale e l'essenza della tecnica: ma Lord la considera un risultato casuale. In genere gli oralisti sembrano delusi da un numero ristretto di formule. Per fortuna si e trovato un modo per aumentare sostanzialmente la quantità di dizione formulare. Questo metodo si chiama "la formula per analogia" o "la frase formulare." Essa significa che contiamo come formulare qualsiasi espressione che assomigli a una formula regolare in qualche modo.[19]

The oral poet uses a traditional formula as a model for fabricating formulaic expressions, which are somehow both traditional and original. He can operate analogy as quickly as he can recall memorized fixed formulae and fit them into orally improvised verse. If, on the other hand, the operation of analogy is not automatic and the bard has time to meditate and compose and memorize, then he would be composing like Milton, and the whole distinction between oral and literate composition, along with the need for the new oral poetics, collapses.[20] Analogy is better suited for constituting formulaic diction than for facilitating versification. Parry's original idea of extensive and economical systems of traditional diction at least has the merit of making extempore oral composition conceivably practicable. Milton had to be "milked" regularly: he did not simultaneously compose and perform. The soft formulae of analogy need to be milked; the hard formulae of systematic traditional diction are pabulum in abundant store.

G. M. Calhoun, too, holds with the hare and hunts with the hounds. Both the tradition and Homer are exalted:

> We have gradually learned that in every part of the text is traditional material that can only be the collective work of ages and in every part are touches that can only be from the hand of a great master.[21]

On the one hand, Homer

> chooses according to his mood and his artistic purpose, but otherwise with entire freedom, from all that the epic tradition has produced and accumulated.[22]

On the other hand, Homer's

> part in the creation, the adaptation, and the polishing of the epic formulas must have been in some measure commensurate with his greatness.[23]

Calhoun believes in "a supremely great poet, working with traditional material,"[22] whereas Parry believes in supremely great traditional material working through traditional bards. For Calhoun, Homer is an oral poet with literate poetics: "His technique can be made out in general outline. It cannot be reduced to a system."[25] If so, then Parry hardly made progress beyond Düntzer and Meillet.

C. M. Bowra is the great expounder of heroic oral poetry, and he closely follows the Parryan line. For him too, however, there is in Homer still a certain something else that is beyond the tradition:

> It is conceivable that, if we had not the *Iliad* and the *Odyssey* but only the work of some uncreative bard who relied entirely on traditional material, we might well be impressed and delighted by it. Yet when we have made every allowance for this, we must still feel that there is something else, not easily defined and in the last resort beyond precise analysis, which reveals a great poet at work.[26]

When Bowra wrote in his posthumous work on Homer, " 'life-giving earth' is a formula, but here it has a noble pathos," he was bearing down to Hades' the laurel for Ruskin.[27] Parry had derided Ruskin for having "contrived" such an "extravagant" notion.[28] Ruskin's Homer has reasserted himself against Parry's tradition.

Of course, some scholars were undeterred by Parry's revolutionary oral poetics and carried on with strictly literary criticism of Homer. S. E. Bassett and K. Reinhardt, literary critics of the first degree and therefore with a following, were far less impressed with the analogy of South Slavic folk poetry than with that of literary genius:

> History has provided us with another analogy. It has shown us that every work of poetic art comparable in greatness to the *Iliad* and *Odyssey* bears the stamp of a single great creative mind. The analogy of Homer to the great historic poets is greater. Since we cannot know, we choose the greater parallel. All the great creators of literature are alike in one respect: they take the old and make of it the new, in ideas and language, in incidents, characters, and action; and they add and invent out of their imagination. We must believe that Homer was no exception.[29]

Bassett at least pays Parry the compliment of a few pages of criticism; Reinhardt rather dismisses Parry with disbelief and dismay:

> Ich kann dieses Buch nicht beginnen ohne zuvor darauf hinzuweisen, dass jene Auffassung [Parry's] darin nicht geteilt wird. Besteht sie zu recht, so wäre diesem Buche besser, dass es nie geschrieben worden wäre.[30]

P. Chantraine reviewed Parry's *thèses* and preconized their epochal significance: "on reconnaîtra que la démonstration est acquise et qu'elle renouvelle la philologie homérique."[31] Nevertheless, four years after Parry's triumph, A. Puech (Parry's thesis adviser) published *L'Iliade d'Homère,* without a mention of Parry.[32] P. Mazon also disregarded Parry in his "L'Origine de l'Iliade" ten years later in Parry's adoptive city.[33]

W. B. Stanford agrees with Bassett's choice of analogy against Parry's:

> No purely oral master-poet, to judge at least from translations, has yet been offered for consideration by oralists, apart from Homer. So there is a logical dilemma: since we cannot compare Homer as an oral master-poet with any other known oral master-poet, we must judge him either in terms of second-rate poets who are oral or master-poets who are literate. Parry prefers the first. But it is hardly unreasonable for others to prefer the second.[34]

Stanford and Bassett do not contest Parry's data on noun-epithet formulae, which high authority has declared *inébranlable* from the beginning.[35] They attempt rather to reduce some of Parry's conclusions to absurdity. Stanford's review, although beginning and ending with complaisant compliments, condemns two general principles in Parry's theory: Homer's unoriginality and the meaninglessness of ornamental epithets.[36] Another interpretation must be sought for Parry's data—or else the data must be discredited also.

Unlike Reinhardt, other German Homerists—W. Schadewaldt, A. Lesky, and A. Heubeck—have carefully taken into account the nature of oral poetry and its relation to Homer. They conclude, however, that although Homer's antecedents were oral bards, Homer certainly surpasses their likes. Homer shows seven *Merkmale* of the older oral poetry and ten of a new conception of epic poetry:

> Durch die Konzeption seines Grossepos hat er das ganze ältere Sängertum, von dem er doch so viel übernommen hat, in den Schatten des Vergessens geworfen.[37]

> Er, der ein Anfang und ein Ende zugleich ist, steht als schaffender Künstler in zwei Welten. Das Beste seiner Kraft holt er aus dem jahrhundertelang mundlich geübten Heldensang seines Volkes, seine Kunst des Bauens und Vertiefens aber weist bereits weit voraus auf die Schöpfungen hellenischer Klassik.[38]

> Homer, equipped with the ample instruments offered to him by tradition, not only continued this tradition, but also went beyond and overcame its set limits in all decisive points.[39]

They can safely proceed, therefore, to analyze Homer by the same principles of literary criticism as they apply to an analysis of Apollonius and Vergil, because the oral tradition had less control over Homer than Parry had thought. Parry's cogent analysis and interpretation are diverted principally to pre-Homeric bards and applied only residually to Homer. *Das homerische in Homer* falls within the jurisdiction of literary poetics.

Parry's theory therefore should have been admirably suited to the work of the *Neoanalytiker,* who have been prospecting for the sources of Homer. On the contrary, "Milman Parry and all his works must be shown the door," because Homer's predecessors, no less than Homer himself, are imagined to have been literary poets.[40]

Thorough studies of Homeric formulae have been made by A.

Hoekstra and J. B. Hainsworth. Like Parry, Hoekstra begins with
an admiration for Homer's formulaic diction:

> Homer's greatness is *partly* due to the magnificent instrument he could
> play, to the highly refined character, that is, of a diction which was
> intensively moulded and fashioned into an immense variety of patterns
> by his forerunners. It is mainly my admiration for this instrument and
> the interest in the history of its development that have induced me to
> examine it more closely.[41]

The difference between Parry and Hoekstra is the qualification
partly, which Parry boldly omitted. For Hoekstra, the other *partly* is
attributable to Homer's originality—not following his predecessors:

> It is the *Posthomerica* of Quintus Smyrnaeus who, in this respect
> [diction], probably imitated Homer more closely than Homer followed
> his predecessors.[42]

Nevertheless, Parry's traditional formulae are fundamental:

> Parry's foremost achievement is that he proved, definitely and irrefu-
> tably, the traditional character of several systems of noun-epithet
> formulae for all the chief characters of the epics.[43]

And traditional formulae are the basis for Hoekstra's investigations:

> It is only the traditional character of a large portion of Homer's diction
> that enables us to draw conclusions concerning its pre-Homeric stages.
> For this traditional nature guarantees that the evolution must have
> proceeded on more or less fixed lines.[44]

The criteria for proving the formulae to be traditional are the
economy and extension of systematic diction. Without the crutches
of economy and extension, the tradition totters.

No one doubts that there is traditional diction in Homer: all
language has traditional diction. Parry has little to say about the
formation and evolution of his traditional diction. His categories are
simplistic: an expression is either traditional or original.[45] Oral
bards employed the former; literate poets, the latter. Traditional
diction somehow came to be in the dim past and was repeated
continuously thereafter. A bard would not voluntarily seek original
expressions. Inadvertent analogical formations create equivalencies,
which are a nuisance in oral composition. Change occurs in
traditional diction if the novel expression prevails over the venerable

formula, for example, if μεγάθυμος Ἀχιλλεύς should overtake πόδας ὠκὺς Ἀχιλλεύς.

Hoekstra has a different view of the development of Homer's formulaic diction. The conclusion of his study makes traditional diction almost as volatile as slang:

> All this clearly shows that in the course of time the formulaic diction must have undergone most drastic changes. It is not only out of the question that, as Parry thought, the Ionian singers merely adapted an inherited repertory to their own dialect. It is also certain that many formulae were lost and partly replaced, that many others were elaborated and that from a date not much anterior to Homer up to the creation of our poems, epic diction as a whole took on a much suppler form and a different colouring.[46]

Indeed, Homeric diction is actually suffering from *decomposition*.[47] Homer himself may well have made many Homeric modifications of formulaic prototypes:

> Why should Homer's contribution to its evolution be regarded as negligible, whereas on this supposition the average singer must have changed it considerably? Of course the extent of Homer's share can by no means be evaluated, but in view of the variety of ideas we find in the *Iliad* and the *Odyssey*, I am not inclined to belittle it.[48]

The way is open for Homer to be as much the creator (and as little the mere transmitter) of his epics as Apollonius and Vergil are of theirs. Hoekstra saves oral composition by objecting to "this equation *oral composition = improvisation*."[49] He thereby risks the equation *oral composition = literate composition*.

If Parry defines formula in a way such that "flexibility is legislated into limbo before the investigation begins,"[50] then Hainsworth defines formula in a way such that flexibility is legislated onto terra firma before the investigation begins. There are subtle ways of inserting or removing what one wishes or does not wish to find in Homer. So many accidental variations are counted as the same formula[51] that it is hardly astonishing to discover that:

> His final conclusion, after much detailed evidence, is that about half of the word-groups whose basic shape is ∪ ∪ – ⌣ are found in other than their basic shape, modified or transmuted in some way, in the Homeric poems, and about a third of those whose basic shape is – ∪ ∪ – ⌣.[52]

Parry's *fixed* formula keeps the meter and the words invariable. Parry's *structural* formula keeps the meter and varies the words. Hainsworth's *flexible* formula keeps the words and varies the meter. Parry showed that the fixed formula is not a factor in literate poetry. Hainsworth criticizes Parry (and his exponents) for failing to show that the structural formula is not a factor in literate poetry. It is curious, therefore, that Hainsworth should have neglected to show that the flexible formula is not a factor in literate poetry, lest there should be anything "vacuously, and so uselessly, true" in the existence of these formulae also.[53] It appears that in order to fit flexible formulae into oral composition Hainsworth had to renounce the idea of improvisation. The flexible formula is evidently better suited to premeditation. Again, oral composition has become hardly distinguishable from literate composition.

The flexible formula is defined as a "repeated word-group" in which "the use of one word created a strong presumption that the other would follow."[54] For Parry, a precise metrical need and an essential idea recalled the formula *swift ships*. For Hainsworth, *swift* suggests *ships* and *ships* suggests *swift* despite the meter. But *swift* also suggests *horses* and *arrows*, while *ships* also suggest *many-benched* and *vermilion-prowed*. Each word has diverse associations that must be sorted out by a thoughtful poet and metrical convenience.

Only the fixed formulae of systematic diction appear to simplify the process of versification in such a way that composition with formulae would be significantly different from composition without them. If this study, however, has hit upon the truth, then Parry's research into systems of noun-epithet formulae is unscientific and untrustworthy, and the *only* clear model of facile versification is undone.

Let Hugh Lloyd-Jones provide my epilogue:

> But if scholars cling to the opinion that the epics were composed orally they do so above all because they are told that, as Kirk puts it, "a large number of crystallised formulas are employed with an astonishing economy and lack of unnecessary variation" (*Homer and the Oral Tradition*, 115–16). He holds that this "suggests strongly, and indeed imperatively, that the oral technique was used in full and undiminished degree for the final main act of composition of each of the two monumental poems." But each of the scholars who have examined the

"formula" in all possible senses of that elusive term has ended by stressing, more strongly than his predecessors, its extreme flexibility and adaptability. The extensive and economic system of formulas revealed by Milman Parry has proved, after close testing, a good deal less tight than people had supposed.[55]

I have tried to help cure Homer of blindness and put a pen in his hand—if only like Milton.[56]

Expressions Signifying Achilles
Nominative Case

Ἀχιλλεύς (*Iliad* 171, *Odyssey* 2)	Iliad	Odyssey
– ⏖ – ⏖ – ⏖ – ⏖ – ⏑ Ἀχιλλεύς	62	2
ὁ Ἀχιλλεύς	2	0
– ⏖ – ⏖ – ⏖ – ⏖ δῖος Ἀχιλλεύς	29	0
ὁ δῖος Ἀχιλλεύς	5	0
ὠκὺς Ἀχιλλεύς	5	0
ὁ ὠκὺς Ἀχιλλεύς	1	0
– ⏖ – ⏖ – ⏖ – πόδας ὠκὺς Ἀχιλλεύς	29	0
μεγάθυμος Ἀχιλλεύς	1	0
ὁ κλυτὸς – ⏑ Ἀχιλλεύς	1	0
– ⏖ – ⏖ – ⏑ ποδάρκης δῖος Ἀχιλλεύς	21	0
ἀρήϊος – ⏑ Ἀχιλλεύς	1	0
ποδώκης – ⏑ Ἀχιλλεύς	1	0
ὁ . . . /διογενὴς Πηλῆος υἱός, πόδας ὠκὺς Ἀχιλλεύς	1	0
Ἀχιλλεύς/ . . . Διὶ φίλος	1	0
– ⏑ Ἀχιλλεύς	7	0
– ⏑ Ἀχιλλεὺς αὐτός	2	0
– ⏑ Ἀχιλλεὺς – δουρικλυτός	1	0
– ⏑ Ἀχιλλεὺς – ⏑ Διὶ φίλος	1	0

Ἀχιλεύς (35,0)		
– Ἀχιλεύς	18	0
– Ἀχιλεύς ⏖ – ⏑ Διὶ φίλος	1	0
– ⏖ – Ἀχιλεύς	12	0
αὐτός – Ἀχιλεύς	1	0
– ⏖ – Ἀχιλεύς, Θέτιδος πάϊς ἠϋκόμοιο	2	0
– ⏖ – ⏖ – Ἀχιλεύς ⏖ – ⏑ δαΐφρων	1	0

Πηλεΐδης (24,0)

Πηλεΐδης	14	0
ὁ . . . / Πηλεΐδης	1	0
– ⏑⏑ Πηλεΐδης	9	0

υἱός (4,0)

– ⏑⏑ – ⏑⏑ υἱός	2	0
– ⏑⏑ Πηλέος υἱός	1	0
διογενὴς Πηλῆος υἱός, πόδας ὠκὺς Ἀχιλλεύς	1	0

πάϊς (2,0)

– ⏑⏑ – Ἀχιλεύς, Θέτιδος πάϊς ἠϋκόμοιο	2	0

ἀνήρ (7,0)

– ⏑⏑ – ⏑⏑ – ⏑ ἀνήρ	1	0
ἀνὴρ ὅ γε	1	0
ἀνὴρ ἆτος πολέμοιο	1	0
οὖλος ἀνήρ	1	0
– ⏑⏑ οὗτος ἀνήρ	1	0
– ὅδ᾽ ἀνήρ	1	0
δεῖνος ἀνήρ	1	0

αὐτός (14,0)

– ⏑⏑ – ⏑⏑ αὐτός	11	0
αὐτός – Ἀχιλεύς	1	0
– ⏑ Ἀχιλλεὺς αὐτός	2	0

ὅδε (2,0)

– ⏑ ὅδε	1	0
– ὅδ᾽ ἀνήρ	1	0

οὗτος (1,0)

– ⏑ ⏑ οὗτος ἀνήρ	1	0

(ἐ)κεῖνος (3,0)

– ⏑ ⏑ – ⏑ ⏑ – ⏑ ⏑ – ⏑ ⏑ – ⏑ ἐκεῖνος	1	0
– ⏑ ⏑ – κεῖνος	1	0
κεῖνος ὅ γε ⏑ ⏑ – ⏑	1	0

ὁ (85,1)

ὁ	53	1

ὅ γε	14	0
ὅ περ	1	0
κεῖνος ὅ γε	1	0
ἀνὴρ ὅ γε	1	0
ὁ διογενής	1	0
ὁ . . . Ἀχιλλεύς	2	0
ὁ γε ἥρως	1	0
ὁ . . . δῖος Ἀχιλλεύς	5	0
ὁ . . . ὠκὺς Ἀχιλλεύς	1	0
ὁ . . . δαίμονι ἶσος	2	0
ὁ κλυτὸς – ◡ Ἀχιλλεύς	1	0
ὁ . . . / Πηλεΐδης	1	0
ὁ . . . / διογενὴς Πηλῆος υἱός, πόδας ὠκὺς Ἀχιλλεύς	1	0

δαίμονι ἶσος (4,0)

– ◡◡ – ◡◡ – ◡◡ – ◡◡ δαίμονι ἶσος	2	0
ὁ δαίμονι ἶσος	2	0
ἶσος Ἐννναλίῳ κορυθάϊκι πτολεμιστῇ	1	0

APPENDIX B

Expressions Signifying Achilles
Genitive Case

’Αχιλλῆος (*Iliad* 26, *Odyssey* 3)	*Iliad*	*Odyssey*
– ∪ Ἀχιλλῆος	17	0
– ∪ Ἀχιλλῆος μεγαθύμου	1	1
– ∪ Ἀχιλλῆος ῥηξήνορος	0	1
– ∪ Ἀχιλλῆος ⏑⏑ – Πηληϊάδαο	0	1
– ∪ Ἀχιλλῆος ⏑⏑ – ⏑⏑ κυδαλίμοιο	1	0
– ⏑⏑ – ∪ Ἀχιλλῆος	1	0
– ⏑⏑ – ⏑⏑ – ∪ Ἀχιλλῆος	4	0
Ἀχιλλῆος θείοιο	2	0

’Αχιλῆος (28,4)		
– ⏑⏑ – Ἀχιλῆος	3	1
χωομένου Ἀχιλῆος	1	0
Πηλεΐδεω Ἀχιλῆος	3	0
Ἀχιλῆος ἀγαυοῦ	1	0
Ἀχιλῆος ἀμύμονος	2	0
Ἀχιλῆος ἀμύμονος Αἰακίδαο	1	0
– ⏑⏑ – ⏑⏑ – ⏑⏑ – Ἀχιλῆος ∪ – –	2	0
– ⏑⏑ – ⏑⏑ – ⏑⏑ – ⏑⏑ – Ἀχιλῆος	7	0
Πηληϊάδεω Ἀχιλῆος	6	2
Πηλεΐδεω Ἀχιλῆος	0	1
κρατεροῦ Ἀχιλῆος	1	0
ποδώκεος – Ἀχιλῆος	1	0

Αἰακίδαο (19,2)		
– ⏑⏑ Αἰακίδαο	1	0
Αἰακίδαο δαΐφρονος	2	0

143

– ‿‿ – ‿‿ – ‿‿ – ‿‿ Αἰακίδαο	6	0
ποδώκεος Αἰακίδαο	8	2
ἀμύμονος Αἰακίδαο	1	0
Ἀχιλῆος ἀμύμονος Αἰακίδαο	1	0

Πηλεΐωνος (11,1)

– ‿‿ Πηλεΐωνος	3	0
Πηλεΐωνος ἀγαυοῦ	1	0
Πηλεΐωνος ὑπερθύμοιο	2	0
– ‿‿ – ‿‿ – ‿‿ Πηλεΐωνος	1	0
– ‿‿ – ‿‿ – ‿‿ – ‿‿ Πηλεΐωνος	2	1
μεγαθύμου Πηλεΐωνος	2	0

Πηλεΐδαο (6,0)

– ‿‿ Πηλεΐδαο	3	0
Πηλεΐδαο ‿ – ‿‿ – θείοιο	1	0
– ‿‿ – ‿‿ – ‿‿ Πηλεΐδαο	1	0
– ‿‿ – ‿‿ – ‿‿ – ‿‿ Πηλεΐδαο	1	0

Πηλεΐδεω (3,1)

Πηλεΐδεω Ἀχιλῆος	3	0
– ‿‿ – ‿‿ – ‿‿ Πηλεΐδεω Ἀχιλῆος	0	1

Πηληϊάδεω (8,2)

– ‿‿ – ‿‿ – Πηληϊάδεω	2	0
Πηληϊάδεω Ἀχιλῆος	6	2

Πηληϊάδαο (1,1)

– ‿‿ – ‿‿ – Πηληϊάδαο	1	0
– ‿ Ἀχιλλῆος ‿ ‿ – Πηληϊάδαο	0	1

ἀνδρός (5,0)

ἀνδρός	2	0
ἀνδρὸς ἀριστῆος	1	0
– ἀνδρὸς θείοιο . . . / – ‿ Ἀχιλλῆος	1	0
– ‿‿ – ‿‿ – ‿‿ – ‿‿ ἀνδρὸς ἑῆος	1	0

ἀνέρος (2,0)

τοίου – ‿‿ – ‿‿ ἀνέρος	1	0
σθένος ἀνέρος	1	0

βασιλῆος (1,0)

– ⏑⏑ – ⏑⏑ – ⏑⏑ – βασιλῆος	1	0

υἷος (2,0)

– ⏑⏑ τοιοῦδ' υἷος	1	0
– ⏑⏑ – ⏑⏑ – ⏑⏑ – ⏑⏑ υἷος ἑοῖο	1	0

υἱέος (1,0)

– ⏑⏑ – ⏑⏑ – οὗ υἱέος	1	0

παιδός (5,1)

παιδός	1	0
παιδὸς ἑοῦ	1	0
– ⏑⏑ – οὗ παιδὸς ἀμύμονος	1	0
οὗ παιδὸς τεθνηότος	0	1
– ⏑⏑ – ⏑⏑ – ⏑⏑ – ⏑⏑ παιδὸς ἑῆος	1	0
παιδὸς ἑοῖο	1	0

αὐτοῖο (3,0)

αὐτοῦ (2,0)

κείνου (3,0)

τοῦ (10,0)

APPENDIX C

Expressions Signifying Achilles
Dative Case

	Iliad	*Odyssey*
'Αχιλλῆϊ (*Iliad* 11, *Odyssey* 0)		
– ∪ Ἀχιλλῆϊ	5	0
Ἀχιλλῆϊ ῥηξήνορι	2	0
– ∪∪ – ∪∪ – ∪ Ἀχιλλῆϊ	3	0
Ἀχιλλῆϊ πτολιπόρθῳ	1	0
'Αχιλλεῖ (1,0)		
– ∪∪ – ∪∪ – ∪∪ – ∪∪ – ∪ Ἀχιλλεῖ	1	0
'Αχιλῆϊ (34,0)		
– Ἀχιλῆϊ	1	0
– ∪∪ – Ἀχιλῆϊ	9	0
Πηλεΐδη Ἀχιλῆϊ	6	0
ὀλοῷ Ἀχιλῆϊ	1	0
Ἀχιλῆϊ δαΐφρονι	3	0
Ἀχιλῆϊ ∪ – ∪ ∪ ποιμένι λαῶν	1	0
– ∪∪ – ∪∪ – ∪∪ – Ἀχιλῆϊ	4	0
Ἀχιλῆϊ ἄνακτι	1	0
– ∪∪ – ∪∪ – ∪∪ – ∪∪ – Ἀχιλῆϊ	7	0
ᾧ παιδὶ ∪ – ∪ ∪ – Ἀχιλῆϊ	1	0
Πηλεΐωνι (8,1)		
Πηλεΐωνι	1	0
– ∪∪ Πηλεΐωνι	4	0
– ∪∪ – ∪∪ – ∪∪ Πηλεΐωνι θανόντι	0	1
– ∪∪ – ∪∪ – ∪ ποδώκεϊ Πηλεΐωνι	2	0
μεγαθύμῳ Πηλεΐωνι	1	0

Πηλεΐδη (9,0)

Πηλεΐδη	3	0
Πηλεΐδη Ἀχιλῆϊ	6	0

ἀνδρί (1,0)

ἀνδρὶ ∪ – κρατερῷ	1	0

ἄνακτι (4,0)

– ⏑⏑ τῷ γε ἄνακτι	1	0
– ⏑⏑ – ⏑⏑ – ⏑⏑ – ⏑⏑ – ∪ ἄνακτι	2	0
Ἀχιλῆϊ ἄνακτι	1	0

ἑταίρῳ (2,0)

– ⏑⏑ – ⏑⏑ – ∪ φίλῳ ⏑⏑ – ∪ ἑταίρῳ	2	0

κεφαλῇ (0,1)

– ∪ Ἀχιλλῆος κεφαλῇ Πηληϊάδαο	0	1

ποιμένι λαῶν (1,0)

– ⏑⏑ – Ἀχιλῆϊ ∪ – ⏑⏑ ποιμένι λαῶν	1	0

υἱεῖ (3,0)

υἱεῖ σῷ	1	0
υἱεῖ ἐμῷ	1	0
υἱεῖ ἐμῷ ὠκυμόρῳ	1	0

παιδί (3,0)

– ⏑⏑ – ∪ φίλῳ παιδί	1	0
– ⏑⏑ – ⏑⏑ – ⏑⏑ – ῷ παιδί	1	0
– ⏑⏑ – ῷ παιδί ∪ – ⏑⏑ – Ἀχιλῆϊ	1	0

τούτῳ (2,0)

αὐτῷ (3,0)

τῷ (12,0)

οἱ (51,1)

APPENDIX D

Expressions Signifying Achilles
Accusative Case

	Iliad	*Odyssey*
Ἀχιλῆα (*Iliad* 24, *Odyssey* 0)		
– Ἀχιλῆα ∪ – ⏖ – ⏖ ὄρχαμον ἀνδρῶν	1	0
– ⏖ – Ἀχιλῆα	8	0
Πηλεΐδην Ἀχιλῆα	1	0
Ἀχιλῆα πελώριον	2	0
Ἀχιλῆα δαΐφρονα	1	0
Ἀχιλῆα πόδας ταχύν	3	0
– ⏖ – ⏖ – ⏖ – Ἀχιλῆα	1	0
– ⏖ – ⏖ – ⏖ – ⏖ – Ἀχιλῆα	4	0
ταχὺν – Ἀχιλῆα	1	0
πόδας ταχὺν – Ἀχιλῆα	1	0
Αἰακίδην Ἀχιλῆα	1	0
Ἀχιλῆ(α) (2,0)		
– Ἀχιλῆ'	2	0
Ἀχιλλῆα (7,0)		
δῖον Ἀχιλλῆα	2	0
Ἀχιλλῆα ῥηξήνορα	1	0
Ἀχιλλῆα ῥηξήνορα θυμολέοντα	1	0
– ⏖ – ⏖ – ∪ Ἀχιλλῆα πτολίπορθον	3	0
Αἰακίδην (2,0)		
Αἰακίδην Ἀχιλῆα	1	0
– ⏖ Αἰακίδην	1	0

Πηλεΐδην (3,0)

Πηλεΐδην	1	0
Πηλεΐδην Ἀχιλῆα	1	0
– ‿‿ *Πηλεΐδην*	1	0

Πηλεΐωνα (24,3)

Πηλεΐωνα	1	0
– ‿‿ *Πηλεΐωνα*	2	0
– ‿‿ – ‿‿ – ‿‿ *Πηλεΐωναδ'*	1	0
– ‿‿ – ‿‿ – ‿‿ – ‿‿ *Πηλεΐωνα*	3	0
ἀμύμονα Πηλεΐωνα	7	3
ποδώκεα Πηλεΐωνα	9	0
– ‿‿ *τόν γε ἄνακτα ποδώκεα Πηλεΐωνα*	1	0

βασιλῆα (1,0)

– ‿‿ – ‿‿ – ‿‿ – ‿‿ – *βασιλῆα*	1	0

ἄνακτα (1,0)

– ‿‿ *τόν γε ἄνακτα ποδώκεα Πηλεΐωνα*	1	0

ποιμένα λαῶν (1,0)

– ‿‿ – ‿‿ – ‿‿ – ‿‿ *ποιμένα λαῶν*	1	0

ὄρχαμον ἀνδρῶν (1,0)

– *Ἀχιλῆα* ∪ – ‿‿ – ‿‿ *ὄρχαμον ἀνδρῶν*	1	0

ἄνδρα (3,0)

– ‿‿ *ἄνδρα φέριστον*	1	0
– ‿‿ – ‿‿ – ‿‿ – ‿‿ *ἄγριον ἄνδρα*	1	0
δήϊον ἄνδρα	1	0

ἀνέρα (2,0)

– ‿‿ *ἀνέρα τοῦτον ἀτάσθαλον ὀβριμοεργόν*	1	0
– ‿‿ – ‿‿ – ‿‿ – ‿‿ *ἀνέρα τοῦτον*	1	0

σθένος ἀνέρος (1,0)

– ‿‿ – ‿‿ – *σθένος ἀνέρος*	1	0

υἱόν (6,0)

υἱὸν ἐμόν	1	0

υἱόν . . . / ἔξοχον ἡρώων   1   0

– ‿‿ – ‿‿ υἱόν   1   0

    φίλον υἱόν   1   0

        υἱὸν ἀμύμονά τε κρατερόν τε   1   0

– ‿‿ – ‿‿ – ‿‿ – ‿‿ ὃν φίλον υἱόν   1   0

υἱέα (1,0)

– ‿‿ – ‿‿ – ‿‿ υἱέα καρτερόθυμον   1   0

παῖδα (2,0)

– ἔνα παῖδα ‿ – παναώριον   1   0

– ‿‿ – ‿‿ παῖδα   1   0

τέκος (1,0)

– ‿‿ – ‿‿ – ‿ φίλον τέκος   1   0

ἄριστον Ἀχαιῶν (2,0)

ἀρχὸν ἀρηίφιλον (1,0)

σε, Πηλῆος υἱέ, μάχης ἀκόρητον (1,0)

Πηλῆος ἀμύμονος ἔκγονον (1,0)

τοῦτον (3,0)

τοῖον (1,0)

κεῖνον (0,1)

αὐτόν (4,0)

τόνδ' (1,0)

τόν (18,0)

μιν (39,1)

ἑ (6,0)

APPENDIX E

Expressions Signifying Achilles
Vocative Case

’Αχιλλεῦ (*Iliad* 16, *Odyssey* 6)	*Iliad*	*Odyssey*
– ‿‿ – ‿‿ – ‿‿ – ‿‿ – ‿ Ἀχιλλεῦ	4	4
ὄβριμ’ Ἀχιλλεῦ	1	0
φαίδιμ’ Ἀχιλλεῦ	3	1
Διὶ φίλε φαίδιμ’ Ἀχιλλεῦ	1	0
θεοείκελ’ Ἀχιλλεῦ	2	0
θεοῖς ἐπιείκελ’ Ἀχιλλεῦ	5	0
ὄλβιε Πηλέος υἱέ, θεοῖς ἐπιείκελ’ Ἀχιλλεῦ	0	1

’Αχιλεῦ (10,1)		
– Ἀχιλεῦ	3	0
ὦ Ἀχιλεῦ	2	0
ὦ Ἀχιλεῦ Πηλῆος υἱέ, μέγα φέρτατ’ Ἀχαιῶν	2	1
ὦ Ἀχιλεῦ ‿‿ – ‿ Διὶ φίλε	1	0
– ‿‿ – Ἀχιλεῦ	1	0
– ‿‿ – ‿‿ – Ἀχιλεῦ	3	0

Πηλεΐδη (7,0)		
Πηλεΐδη	3	0
Πηλεΐδη μεγάθυμε	1	0
– ‿‿ Πηλεΐδη	1	0
Πηλεΐδη, πάντων ἐκπαγλότατ’ ἀνδρῶν	2	0

Πηλέος υἱέ (7,2)		
– ‿‿ Πηλέος υἱέ	3	0
Πηλέος υἱὲ δαΐφρονος	1	0

σχέτλιε Πηλέος υἱέ	1	0
ὄλβιε Πηλέος υἱέ, θεοῖς ἐπιείκελ' Ἀχιλλεῦ	0	1
ὦ Ἀχιλεῦ Πηλῆος υἱέ, μέγα φέρτατ' Ἀχαιῶν	2	1

τέκνον (8,0)

τέκνον	4	0
τέκνον ἐμόν	4	0

τέκος (4,0)

τέκος	2	0
φίλον τέκος	2	0

ὄρχαμε λαῶν (1,0)

ἄναξ (2,0)

φίλος (3,0)

διοτρεφές (4,0)

ὦ τέπον (1,0)

αἰναρέτα (1,0)

νηλεές (2,0)

Notes

Preface

1. Adam Parry, "Language and Characterization in Homer," *Harvard Studies in Classical Philology* 76(1972):1–22. Anne Amory Parry, "Homer as Artist," *Classical Quarterly* New Series 21(1971):1–15.
2. Before the colon, J. Griffin; after the colon, R. Janko—at a conference on Homer at the University of Pennsylvania, Spring 1984.
3. In his review of *The Epithets of Homer* by P. Vivante, *Classical Philology* 80 (1985): 67.

Chapter I

1. "In any field the essence of a formula is repetition." J. B. Hainsworth, *The Flexibility of the Homeric Formula* (Oxford, 1968), p. 35.
2. It need not be significant that Aristotle does not mention them in the *Poetics,* where epic largely serves to illustrate tragedy. Moreover, one need not wonder that epic formulae are not discussed in treatises on rhetorical style, viz. "Longinus" and Demetrius. Neither tragedy nor rhetoric has much use for Homer's formulae. Grammarians and scholiasts recognize noun-epithet phrases, e.g., apud II 45:

> ξίφος ἀργυρόηλον: ὅτι τὸ Ἀγαμέμνονος ⟨ξίφος⟩ νῦν μὲν ἀργυρόηλον, ἐν ἄλλοις δὲ χρυσόηλον. . . . τὰ τοιαῦτα δὲ κυρίως οὐ λέγεται, ἀλλὰ κατ' ἐπιφοράν ἐστι ποιητικῆς ἀρεσκείας. ὥσπερ δὲ τὰ περὶ τὸν θώρακα καὶ τὴν ἀσπίδα διαφορώτερον φράζει, οὕτω καὶ τὸ ξίφος κοσμεῖ,

and apud X 220,

> θυμὸς ἀγήνωρ: παρέλκει τὸ ἐπίθετο⟨ν⟩, καὶ ἔστιν Ὁμηρικόν, ὡς τὸ Ἀνδρομάχη λευκώλενος.

These are cited from *Scholia Graeca in Homeri Iliadem,* ed. H. Erbse, (Berlin, 1969–1983), 1:186 and 3:42.

3. *Les Essais,* III ix. Compare Oliver Goldsmith in *The Vicar of Wakefield,* 2d ed., vol. 1 (London, 1766), p. 69:

> "It is remarkable," cried Mr. Burchell, "that both the poets you mention have equally contributed to introduce a false taste into their respective countries, by loading all their lines with epithet. Men of little genius found them most easily imitated in their defects, and English poetry, like that of the latter empire of Rome, is nothing at present but a combination of luxuriant images without plot or connexion; a string of epithets that improve the sound without carrying on the sense.

And contrast Jean d'Ormesson in *Le Vagabond qui passe sous une ombrelle trouée* (Paris, 1978), p. 149:

> J'aimais et j'aime toujours ces naïvetés, ces répétitions, ces signes de reconnaissance qui sont comme les tics d'un écrivain et qui donnent à un style sa saveur incomparable. Le modèle en est chez Homère où chaque personnage est invariablement accompagné de sa petite musique personnelle.

4. *Discours sur Homere* (Paris, 1754), pp. 49–50. The essay was first published in 1714.

5. *Prolegomena ad Homerum,* ed. R. Peppmüller (Hildesheim, 1963). There is now an English translation of the *Prolegomena* with introduction and notes by A. Grafton, G. W. Most, and J. E. G. Zetzel (Princeton, 1985). A. Lang badgers Wolf in four chapters of *Homer and the Epic* (London, 1893), pp. 13–78. Had I known that H. Lloyd-Jones was writing his "Remarks on the Homeric Question," in *History and Imagination: Essays in Honour of H. R. Trevor-Roper* (New York, 1982), pp. 15–29, I could have improved my chapter or discarded it. My writing was complete by then: the rigors of a University of Toronto dissertation and the discovery of word processing occasioned delays and detours.

6. S. A. Naber, *Quaestiones Homericae* (Amsterdam, 1877), p. 210.

7. Majuscule Roman numerals refer to books of the *Iliad;* minuscules, *Odyssey,* in the editions of D. B. Monro and T. W. Allen: *Iliad* 3d ed. (Oxford, 1920), *Odyssey* 2d ed. (Oxford, 1917), *Hymns* (Oxford, 1912). An asterisk precedes my own hypothetically Homeric Greek. Milman Parry is cited from Adam Parry's edition, *The Making of Homeric Verse: The Collected Papers of Milman Parry* (Oxford, 1971), hereafter *MHV.* M. Parry's major *thèse* is entitled *L'Epithète traditionnelle.*

8. Scholion apud XV 265 ἀθετοῦνται στίχοι τέσσαρες καὶ ἀστερίσκοι παράκεινται, ὅτι οἰκειότερον ἐπ' Ἀλεξάνδρου. *Scholia,* ed. Erbse, 4:69. W. Leaf writes eloquently on this passage in his commentary, *Iliad,* vol. 2 (London,

1902), p. 122:

> This simile, so fine when applied to the vain and handsome Paris loses much of its force here, where it is inserted to illustrate not the exultant beauty but merely the speed of Hector. ... We have here, as at the end of Θ (557–58), a clear plagiarism of a passage whose intrinsic beauty marked it out for plunder. How a single "Homer" could have thus repeated his own best passages, careless of their appropriateness, it is for the defenders of the unity of the *Iliad* to say. But we have no right to talk of interpolation; the simile is embedded in the structure of the book and has doubtless been so from the first, like the drums from older temples in the wall of Themistokles.

9. "Vss. 39.40 sind über Π 775.776 gemacht" is the succinct comment of A. Kirchhoff, *Die Homerische Odyssee* (Berlin, 1879), p. 534.

10. Notable instances are: A. Shewan, *The Lay of Dolon* (London, 1912) and J. A. Scott, *The Unity of Homer* (Berkeley, 1921).

11. *Conjectures académiques ou Dissertation sur l'Iliade* (Paris, 1715). The abbot might have been genuinely disturbed by the immorality of the pagan gods and heroes. The offensive evidence could be removed from circulation if it were mere trash. Homer was the great educator of Hellas; amiss, thought some. At any rate, disinterested scholarship is not apparent here, and one suspects that d'Aubignac cared more to preach than to prove. Anne Dacier was obliged to expose in *L'Escriture sainte* the same censured Homeric practices, in order to exonerate them. This is a major concern of her seventy-two page preface in *L'Iliade d'Homere traduite en françois avec des remarques* (Paris, 1711).

12. In the midst of the battle was Charles Perrault, *Parallèle des anciens et des modernes,* 4 vols. (Paris, 1692–97; reprinted Geneva, 1979). Vol. 3 defends Chapelain against Homer.

13. Ibid., 3:110–11.

14. *Remarks upon a Late Discourse of Free-Thinking* (London, 1713) is included in A. Dyce's edition of *The Works of Richard Bentley,* vol. 3 (London 1836–38). There is a good account in R. C. Jebb's, *Bentley* (London, 1902), pp. 142–51.

15. B. Croce, *The Philosophy of Giambattista Vico,* tr. R. G. Collingwood (New York, 1913), pp. 183–96. Compare also J. G. Herder, *Abhandlung über den Ursprung der Sprache* [1772], ed. W. Pross (Munich, 1978), and J.-J. Rousseau, "Essai sur l'origine des langues," in *Oeuvres Postumes de Jean-Jaque Rousseau,* vol. 3 (Geneva, 1781), pp. 211–327.

16. R. Wood, *An Essay on the Original Genius and Writings of Homer,* (London, 1775). Compare Anne Dacier (Preface to *L'Iliade,* p. xxv): "je trouve ces temps anciens d'autant plus beaux, qu'ils ressemblent moins au nostre." An excellent biography is Fern Farnham's *Madame Dacier: Scholar and Humanist* (Monterey, 1976).

17. Plato explicitly puts Homer into a class with Solon and Lysias as writers (278c1–3). If Plato had any knowledge at all of an oral tradition of Homeric poetry, then the final section of the *Phaedrus* would have been the perfect place for it. Not so E. Havelock, *Preface to Plato* (Cambridge, MA, 1963) and *The Literate Revolution in Greece and Its Cultural Consequences* (Princeton, 1982) and finally "The Linguistic Task of the Presocratics" in *Language and Thought in Early Greek Philosophy*, ed. K. Robb (La Salle, 1983), pp. 7–84. A. W. H. Adkins thoroughly rebuts Havelock in the same volume: "Orality and Philosophy," pp. 207–27.

18. Wood's emphasis, however, on "the fidelity of oral tradition and the powers of memory" in nonliterate composition, as opposed to the "Poet's knowledge" (*Original Genius*, p. 259), later led others to deny Homer's original genius and discover many Homers.

19. *Original Genius*, pp. v, vi, ix ("he wrote": *lapsus calami* common in oral composition). M. Parry was of the same school as Wood. He opens *L'Epithète traditionnelle* with a citation of E. Renan (*MHV*, p. 2):

> How can we grasp the physiognomy and the originality of a primitive literature unless we enter into the personal and moral life of the people who made it; unless we place ourselves at the point of humanity which was theirs, so that we see and feel as they saw and felt; unless we watch them live, or better, unless for a moment we live with them?

Compare Parry's essay: "The Historical Method of Literary Criticism" (*MHV*, pp. 408–13).

20. *Original Genius*, p. 281.

21. "Of Poetry and Musick" (1762) cited by D. M. Foerster, *Homer in English Criticism* (New Haven, 1947, repr. 1969), pp. 103–4.

22. *MHV*, p. 1. Parry pays tribute to Düntzer's ideas, to Berard's bibliographies, and then to three of his teachers. Recognition of Düntzer here is significant: it cannot be perfunctory and formulaic.

23. *MHV*, p. 124. In Parry's French *thèse*, Düntzer's title and sentence are translated into French from the original German. This explains the English of A. Parry's edition.

24. *MHV*, pp. 124–25.

25. A. Meillet, *Les Origines indo-européennes des mètres grecs* (Paris, 1923), p. 61, cited by Parry: *MHV*, p. 9. Meillet's book was published in the year of Parry's arrival in Paris.

26. *MHV*, p. 20. According to A. Parry, "our" must be an authorial plural. The impression is M. Parry's own; he does not owe it to Meillet (A. Parry, Introduction to *MHV*, p. xxiii):

> Meillet gave Parry confidence in following out his intuition that the structure of Homeric verse is altogether formulary; but he cannot be said to have vitally affected the direction of his thought.

The last clause, at least, is flatly contradicted by M. Parry himself (*MHV,* p. 439): "It was largely due to the remarks of my teacher M. Antoine Meillet that I came to see, dimly at first ..." As for formulae, the standard work on French medieval literature a generation before Meillet, Gaston Paris's *La Littérature française au moyen age* (Paris, 1888), has this to report on page 63:

> Il y a déjà dans le *Roland* beaucoup de formules toutes faites, héritage de l'épopée antérieure, qui facilitent au poète l'expression de ses idées, mais la rendent fréquemment banale, et qui l'empêchent trop souvent de voir directement et avec une émotion personnelle les choses qu'il veut peindre.

Here already there is mention of many traditional convenient formulae. Meillet and Parry need only have changed *Roland* to *Iliade* and *beaucoup* to *cent pour-cent.* They need not, however, have gone beyond the Homeric Question to have an account of this insight. A. van Gennep anticipated Parry's discoveries in *La Question d'Homère: Les Poèmes homériques, l'archéologie et la poésie populaire* (Paris, 1909), pp. 13–14:

> Le repos des auditeurs, et cette fois aussi du récitant, est encore obtenu par l'emploi des célèbres épithètes. ... Les "épithètes homériques" sont des clichés et des chevilles de repos, comparables aux clichés verbaux des bylines russes et des chansons épiques des slaves méridionaux. D'où leur automatisme. ... Mais l'épithète et le substantif forment un seul mot, une seule aspiration pour le chanteur, un seul harmonique pour l'auditeur. Les épithètes également stéréotypées de nos Chansons de Geste, nos "Empereur à la barbe fleurie" s'explique de la même manière. Et ce procédé se rencontre dans tous les poèmes d'une certaine longueur destinés à être récités. Un aède n'est pas un phonographe. ... [Quoting M. Bréal, *Pour mieux connaître Homère* (Paris, 1906):] "Les auditeurs d'Homère ne les percevaient pas plus que nous ne percevons l'adjectif quand nous disons le brave Dunois, le grand Corneille."

Indeed, Parry himself admits that formulae were common knowledge (*MHV,* p. 440):

> Thus my first work on the formulas of Homer thoroughly developed a familiar enough theme, since it was generally said that the Homeric style was formulaic.

Consider the *haute vulgarisation* of A. Thérive in *Le Retour d'Amazan* (Paris, 1926), pp. 58–59:

> Les vers y [*Chanson de Roland*] sont très bien faits, malgré les clichés un peu fades comme dans Homère, ce qui prouve toujours une longue tradition préalable. Evidemment le tort de ces oeuvres, quand elles languissent un peu, c'est d'avoir été faites pour la récitation et non l'édition imprimée. La diction orale autorise dans la forme trop de nonchalance et trop de facilité.

27. *MHV,* pp. 246, 106.
28. Ibid., p. 439.

29. Ibid., p. 329.

30. Ibid., p. 377. (All) oral poetry uses traditional formulae; Homer uses traditional formulae: Homer is oral poetry.

31. Ibid., p. 378.

32. Ibid., p. 440.

33. Ibid., p. 444.

34. Ibid., p. 439.

35. M. Murko, *La Poésie populaire épique en Yougoslavie au début du XXe siècle* (Paris, 1929), p. 19. Murko had previously published *Bericht über eine Reise zum Studium der Volksepik in Bosnien und Herzegowina im Jahre 1913* (Vienna, 1915) and "Neues über südslavische Volksepik," *Neue Jahrbücher für das klassische Altertum* 22 (1919):273–96.

36. *La Poésie populaire*, pp. 18, 20. Parry was particularly impressed by Murko's comments on the unfixed text of orally improvised songs. He cites Murko at length on this point (*MHV*, p. 336).

37. Paris: Beauchesne, 1925.

38. *MHV*, p. 270n.

39. J. Marouzeau, Review of *Le Style oral* by M. Jousse, *Revue des études latines* 6(1928):234–36. Adam Parry attributes to Jousse "a sharp differentiation of that kind of poetry [oral] from anything composed in writing" (*MHV*, p. xxii). Marouzeau's review of Jousse seems to contradict this (p. 235):

> Tout style est d'abord style oral. Le style écrit lui-même est oral à deux degrés, car l'écrivain en composant prononce à la fois et écoute ce qu'il écrit; il en fait, conscient ou non, l'expérience orale.

(Jousse needs reprinting: only two copies are listed in the National Union Catalog.)

40. *MHV*, p. 361.

41. R. Finnegan, *Oral Poetry: Its Nature, Significance, and Social Context* (Cambridge, 1977) p. 272. Not so R. Beaton, *Folk Poetry of Modern Greece* (Cambridge, 1980) and D. G. Miller, *Improvisation, Typology, Culture, and "the New Orthodoxy": How "Oral" Is Homer?* (Washington, DC, 1982).

42. J. L. Myres, *Homer and His Critics* (London, 1958), p. 2:

> All that any critic of Homer can do is to bring his knowledge and interpretation up to date, abreast of his generation's outlook—perhaps in some particular a little ahead of it, as a few great critics have done.

43. *MHV*, p. 440.

44. A. Shewan, "Repetition in Homer and Tennyson," *Classical Weekly* 16(1923):154.

45. A. Lang, *The World of Homer* (London, 1910), pp. 293–94. Lang and Shewan played golf at St. Andrews. Formulae are like golf clubs: a golfer

needs no more than one of each kind; one does not fashion a new club for every shot. And "not to use them would be not to play the game."

46. A. Shewan, "The Homeric Repetitions Again," *Philological Quarterly* 8(1929):115.

47. D. B. Monro, *Odyssey XIII–XXIV* (Oxford, 1901), p. 326.

48. J. A. Scott, "Repeated Verses in Homer," *American Journal of Philology* 32(1911):321.

49. *MHV,* p. 8.

50. See Parry's note at *MHV,* pp. 26–27, especially the following sentence:

> However, the *Lexicon* is particularly explicit in giving the epithets that occur with each noun, and hence has been of great value for the purposes of this essay.

51. Ibid., p. 130. Surely story telling (and possibly also epic poetry) existed in the Dark Ages. There was an oral tradition; otherwise, Homer could not have known about Troy, let alone *windy Ilion* or *steep Wilusa.* On the extent of Homer's knowledge of the past, see G. S. Kirk, "The Homeric Poems as History," in *Cambridge Ancient History,* 3d ed., vol. 2, pt. 2 (Cambridge, 1975), pp. 820–50, and M. I. Finley, "Lost: The Trojan War," revised in *Aspects of Antiquity,* 2d ed. (Harmondsworth, 1977), pp. 31–42.

52. *Poems of Alexander Pope,* ed. M. Mack (London and New Haven, 1967), 7:3. Italics in edition of London: Temple-Gates, 1720.

53. *L'Iliade d'Homère* (Paris, [1932]), p. 7.

54. A. Parry, Introduction to *MHV,* p. xlix.

55. *MHV,* pp. 8, 16.

56. Ibid., pp. 82, 106.

57. Ibid., pp. 206, 220.

58. F. M. Combellack, "Homer the Innovator," *Classical Philology* 71(1976):54.

59. Ibid., p. 55.

60. Ibid.

61. *MHV,* p. 189.

62. Ibid., p. 190.

63. Tables of Homeric diction with frequencies of occurrences are provided in appendixes A to E. I am here concerned with only one essential idea—*Achilles.* By *extension,* I mean the variety of metrical shapes in which Homer expresses that essential idea. By *economy* or *thrift,* I mean the lack of variety in which Homer expresses that essential idea in each of these metrical shapes. This is what Parry too means by *extension* and *economy.* In addition, however, Parry unduly confuses the term *extension* by applying it also to the variety of essential ideas (e.g., names of different gods and heroes) that are expressed in any given metrical shape. In restricting myself to Achilles, I avoid this ambiguity. I have, however, compared my appendixes naming Achilles with lists of the names of Zeus and Odysseus. They are agreeable.

Chapter II

1. A Greek bard need not have fastidiously fashioned and produced ἕζετο δ' ἥρως, in the mould of ἥλυθε δ' ἥρως. Much has been made of Homer's artificial language (*Kunstsprache*), but many phrases were doubtless composed in ordinary Greek and would have been spoken daily by ordinary Greek speakers. Compare Anne Dacier, (Preface to *L'Iliade*, p. xl):

> Aristote mesme a reconnu que la prose n'est pas ennemie du Poëme Epique, puisqu'il a escrit que l'Epopée se sert de la prose comme des vers.

Presumably, she refers to *Poetics* 1458a18–1459a16.

2. Αὐτός "sert à souligner une personne ou un objet par opposition à ce qui l'entoure." P. Chantraine, *Grammaire homerique*, Vol. 2: *Syntaxe* (Paris, 1953), p. 156.

3. Homer has it only twice: iv 224, viii 550; it is not in Hesiod or the *Hymns*. With all the talk of parents in the poems, one might have expected these phrases to occur as frequently as our formulaic *Papa et Maman*.

4. Alternative phrases are easily conceived:

*ἐν νηῶν ἀγύρει Θέτις ἀργυρόπεζα / Πηλεΐδης τε

*ἐν νηῶν ἀγύρει Θέτις Αἰακίδης τε.

5. That is, since 811 ὣς ἔφατ'. Aristophanes and Aristarchus athetize the lines, perhaps considering the reference to Achilles unclear. The grammarians are distrusted, however, in questions of formulaic diction.

6. If indeed there was a normal way.

7. Leaf comments at XXIII 896: "δῶκε: Achilles.—ὅ γ' marks a fresh act of the same subject, as often." Ambiguity is denied.

8. A third can be ὅ γ' ἤδη.

9. Sthenelus V 327, Diomede X 154, Meriones XIII 164.

10. Teucer VIII 268, Odysseus XI 483, Meriones XIII 164.

11. Αὐτὰρ 'Οδυσσεύς 25 times, αὐτὰρ Ἀθήνη 6 times, αὐτὰρ Ἀπόλλων 2 times.

12. At IX 628, ὅ γ' ἥρως would have been effective sarcasm.

13. XI 482–83 'Οδυσῆα . . . αὐτὰρ ὅ γ' ἥρως, XX 422–23 Ἀχιλῆϊ . . . αὐτὰρ Ἀχιλλεύς.

14. VI 414, IX 199, IX 663, XVIII 228, XXI 39, XXIII 136, XXIV 151, 180, 596.

15. The most notorious example of overlengthening is ποδάρκης δῖος Ἀχιλλεύς. If overlengthening was reprehensible, ποδάρκης δῖος Ἀχιλλεύς would have been or become ποδάρκης ὠκὺς Ἀχιλλεύς, even if this amounted to *foot-swift swift Achilles:* for Homer is thought to have been indifferent to the particular meaning of epithets and glosses.

16. It occurs four times: V 438, XVI 705, 786, XX 447.

17. I should like to use the terms *pronoun* and *pronominal* loosely for any expression that takes the place of a noun. Moreover, in order to avoid cumbersome expressions, when speaking of formulae, let *vocalic* mean beginning with a vowel, and let *consonantal* mean beginning with a consonant.

18. Homer might have been well advised to avoid two comparisons in one line: like fire *(ὥς)* . . . like (equal to) a god. If δαίμονι ἶσος was essentially equivalent to δῖος Ἀχιλλεύς, Homer might not have noticed the literal double comparison that a literate poet could have guarded against. This case militates against always taking δαίμονι ἶσος as a significant adverbial phrase.

19. The following verbs are found with δαίμονι ἶσος: ἐπέσσυτο (six times), θῦνε (once), ἔσθορε (once). Δαίμονι ἶσος appears never to be used merely for its pronominal quality. For variation, compare ἐπέσσυτο οἴδματι θύων seven lines after ἐπέσσυτο δαίμονι ἶσος (XXI 227).

20. The first is good if ἥρως regularly refers to Achilles in the sixth foot. The second and third need the antique dual. Ἀγαλείος Ἀχιλλεύς is literally apt, but a jingle. Ἴφθιμος is out of its regular place. There are doubtless others.

21. The great paradox is that words "holy and sweet and wondrous" (*MHV*, p. 374) should elicit *indifference*.

22. Likewise XXIII 776.

23. If Homer had consistently chosen the forms with *nu* or without *nu*, one could conclude that this element determined his choice.

24.

XVIII 203

αὐτὰρ Ἀχιλλεὺς ὦρτο Διὶ φίλος· ἀμφὶ δ' Ἀθήνη

might have been

*ἂν δ' ἄρα διογενὴς ὦρτο κλυτὸς ὠκὺς Ἀχιλλεύς.

Without *κλυτὸς ὠκὺς Ἀχιλλεύς, Homer would likewise be unable to say *Achilles* after the conjunctions δέ, ἠδέ, οὔτε, τε.

25. It is a short step from *ἠδὲ (μ)μεγάθυμος Ἀχιλλεύς to *ἠδὲ πόδας ὠκὺς Ἀχιλλεύς.

26. ἠδ' ὁ is a correction for ἠδέ: the same precedes πτολίπορθος Ὀδυσσεύς at II 278 and X 363.

27. Κλυτός is found only in this position, if ὀνομάκλυτος, which is sometimes written separately, is excepted. Four other names have the epithet κλυτός.

28. Compare the one occurrence of θρασύς:

x 436–37

ἡμέτεροι ἕταροι, σὺν δ' ὁ θρασὺς εἶπετ' Ὀδυσσεύς·
τούτου γὰρ καὶ κεῖνοι ἀτασθαλίῃσιν ὄλοντο.

29. Or the corpse's being swift-footed: νέκυν πόδας ὠκύν.

30. For example, *πόδας ὠκὺς Ἀχιλλεύς / ἐς σκέλος ἐκ κεφαλῆς.

31. Or great-hearted corpse: νέκυν μεγάθυμον.

32. One might try to infer the relative ages of the story of *swift feet* (πόδας ὠκὺς Ἀχιλλεύς) and the story of *great anger* (μεγάθυμος Ἀχιλλεύς). The story of Achilles' *anger* is too recent for μεγάθυμος Ἀχιλλεύς to be firmly established in Homer's formulaic diction. Did Statius have this epic source for his *Achilleid*, which begins: "magnanimum Aeaciden ... diva, refer"?

33. Analogy is Parry's important contribution to Düntzer: it is supposed to account for equivalencies (*MHV*, p. 175):

A large portion of the equivalent noun-epithet formulae which disturbed Düntzer actually attest it [the influence of metre i.e. traditional diction].

34. *MHV*, p. 179.

35. It seems reasonable that, Achilles being the hero that he was and the subject of songs, one would sooner find fifty examples of μεγάθυμος Ἀχιλλεύς in lost epics than five of μεγάθυμος Ἀγήνωρ.

36. Parry is so often black and white; the truth, however, would seem to be gray. For example, a traditional bard is *never* searching for new words; apparently a literate poet *always* does. Compare W. B. Stanford, "Remarks on the Collected Works of Milman Parry," *Hermathena* 112(1971):43:

One may note in passing how fond Parry was of using words like "must," "invariably," "inevitably," "unquestionably," "it is certain that," symptoms partly, no doubt, of youth's generous yearning for intellectual absolutes.

37. Parry noticed this problem (*MHV*, pp. 188–89) and explained it by an unenlightening truism: its fixity prevents it from changing. Habitual use and lack of an alternative condone it, whereas Ἥρης χρυσοπεδίλου is condemned because it is not often used and because it has a flawless equivalent, Ἥρης ἠϋκόμοιο. But flawless equivalents of ποδάρκης δῖος Ἀχιλλεύς are easily found, and habitual use of an overlengthened phrase justifies extension of the practice (by analogy) and finally exculpates overlengthening.

38. The hypothetical formulae are derived by analogy from formulae for Achilles in the other cases.

39. Generic epithets and the principle of analogy suggest many possibilities.

40. Only ἔπειτα (twice), ἄκοντι, and δέ require a consonantal formula—unless γ' can close the vowels, in which case ποδάρκης δῖος Ἀχιλλεύς would never be needed.

41. Homer uses this same image, but not *ad nauseam*. Vergil here is more like the unimaginative formulaic bard, frequently reusing the same device: *Aeneid* II 222, 338, 488; IV 665, V 140, 451; X 262, 895; XI 192, 745, 832, 878; XII 409, 462.

42. Ἄρης ἆτος πολέμοιο occurs three times in Homer: V 388, V 863, VI 203.

43. The two uses of vocalic formulae for Achilles in this position are made possible by paragogic *nu:* XIII 746, XVI 166. In three cases, however, the poet stops short of the vocalic formula.

XX 467

οὐ γάρ τι γλυκύθυμος ἀνὴρ ἦν οὐδ' ἀγανόφρων.

Here is a line worthy of Herodotus. A formulaic bard might have been expected to use the vocalic formula for Achilles in the second hemistich:

*οὐ γάρ τι γλυκύθυμος ἀνὴρ ἆτος πολέμοιο

*οὐ γάρ τι γλυκύθυμος ἀρήϊος ὠκὺς Ἀχιλλεύς

*οὐ γάρ τι γλυκύθυμος ἀμύμων ὠκὺς Ἀχιλλεύς.

A verb might easily have been substituted for an epithet:

*οὐ γάρ τι γλυκύθυμος ἀρήϊος ἦεν Ἀχιλλεύς

*οὐ γάρ τι γλυκύθυμος ἀμύμων ἦεν Ἀχιλλεύς.

XXI 536

δείδια γὰρ μὴ οὖλος ἀνὴρ ἐς τεῖχος ἅληται.

The place for a noun-epithet formula is not between the second diaeresis and hephthemimeris.

*δείδια γὰρ μὴ ἐς τεῖχος ἅληται δῖος Ἀχιλλεύς

*δείδια μὴ κατὰ τεῖχος ἅληται δαίμονι ἶσος.

Since the predicate is postponed, it could have fallen after

*δείδια γὰρ μὴ οὖλος ἀνὴρ ἆτος πολέμοιο

or the like.

XXIV 207

ὠμηστὴς καὶ ἄπιστος ἀνὴρ ὅ γε, οὔ σ' ἐλεήσει.

Again the poet resists the inclination to fill the hemistich with the vocalic formula for Achilles:

*ὠμηστὴς καὶ ἄπιστος ἀνὴς ἆτος πολέμοιο

or the like. Formulae are often best unused.

44. Paradoxically, the very fixity of ποδάρκης δῖος Ἀχιλλεύς can hinder facile versification; for it does not allow substitution of essential words for inessential ones. Formulaic phrases are more useful if they are flexible.

45. The economic and extensive system of pronominal expressions, like that of nominal expressions, should consist of three unique phrases: vocalic, consonantal, and double consonantal. The number of noun-epithet formulae of gods and heroes is therefore doubled. Alternatively, the formulary bards may have foregone the nicety of pronominal formulae and always used nominal formulae. Homer did not.

46. The preceding line ends with ποδώκεος Αἰακίδαο. The poet's semantic sensitivity might have led him to avoid representing Achilles as *foot-swift* while standing. But since such semantic illogicalities do remain in Homer, perhaps his more refined musical sensitivity was responsible for rejecting ποδώκης here. One might hypothesize stages in the hermeneutics of epithets and the development of style: (1) insensitivity to epithets, (2) musical sensitivity to epithets, (3) semantic sensitivity to epithets.

47. Homer's musical composition may be responsible for the parechesis of ἄρα ἀρήϊος.

48. Achilles is twice *dear to Zeus* when meter prohibited *foot-swift:*

I 74

ὦ Ἀχιλεῦ, κέλεαί με, Διὶ φίλε, μυθήσασθαι

XXII 216

νῦν δὴ νῶι ἔολπα, Διὶ φίλε φαίδιμ' Ἀχιλλεῦ.

Analogy rather excuses than justifies the use of Διὶ φίλος with Ἀχιλλεύς in other cases; so does the mere fact that Διὶ φίλος is a generic epithet of a hero and Achilles is a hero.

49. Strunk and White, *The Elements of Style,* 3d ed. (New York, 1979), p. 71.

50. Achilles and Hector are clearly Zeus's favorites in the story itself. Only Achilles, Hector, and Odysseus have the epithet more than once. Apollo, Patroclus, κήρυκες, Phoenix, and Phyleus have the epithet once each. Phonic reasons may be suspected in the last two instances.

51. Parry would evoke analogy to explain Homer's use of the unfamiliar expression. Three other lines are similar:

XXIV 325

τὰς 'Ιδαῖος ἔλαυνε δαΐφρων· αὐτὰρ ὄπισθεν

viii 373

πορφυρέην, τήν σφιν Πόλυβος ποίησε δαΐφρων

xxii 243

Πείσανδρός τε Πολυκτορίδης Πόλυβός τε δαΐφρων.

Although *Polybus the skillful Phaeacian* is not *Polybus the fiery suitor,* the repeated noun-epithet combination may claim formulaic status. Then somehow (doubtless in the flush of hectic composition) where ordinary

Homeric usage and traditional diction calls for *foot-swift Achilles:*

*χρυσὸν δὲ ποδώκης εἷλεν Ἀχιλλεύς

*χρυσὸν δὲ λάβεν πόδας ὠκὺς Ἀχιλλεύς

(as, too, does the Homerist who hastily supplies formulae for lacunae in mutilated papyri), Πόλυβος δαΐφρων comes to mind as if by lapse of synapse and serves as a model for the creation of Ἀχιλεὺς δαΐφρων. Analogy explains how other formulae can be constructed, but not why in any given line a familiar formula is or is not replaced by an intrusive and otiose analogical formation. Another theory compares the use of names with and without an epithet. Δαΐφρων might have been used in these lines:

V 11
    Φηγεὺς Ἰδαῖός τε, μάχης εὖ εἰδότε πάσης

V 20
    Ἰδαῖος δ' ἀπόρουσε λιπὼν περικαλλέα δίφρον

*Ἰδαῖός τε δαΐφρων at V 11 would have allowed the poet to begin the next sentence at the fourth diaeresis, as at XXIV 325. Alternatively, both sentences could have been stopped at the main caesura and adjectival development neglected, as at VII 416. At V 20 Idaeus plays the coward; the poet, avoiding inconsistency, has him dash off without δαΐφρων. At viii 373 the poet might have been thinking of δαιδάλλων; he ingeniously shortened it by a breve to δαΐφρων, which can be understood as synonymous. At xxii 243 the poet might have preferred to give Polybus a patronymic to balance the line, but since neither Polybus nor a patronymic fits the meter of the sixth foot he settled for a convenient epithet, although he might have recomposed the line entirely. In these instances the poet appears to be composing a word at a time, not in formulae: he is not wholly dependent upon traditional diction and analogical models. Some of Homer's phrases are just as much *his own* as Pindar's are.

52. The possibility of elision allows the caesura to be either masculine or feminine. The former is rarer and not classified by Parry as a principal type (*MHV*, p. 39).

53. The mindless repetition of familiar formulae might have been stodgy and stuffy. Those who admire traditional diction in Homer might have loathed it in doggerel as in caricature. If all bards were singing the same myths and legends, something in Homer's freer style might have distinguished him from the rest.

54. The first two are most notable; the others are defensible by analogy. For ἐκομίσσατο, compare VIII 284. Δὲ λάβεν/ δ' εἷλεν and εἷλεν/ αἴνυτ' are equivalencies. Here and hereafter, the long lists of possible substitutions

offered in my doctoral dissertation (University of Toronto, 1985) are curtailed.

55. Μενέλαε δαΐφρον is not in Homer; an equivalent φίλος ὦ Μενέλαε is found once. Homer has Μενέλαος ἀμύμων once; ξανθὸς Μενέλαος is the regular phrase, although it often commits the fault of overlengthening where Μενέλαος ἀμύμων would be blameless. There is reason to infer that Homer cared nothing for overlengthening, was careful to keep Menelaus ξανθός, and failed to perceive the utility of the formulaic system of δαΐφρων and ἀμύμων.

56. Parry disapproves overlengthening at the bucolic diaeresis, "where the rapidity of movement is essential to the rhythm" (MHV, p. 41). Ἥρης χρυσοπεδίλου is condemned as "the work of a poet who had lost the sense of the ancient heroic rhythm" (MHV, p. 189). The equivalent Ἥρης ἠϋκόμοιο is approved. Nothing is said of overlengthening at the main caesura, but consistency doubtless requires that Parry should condemn Ἑρμείας χρυσόρραπις and approve the equivalent Ἑρμείας ἐριούνιος. Analogy would presumably generalize the use or disuse of overlengthening.

57. This formula, along with Ἀχαιῶν χαλκοχιτώνων and ποδάρκης δῖος Ἀχιλλεύς and others, must have become established before any prohibition of overlengthening. With the retention of old formulae, the force of analogy would be working against the new prohibition. Oral composition could hardly benefit by uncertainty and inhibition.

58. This contravenes Parry's one condemnation. According to this argument Ἥρης χρυσοπεδίλου is ancient, whereas Ἥρης ἠϋκόμοιο is a recent correction easily perpetrated by supplanting the distinctive χρυσοπεδίλου in favor of the generic ἠϋκόμοιο, a weak substitute. The principle is lectio difficilior.

59. When overlengthening was permitted, bards sang

*οὐ μὰν οὐδ' Ἀχιλεὺς μίσγει χεῖράς τε μένος τε.

60. Some will be quick to remark that the story of Achilles' invulnerability is first read in Statius (Achilleid 1.134). It is in fact a motif of folk-tale. It is as absurd to suppose that Homer knew no more than what we see in print in our texts as it is to suppose that Aeschylus knew no more than what appears in the extant plays. The Iliad is not an encyclopaedic article on the subject of Achilles. It is simply impossible to say when the motif was first applied to Achilles. Homer's invulnerable Achilles need not disdain Hephaestus' panoply and charge into battle naked, in folk-tale fashion; for epic has a capacity of viewing things separately, combining incompatibles. Invulnerability is like fate—Hector and Troy are bound to fight invincible foes, tragically.

61. Pronouns are developed by appositives rather than by epithets.

62. These are Parry's rubrics (*MHV*, pp. 37, 63).

63. Parry's rubrics: ibid., p. 39.

64.

*Πηλεΐδης Ἀχιλεύς	8 × Πηληϊάδεω Ἀχιλῆος
*διογενὴς Ἀχιλεύς	I 489 διογενὴς Πηλῆος υἱός
	6 × διογενὴς Ὀδυσεύς
*αἰχμητὴς Ἀχιλεύς	ii 19 Ἄντιφος αἰχμητής
*δῖος Πηλεΐδης (δ' Αἰακίδης)	XXI 250 δῖον Ἀχιλλῆα
*διογενὴς (αἰχμητὴς) ἥρως	4 × γέρων ἥρως
	2 × φαίδιμος ἥρως (Allen: Φαίδιμος)
*δουρικλειτὸς ἀνήρ	XVII 520 αἰζήϊος ἀνήρ
	I 144 ἀνὴρ βουληφόρος
*Πηλεΐδης δ' ἥρως	2 × Τηλέμαχος θ' ἥρως
	3 × Λαέρτῃ ἥρωϊ (also gen., acc.)
*ἥρως Πηλεΐδης (Αἰακίδης)	5 × ἥρως Ἀτρεΐδης

65. There is something illiberal here; Homer's expressions lack Homeric fullness.

66. That there is no pronominal reference to Hector in the fourth line shows that it could be absent in the third. Its absence in the fourth would make probable its presence in the third only if Homer knew before he composed the third that it would be absent in the fourth, i.e., if he composed the fourth before the third, as a premeditative poet often does.

67. The verb is otiose, besides being pedestrian. After θεῖον γένος (Homer's phrase at VI 180), the poet would have turned the line differently.

68. Πατέρα is clearly ἑὸν πατέρα, just like unmodified πατρός four lines before.

69. Why did Homer not compose XXIV 631 on the model of

XXIV 483

   ὡς Ἀχιλεὺς θάμβησεν ἰδὼν Πρίαμον θεοειδέα

   *ἀλλ' Ἀχιλεὺς θάμβησεν ἰδὼν Πρίαμον θεοειδέα.

Instead of repeating this formulaic line, Homer declined names:

XXIV 629

   ἤτοι Δαρδανίδης Πρίαμος θαύμαζ' Ἀχιλῆα

XXIV 631

   αὐτὰρ ὁ Δαρδανίδην Πρίαμον θαύμαζεν Ἀχιλλεύς.

Homer seems to have the last few lines of text before him.

70. Long closed παίζειν requires Πηλέος υἱός; otherwise, either phrase will do:

*παίζει Πηλέος υἱός	παίζει Ἀχιλλεὺς αὐτός
*παίζεν Πηλέος υἱός	παίζεν Ἀχιλλεὺς αὐτός
*αἶψε δὲ Πηλέος υἱός	αἶψε δ' Ἀχιλλεὺς αὐτός.

71. The force of analogy might account for these phrases.

*Πηληΐδης μεγάθυμος	XXI 153 Πηλεΐδη μεγάθυμε
*Πηλεΐδης πτολίπορθος	3 × Ἀχιλλῆα πτολίπορθον
*Πηλεΐδης πόδας ὠκύς	xiii 260 Ὀρσίλοχον πόδας ὠκύν
*δῖος Πηλέος υἱός	2 × δῖον Ἀχιλλῆα
*ἥρως Πηλέος υἱός	5 × ἥρως Ἀτρεΐδης
*ἥρως δουρικλειτός	xv 52 ἥρως Ἀτρεΐδης, δουρικλειτὸς Μενέλαος

72.

*ἰδ' Ἀτρεΐδης Ἀγαμέμνων	XIV 380 καὶ Ἀτρεΐδης Ἀγαμέμνων
*καὶ ἄναξ ἀνδρῶν Ἀγαμέμνων	
*ἄναξ τ' ἀνδρῶν Ἀγαμέμνων	viii 77 ἄναξ δ' ἀνδρῶν Ἀγαμέμνων
*εὐρυκρείων τ' Ἀγαμέμνων	

73. *MHV*, p. 18:

A study of the noun-epithet formula in Apollonius and in Virgil will show us in the most conclusive manner that it is impossible for a poet by himself to create more than an insignificant number of noun-epithet formulae.

74. Of course, some of these could hardly be acceptable, unless perhaps the special effect of anadiplosis or anastrophe is desired, as in

*Πηλεΐδης Ἀχιλεύς, Ἀχιλεὺς ἦύς τε μέγας τε.

Moreover, the lists consist only of lines built round the penthemimeral and tritotrochaic caesurae. Homer or the tradition went to the trouble to build a phrase round the hephthemimeral caesura, with the help of synizesis:

I 489

διογενὴς Πηλῆος υἱός, πόδας ὠκὺς Ἀχιλλεύς.

A line divided at the trithemimeral caesura is guaranteed by analogy with the thrice-repeated line

VII 166, VIII 264, XVII 259

Μηριόνης, ἀτάλαντος Ἐννυαλίῳ ἀνδρειφόντῃ

*Πηλεΐδης, ἀτάλαντος Ἐννυαλίῳ ἀνδρειφόντῃ.

We are asked to believe that tradition chose the optimal line and Homer acquiesced. Compare C. R. Beye, *The Iliad, the Odyssey, and the Epic Tradition* (London, 1968), p. 11:

> Once the formula came into being and was accepted as the optimum phrase in terms of semantics, meter, and aesthetics, it stood—there was no alternative.

I 489 might rather be found somewhat forced: Homer approved the oxymoron in the previous verse *(παρήμενος ὠκυπόροισι)* and enhanced it with *πόδας ὠκύς* mirroring *ὠκυπόροισι* (which is repeated from I 421).

75. The line might demonstrate by contextual irrelevance that it was merely a tag.

76. This line would allow the poet to repeat the pun on Peleus and Pelion *(Πηλιάδα μελίην* XXII 133), which would then confidently be pronounced traditional.

77. There are other ways to make the comparison with Ares:

Πηλείδης, ἀτάλαντος Ἐνυαλίῳ ἀνδρειφόντῃ

Πηλείδης Ἀχιλεύς, βροτολοιγῷ ἶσος Ἄρηϊ

ὄρμενος αἰεὶ ῥίμφα, θοῷ ἀτάλαντος Ἄρηϊ

Πηλείδης Ἀχιλεὺς ἥρως, ἀτάλαντος Ἄρηϊ

Πηλείδης Ἀχιλεὺς δουρικλυτός, ἶσος Ἄρηϊ.

78. To admit that it was reserved for special use is to admit that it had special force i.e., it did not merely name the subject and get the poet to the end of the verse.

79. Here are four examples at the beginning of XXIII:

*4–5 *εἴα ἀποσκίδνασθαι ἐκεῖνος/διογενὴς Πηλῆος υἱός*

*12–13 *ἦρχε δ' ὅ γ' ἥρως/διογενὴς Πηλῆος υἱός*

*29–30 *δαίνυ/διογενὴς Πηλῆος υἱός*

*42–43 *ἐπὶ δ' ὅρκον ὅμοσσεν/διογενὴς Πηλῆος υἱός.*

Chapter III

1. If it is just a matter of getting Achilles into the line, then *him, that one,* and *that man* are undifferentiated in meaning and therefore may be classified together and called (loosely) pronominal.

2. *Φωτὸς ἐῆος* (xiv 505) is *ἀνδρὸς ἐῆος* with an initial consonant.

3. *Υἷος ἐῆος her goodly son* is also attested in the first line and *ἀνδρὸς ἐοῖο your man* in the second. This is another small instance of superfluity of expression, if all either does is to signify Achilles in so much metrical space.

4. Presumably *χάλκεον τοῖο ἄνακτος* with synizesis, easily mistaken by a dull scribe and emended by a formulary scribe. *Τοῖο ἄνακτος* occurs at iii 388 and xxi 62.

5. A more professional bard would remember regular formulae and therefore not require analogy and equivalence.

6. Extempore oral composition is expedited by a lack of such alternatives: nice nuances are niggling minutiae. Repetition of irrelevancies is the stuff of oral style. Thetis caressing *Peleides* would correspond well with Penelope's *heavy hand*.

7. In the first case, Homer is always nodding; in the second, he never nods; in the third, he is at least a credible genius.

8. In its only other occurrence, Πηληϊάδαο follows the main caesura (XVI 686).

9. Substituting ἥρωος or βασιλῆος for Ἀχιλῆος provides two more series of formulae. The forms with hiatus might originally have contained a conjunction: κρατεροῦ τ᾽ Ἀχιλῆος.

10. *MHV*, p. 57. The pair is therefore ignored also in Parry's lists of equivalent formulae justified by analogy (ibid., pp. 177–89). Patronymics used as *epithets* before a proper name show up in Ebeling under the name of the hero; and they figure, of course, in Parry's tables, e.g., Πηληϊάδεω Ἀχιλῆος. Other expressions are occasionally noted (ibid., p. 38):

> The expressions given in square brackets are those which do not actually contain the name of the god or hero, but can take its place; for example, πατὴρ ἀνδρῶν τε θεῶν τε for Zeus and Τυδέος υἱός for Diomedes.

These are precisely the types of formulae that would produce a considerable number of equivalent formulae. When Parry reports them, it is for the benefit of extension, not to the detriment of economy.

11. In different circumstances, therefore, one could perhaps expect one of these:

*ἀρηΐου Αἰακίδαο
*Ἀχιλῆος μεγαθύμου
*Ἀχιλῆος βασιλῆος
*Ἀχιλῆος κρατεροῖο
*Ἀχιλῆος πτολιπόρθου
*ἀγακλειτοῦ βασιλῆος
*ὑπερθύμου βασιλῆος
*ἀρηϊφίλου βασιλῆος
*ἐϋμμελίω βασιλῆος
*διοτρεφέος βασιλῆος
*ἀγακλῆος βασιλῆος
*ὑπερθύμοιο ἄνακτος
*ἄνακτος κυδαλίμοιο.

12. A chief virtue of Parry's brilliant theory is to be rid of premeditation—thereby explaining and condoning the Homeric anomalies and inconsistencies. Now oralists reinstate premeditation to explain and extol Homeric niceties. τὰ ἐναντία τῶν ἐναντίων ἐστὶν ἰήματα.

13. Uniqueness is reinstated if the latter was devised as μμεγαθύμου Πηλεΐωνος and strictly used by the formulary bards to lengthen a short syllable. In this case, Homer fails to appreciate this elementary point.

14. *MHV*, p. 57.

15. See μεγάθυμος in chap. II.

16. Plato, *Cratylus* 419e.

17. Μεγαθύμῳ Πηλεΐωνι is also well attested here; Zenodotus preferred Πηληϊάδεω Ἀχιλῆος. Family i also has this line in place of

XVII 199

τεύχεσι Πηλεΐδαο κορυσσόμενον θείοιο.

18. Θυμός and *fumus* are cognates (Boisacq, *Dictionnaire étymologique de la langue grecque,* p. 356). Athena's fire represents Achilles' anger as Athena's hair-pulling represents Achilles' second thoughts. The poet is characteristically ambivalent about human and divine responsibility: poetic truth is served by both explanations. The different levels of reality are discussed by A. Lesky, *Göttliche und menschliche Motivation im homerischen Epos* (Heidelberg, 1961), and M. M. Willcock, "Some Aspects of the Gods in the *Iliad*," *Bulletin of the Institute of Classical Studies* 17(1970):1–10, and idem, "Ad hoc Invention in the *Iliad*," *Harvard Studies in Classical Philology* 81(1977):43–53.

19. This is not a case of

*μῆνιν ἀπειπόντος F' ἀγαπήνορος Αἰακίδαο

or

*μῆνιν ἀπειπόντος μεγαλήτορος Αἰακίδαο

but of Achilles forgoing a now trivial anger because he is furious, μεγαθύμου.

20. Compare ἄστυ μέγα Πριάμοιο ἄνακτος (four times) and ἄστυ μέγα Πριάμοιο ∪ – – (twice).

21. This is the common theme of the *Greek genius*. The Egyptians repeated formulae of statuary over millennia, whereas the Greeks mastered the style and surpassed mere stylization in a century. Tragedy and Comedy, from boorish ritual to high art in a century; History, from annals to Thucydides in a century; Philosophy, pre-Socratic to Plato in a century; Rhetoric, from Gorgias to Demosthenes in a century. Man's boast: to transcend the slow evolution of pithecanthropes.

22. It is the convenient linkage of formulae (vocalic, consonantal, and biconsonantal) that led Parry to the idea of extemporary composition. The

bard need not worry about the adaptability of the fourth colon when composing the third. In turn, extemporization was blamed for faulty linkages—which must go unexplained if Homer could plan ahead. Oralists who grant Homer premeditation *must forfeit* Parry's considerable success in explaining Homer's anomalies by unpremeditation.

23. Πηλείδεω Ἀχιλῆος also occurs once at the end of the verse:

viii 75
   νεῖκος Ὀδυσσῆος καὶ Πηλείδεω Ἀχιλῆος,

where it should have been especially useful with conjunctions and prepositions. An equivalent noun-epithet formula is also available:

X 392
   ὅς μοι Πηλείωνος ἀγαυοῦ μώνυχας ἵππους
  *ὅς μοι Πηλείδεω Ἀχιλῆος μώνυχες ἵππους
  *νεῖκος Ὀδυσσῆος καὶ Πηλείωνος ἀγαυοῦ.

24. Achilles is still angry in Book XV, but

XV 63–4
   φεύγοντες δ' ἐν νηυσὶ πολυκλήϊσι πέσωσι
   Πηλείδεω Ἀχιλῆος.

25. Combellack, "Homer the Innovator," *Classical Philology* 71(1976):54.

Chapter IV

1. The corresponding form Ἀχιλεῖ does not occur in the *Iliad* or *Odyssey*, but Parry would be unwilling to exclude it from formulaic diction (*MHV*, p. 174):

> Except in the case of an expression which by its very nature could not be of use in the making of verse—and it is doubtful that any such could be found in Homer—we cannot claim to be so familiar with bardic diction that we could with confidence refuse to recognize as traditional any element which would add flexibility in composition.

2. Adverbial expressions might replace epithets as metrical filler. Homer often fills the line with punctuation and an ongoing clause.

3. The pronominal use of ποιμένα λαῶν is well illustrated in the following passage:

XIX 384–86
   πειρήθη δ' ἕο αὐτοῦ ἐν ἔντεσι Ἀχιλλεύς
   εἰ οἷ ἐφαρμόσσειε καὶ ἐντρέχοι ἀγλαὰ γυῖα·
   τῷ δ' εὖτε πτερὰ γίγνετ', ἄειρε δὲ ποιμένα λαῶν.

To him they became as wings and lifted him. Both τῷ and ποιμένα λαῶν have the same function: to stand for Achilles.

4. Τῷ γε ἄνακτι is metrically interchangeable with ποιμένι λαῶν here, but its connotation probably differs:

XXIII 173

ἐννέα τῷ γε ἄνακτι τραπεζῆες κύνες ἦσαν.

5.

*διδοῖς οἶκόνδε φέρεσθαι

XXIV 581

δοίη οἶκόνδε φέρεσθαι.

*διδοῖς ἥρωϊ ἄνακτι

XIII 582

ἥρωϊ ἄνακτι.

*διδοῖς Ἀχιλῆϊ γ᾽ ἄποινα

II 229–30

. . . . . . χρυσοῦ ἐπιδεύεαι, ὅν κέ τις οἴσει
Τρώων ἱπποδάμων ἐξ ᾽Ιλίου υἷος ἄποινα

and

IX 120

ἄψ ἐθέλω ἀρέσαι δόμεναι τ᾽ ἀπερείσι᾽ ἄποινα.

*διδοῖς, κρείων Ἀγάμεμνον

II 362

κρῖν᾽ ἄνδρας κατὰ φῦλα, κατὰ φρήτρας, Ἀγάμεμνον.

*διδοῖς ἀρέσαι γ᾽ Ἀχιλῆϊ

XVI 40

δὸς δέ μοι ὤμοιιν τὰ σὰ τεύχεα θωρηχθῆναι.

*διδοῖς ᾧ Ζεύς γε φιλήσῃ

IX 116–17

. . . . . . ἀντὶ νυ πολλῶν
λαῶν ἐστιν ἀνὴρ ὅν τε Ζεὺς κῆρι φιλήσῃ.

Homer might also have punctuated after διδοῖς and proceeded to the expression of the next sentence.

6. Unbalanced expressions and a spondaic beginning of the succeeding sentence would make a poor verse:

*Ἕκτορος ἀμφὶ νέκυι καὶ Ἀχιλλῆϊ· κλέψαι δέ.

7. It seems that Parry would also have neglected it if he had made a table of noun-epithet formulae for gods and heroes in the dative case; for it is a patronymical formula. Inadequate extension prevented Parry from showing tables of the dative, accusative, and vocative cases—which patronymical formulae could have helped to fill.

8. Another example might be:

XX 356

ἀργαλέον δέ μοί ἐστι καὶ ἰφθίμῳ περ ἐόντι
*ἀργαλέον δέ μοί ἐστι ποδώκεϊ Πηλεΐωνι
*ἀργαλέον δέ μοί ἐστιν Ἀχιλλῆϊ πτολιπόρθῳ.

9. It might be objected that κάρη κομόωντες Ἀχαιοί inexactly represents the chief Achaeans whom Achilles is addressing (XXIII 236 ἀριστῆες Παναχαιῶν). But such inexactitude and trifling inconsistency is supposed to be characteristic of Homeric composition.

10. Compare the following equivalencies:

*δῶρα μέγας	δῶρ' ἀγαθός
*κακὰ φαίδιμος	κάκ' ἀρήϊος
*κακὰ διογενής	κάκ' ἀρηΐφιλος
*δῶρα θοῷ ἀτάλαντος Ἄρηϊ	δῶρ' ἐπιείκελος ἀθανάτοισι
*πείθετο Πηλεΐωνι δαΐφρονι δῖος ἑταῖρος	πείθετ' Ἀχιλλῆϊ ῥηξήνορι δῖος ἑταῖρος.

11. Homer was able to put four datives (one implied) into one verse:

XXIII 791–92

. . . . ἀργαλέον δὲ
ποσσὶν [Ὀδυσῆϊ] ἐριδήσασθαι Ἀχαιοῖς, εἰ μὴ Ἀχιλλεῖ.

12. If λίσσομαι must have an accusative object, then Ἀχιλλῆϊ must go with the following clause.

13.

*λῆγε χόλοιο	I 224 λῆγε χόλοιο
*μῆνιν ἀφεῖναι	XIII 444 ἀφίει μένος ὄβριμος Ἄρης
*ἐξ ἔρον εἶναι	XIII 638 ἐξ ἔρον εἶναι
*χωόμενός περ παύε'	XIV 260 ὁ δὲ παύσατο χωόμενός περ
*παύε', ἔα δέ	IX 260 παύε', ἔα δὲ χόλον θυμαλγέα
*λίσσομ' . . . παύε', ἔα δέ	XXII 338–39 λίσσομ' . . . μή με ἔα.

14. If the bard composes, memorizes, and then performs, he hardly differs from the literate poet (who may write or memorize), and Parry's formulaic

diction becomes the casual result of poetic composition rather than its means and cause.

15.

κράτος τε μένος τε   3 × *ψυχή τε μένος τε*

     2 × *χείράς τε μένος τε*

     XVII 476 *δμήσίν τε μένος τε*

κῦδος ὑπέρτερον ἐγγυαλίζω   2 × *κῦδος ὑπέρτερον ἐγγυαλίξειν*

The formula for Achilles could conveniently be extended:

Πηλείδη κρατερῷ ῥηξήνορι θυμολέοντι.

16. At XVIII 143, *αἴ κε διδοίη* could also be *αἴ κε πόρῃσιν* (ii 186). At XXII 110 *αὐτόν* clarifies the subject of the infinitive. Leaf, in fact, prints *αὐτόν*.

17. At XXII 58, instead of glorifying Achilles with a heroic formula, Priam feels intensely for his son, even at the cost of hiatus. At XXIV 39, Apollo is uncomplimentary and so is Achilles' epithet, even at the cost of hiatus, which would have been permissible in a traditional formula: *Πηλείδη Ἀχιλῆϊ.* At XXII 277, *Ἕκτορα, ποιμένα λαῶν* occurs twice, *Ἕκτορα δῖον* twenty-seven times:

XV 583

τεύχεα συλήσων· ἀλλ᾿ οὐ λάθεν Ἕκτορα δῖον.

At XXII 40, with parataxis:

Πηλείδη Ἀχιλῆϊ δαμείς· ὁ δὲ φέρτερός ἐστι.

At XXIII 173, Achilles need not have been mentioned at all:

xiv 21

πὰρ δὲ κύνες θήρεσσιν ἐοικότες αἰὲν ἴαυον / τέσσαρες.

At XI 783, *πατὴρ ἐπετέλλετο Πηλεύς* occurs at IX 252. The use of formulae would excuse *Πηλείδη . . . Πηλεύς.* At XXI 569, *ψυχή τε καὶ αἰών* occurs at XVI 453. Compare also:

XVI 441, XXII 179

ἄνδρα θνητὸν ἐόντα, πάλαι πεπρωμένον αἴσῃ.

At XXI 570, Achilles has only been named by pronouns since XXI 557.

Chapter V

1. Compare XI 772 *πὰρ δ᾿ Ἀχιλῆα.*

2. Compare xv 243 *Ἀντιφάτης*, xv 242 *Ἀντιφάτην*, x 106, 199 *Ἀντιφάταο*, x 114 *Ἀντιφατῆα.*

3.

*Ἀχιλῆα ἄνακτα	iii 163 Ὀδυσῆα ἄνακτα
*ἥρω' Ἀχιλῆα	VI 63 ἥρω' Ἄδρηστον
*κρείοντ' Ἀχιλῆα	XXIII 630 κρείοντ' Ἀμαρυγκέα.

4. Each hemistich occurs in Homer:

iii 41

χρυσείῳ δέπαϊ· δειδισκόμενος δὲ προσηύδα

xviii 121

καὶ δέπαϊ χρυσέῳ δειδίσκετο φώνησέν τε.

5. Of the three phrases, only ἀμύμονά τε κρατερόν τε recurs: IV 89 and V 169 for Pandarus, XXI 546 for Agenor.
6. The subject of ἐκπέρσει is probably Achilles, not σθένος ἀνέρος.
7. If this apostrophe is intentional, others may well be too.

Chapter VI

1. There are other possibilities:

*εἰ μὲν δὴ νόστον γε μετὰ φρεσὶ σῇσι τίθησθα

*εἰ μὲν δὴ νόστος γε μετὰ φρεσὶ σῇσι μέμηλε.

2. Υἱὲ μέγα indicates an original double consonant—to the benefit of extension. But Homer never takes advantage of the device, beyond this repeated verse. Homer overlengthens and underlengthens.
3. *MHV*, p. 272.
4. The epithet, far from being metrical filler, expresses an essential idea of the whole plot:

X 45–49

. . . . ἐπεὶ Διὸς ἐτράπετο φρήν

. . . .

ὅσσ' Ἕκτωρ ἔρρεξε Διὶ φίλος υἷας Ἀχαιῶν.

Compare VI 318, VIII 493, XIII 674, XV 610–12, 637.
5. Compare *Πηλέος υἱέ, θεοῖς ἐπιείκελ' Ἀχιλλεῦ with Homer's

XVIII 18

ὤ μοι, Πηλέος υἱὲ δαΐφρονος, ἦ μάλα λυγρῆς

XVI 203

σχέτλιε Πηλέος υἱέ, χόλῳ ἄρα σ' ἔτρεφε μήτηρ, | νηλεές

XX 2

ἀμφὶ σέ, Πηλέος υἱέ, μάχης ἀκόρητον Ἀχαιοί.

6. The nominative for vocative is an expedient that makes the formula more versatile and convenient. On the other hand, hiatus at the caesura would be attributed to mechanical juxtaposition of formulae.

7. The whole-verse formula (XVI 21, XIX 216, xi 478) is an extension of the polite form ὦ Ἀχιλεῦ.

8.

XVI 596

ὄλβῳ τε πλούτῳ τε μετέπρεπε Μυρμιδόνεσσι

XXIV 536

ὄλβῳ τε πλούτῳ τε, ἄνασσε δὲ Μυρμιδόνεσσι.

9.

VI 382

Ἕκτωρ, ἐπεὶ μάλ' ἄνωγας ἀληθέα μυθήσασθαι.

10. See Διὶ φίλος in chap. II.

Chapter VII

1. C. M. Bowra, "The Comparative Study of Homer," *American Journal of Archaeology* 54(1950):187.

2. G. F. Else, "Homer and the Homeric Problem," *University of Cincinnati Classical Studies* (Semple Lectures) 1(1967):336.

3. J. B. Hainsworth, "Structure and Content in Epic Formulae: The Question of the Unique Expression," *Classical Quarterly* 14(1964):157.

4. A. B. Lord, *The Singer of Tales* (Cambridge, MA, 1960), p. 144.

5. A. Parry, Introduction to *MHV*, p. xxvii.

6. G. Nagy, "An Evolutionary Model for the Text Fixation of Homeric Epos," in *Oral Traditional Literature: Festschrift for A. B. Lord,* ed. J. M. Foley (Columbus, OH, 1981), p. 390.

7. N. Austin, Review of *The Epithets of Homer* by P. Vivante, *Classical Philology* 80(1985):67. Nor are extension and economy merely an Anglo-American dogma. Consider G. Broccia in *La Questione omerica* (Florence, 1979), p. 71:

> Accurate statistiche confermano l'ampiezza del sistema e l'economia che lo governa, e dimostrano come soltanto molti cantori nel corso di molte generazione avrebbero potuto produrre un tale linguaggio, che è dunque tradizionale. La differenza rispetto all'epica letteraria di Apollonio Rodio e Virgilio è completa.

8. F. M. Combellack, "Homer the Innovator," *Classical Philology* 71(1976):54.

9. *MHV*, p. 19.

10. Parry mentions these equivalencies at *MHV*, pp. 178–79.

11. He does, of course, catch patronymics used epithetically with personal names, e.g., Πηληϊάδεω Ἀχιλῆος. 45 is a fair count of expressions containing a form of Ἀχιλ(λ)εύς in all cases.

12. *MHV*, p. 38.

13. Ibid., p. 57.

14. This is admitted by G. P. Edwards in *The Language of Hesiod in Its Traditional Context* (Oxford, 1971), p. 58:

> The extent to which breaches of the principle of economy occur in Homer is perhaps greater than is generally supposed, and too strong an insistence on the strictness with which the principle is observed is in danger of obscuring the real range of choice which is frequently open to the poet.

After examining a few examples of equivalencies (so-called doublets), he concludes that oral poets can handle them (ibid., p. 60):

> Alternative expressions can arise from causes which have nothing to do with the use of writing and the more deliberate choice of language which writing makes possible, so that a breach of the principle of economy cannot invariably be interpreted as an indication of written composition.

After extensively examining Achilles' equivalent formulae, I doubt that oral poets can handle them. B. Alexanderson examines "Homeric Formulae for Ships" in *Eranos* 68(1970):1–43, and he draws the opposite conclusions. N. Austin studied "the utility, range, and necessity of the formulaic system" for Odysseus and failed it on all three counts in *Archery at the Dark of the Moon* (Berkeley, 1975), chap. 1. M. W. Edwards investigated some "striking violations of the principle of formulaic economy" in his article "On Some 'Answering' Expressions in Homer," *Classical Philology* 64(1969):81–87. Some instances possibly show "signs of a liking of variations," some "a special note of poignancy" (p. 87). In his "Homeric Speech Introductions," *Harvard Studies in Classical Philology* 74(1970):1–36, Edwards concludes that "the formulaic system itself [of speech introductions] maintains the principle of economy to a certain extent," but "flexibility seems to indicate a considerable level of sophistication ... in his [oral] technique" (pp. 35–36). Robert Garland finds "some 60 ways of conveying the idea that 'X died' in the *Iliad*" in "The Causation of Death in the *Iliad*," *Bulletin of the Institute of Classical Studies* 28(1981):50.

15. P. Vivante's extreme postion seems no less untenable than Parry's. He largely develops, somewhat poetically, the ideas of W. Whallon: "The Homeric Epithets," *Yale Classical Studies* 17(1961):97–142 and *Formula, Character, and Context* (Washington, DC, 1969). Whallon's publications are derived from his doctoral dissertation (Yale, 1957), for which he

expresses his indebtedness to Adam Parry—that great source of revisionism.

16. *MHV*, p. 18.

17. A. Parry citing M. Parry, Introduction to *MHV*, p. lii.

18. J. A. Notopoulos, "Studies in Early Greek Oral Poetry," *Harvard Studies in Classical Philology* 68(1964):60–62.

19. J. B. Hainsworth, "Criteri di oralità nella poesia non omerica," in *I poemi epici rapsodici non omerici e la tradizione orale,* (Padua, 1981), p. 6.

20. This point is vigorously argued by D. C. C. Young: "Miltonic Light on Prof. D. Page's Homeric Theory," *Greece and Rome* 6(1959); "Was Homer an Illiterate Improvisor?" *Minnesota Review* 5(1965); "Never Blotted a Line? Formula and Premeditation in Homer and Hesiod," *Arion* 6(1967).

21. G. M. Calhoun, "Homeric Repetitions," *University of California Publications in Classical Philology* 12(1933):25.

22. Ibid., p. 18.

23. Ibid., p. 25.

24. Ibid.

25. Ibid., p. 18.

26. C. M. Bowra, "Composition," in *A Companion to Homer* (London, 1962), p. 73.

27. Idem., *Homer* (London, 1972), p. 24.

28. *MHV*, pp. 125, 129.

29. S. E. Bassett, *The Poetry of Homer* (Berkeley, 1938), p. 18. H. Fränkel, on the contrary, was quite impressed with the Slavic analogy. He cites Murko extensively and relegates Parry to an inglorious footnote in *Dichtung und Philosophie des frühen Griechentums,* 2d ed. (Munich, 1962), p. 9 n. 1:

Murkos Arbeit wurde von H. Geseman, Milman Parry und A. B. Lord (*Trans. Amer. Philol. Ass.* 67; 69; 79) forgesetzt, und die Untersuchungen werden zur Zeit weiter vorangetrieben.

30. K. Reinhardt, *Die Ilias und ihr Dichter* (Göttingen, 1961), p. 16.

31. P. Chantraine, "Sur un trait du style homérique," *Revue de Philologie* 3(1929):299.

32. A. Puech, *L'Iliade d'Homère* (Paris, [1932]).

33. In *Introduction à l'Iliade* (Paris, 1942).

34. W. B. Stanford, "Remarks on the Collected Works of Milman Parry," *Hermathena* 112(1971):47. Compare L. A. Stella in *Tradizione micenea e poesia dell'Iliade* (Rome, 1978), p. 324: la distanza fra la poesia orale e l'Iliade si rivela (a me sembra) un incolmabile abisso."

35. Chaintraine, "Style homérique," p. 294.

36. Stanford, "Remarks," p. 36.

37. W. Schadewaldt, "Die epische Tradition," in *Homer: Tradition und Neuerung,* ed. J. Latacz (Darmstadt, 1979), pp. 536–37. The lists of *Merkmale* are on pages 532–35.

38. A. Lesky, "Mündlichkeit und Schriftlichkeit im homerischen Epos," In *Festschrift Kralik* (Vienna 1954), p. 9.

39. A. Heubeck, "Homeric Studies Today," in *Homer: Tradition and Invention,* ed. B. Fenik (Leiden, 1978), p. 15. So also L. A. Stella, in *Tradizione micenea e poesia dell'Iliade,* Pt. 3: "Continuità di tradizione epica" (Rome, 1978), pp. 239–414.

40. D. Page, Review of *Ilias und Aithiopis* by G. Schoeck, *Classical Review* New Series 13(1963):22. There is a good comparison of the two schools of thought by W. Kullmann, "Oral Poetry Theory and Neoanalysis in Homeric Research," *Greek Roman and Byzantine Studies* 25(1984):307–23.

41. A. Hoekstra, *Homeric Modifications of Formulaic Prototypes* (Amsterdam, 1965), p. 7 (my emphasis).

42. Ibid., 17.

43. Ibid., 9.

44. Ibid., 25. R. Janko goes so far in the assumption of regularity in the evolution of epic diction that he needs only to "count archaisms and innovations" to give "relative dates to the poems" in *Homer, Hesiod, and the Hymns* (Cambridge, 1982), p. 189. But then, of course, one must distinguish between Homer's archaisms and those of the *Shield* in order that the latter should not be contemporary with the former.

45. Compare *MHV,* p. 1:

> It is not enough to know that the style of Homer is more or less traditional; we must know which words are traditional, which expressions.

46. Hoekstra, *Homeric Modifications,* p. 137.

47. W. E. McLeod, in his review of *Homeric Modifications, Phoenix* 20(1966):333, remarks on Hoekstra's use of the word *decomposition:*

> (a key-word; 8, 27, 28, 41, 61, 75, 77, 83, 110, 131)—a process which continued until Hesiod and the earlier hymns (8, 26, 75–87).

48. Hoekstra, *Homeric Modifications,* p. 16.

49. Ibid., 18.

50. J. B. Hainsworth, *The Flexibility of the Homeric Formula* (Oxford, 1968), p. 36.

51. Ibid.: "I postulate that for present purposes the following accidents permit words and word-groups to be counted the same."

52. M. M. Willcock, Review of *Flexibility* by J. B. Hainsworth, *Classical Review* New Series 20(1970):144.

53. J. B. Hainsworth, "Structure and Content in Epic Formulae,"

Classical Quarterly 14(1964):157. See also Hainsworth's "The Criticism of an Oral Homer," *Journal of Hellenic Studies* 90(1970):91.

54. Idem., *Flexibility,* pp. 35–36.

55. "Remarks on the Homeric Question" in *History and Imagination: Essays in Honour of H. R. Trevor-Roper* (New York, 1982). G. S. Kirk still admires Homer's remarkable extension and remarkable economy in *The Iliad: A Commentary,* Vol. 1, Books 1–4 (Cambridge, 1985), pp. 24–25:

> It is now generally agreed that oral poetry tends to develop a conventional phraseology amounting in many cases to a systematic corpus of phrases for different characters, objects and functions, much more markedly than literate poetry or ordinary speech; and that a highly developed system like the Homeric one maintains both remarkable coverage ("scope") [or extension] and remarkable avoidance of duplication ("economy" or "thrift") in the creation, preservation and deployment of these fixed, traditional or conventional phrases known as formulas. ... It was the publication in 1928 of Milman Parry's Paris dissertation *L'Epithète traditionnelle dans Homère* that first made almost complete sense of this aspect of Homeric style. Milman Parry both demonstrated in detail the systematic nature of an important part of Homeric phraseology, and drew the convincing if not wholly provable conclusion that such a system could only be developed for the purposes of specifically oral poetry. That is common knowledge by now.

I have sought to assail what by now is common knowledge.

56. G. S. Kirk compares *"deliberate, self-conscious composition in a formular style"* with *"natural composition in a formular tradition"* in "Formular Language and Oral Quality," *Yale Classical Studies* 20(1966):174, but he puts Homer into the wrong category. The following scholars have put Homer into the right category: the Germans; S. Bassett, *The Poetry of Homer* (Berkeley, 1938), pp. 14–19; H. T. Wade-Gery, *The Poet of the Iliad* (Cambridge, 1952), p. 39. Others put Homer in both categories or between the two: Adam Parry, "Have we Homer's *Iliad?*" *Yale Classical Studies* 20(1966):215–16; J. A. Russo, "Homer Against his Tradition," *Arion* 7(1968):276, and his review of Hoekstra's *Homeric Modifications* in *American Journal of Philology* 88(1969):344; and now probably most scholars.

C. O. Pavese, in *Studi sulla tradizione epica rapsodica* (Rome, 1974), p. 30, writes that "la dizione di un autore recente si tradirebbe per il fatto di sostrarsi all'influenza semplificante dell'esametro che opera nella dizione tradizionale." Primitivists have made Homer a primitive bard. For me Homer is *un autore recente.* For the past two hundred years (Vico, Herder, Rousseau, Wood, Wolf, Parry, and Parryans) Homerists have been developing a new conception of Homer and Homeric heroic epic as *oral poetry:* which is meant to correct the anachronistic misconception of Aristotle's *Poetics* that Homer composed like Sophocles. Milman Parry consummated this new conception. Even revisionism is truly Parryan, as indicated by the remarks of N. Austin cited at the beginning of this chapter and B. Fenik's question in his preface to *Homer: Tradition and Invention* (Leiden, 1978), p. viii:

> How shall we give full recognition to the large areas of Homer's style that came to him ready-made, and interpret them properly, but also account for the powerful and obviously unique artistry of the Iliad and Odyssey? In short, how shall we discover Homer's invention within his tradition?

If, however, the myths of economy and extension are dispelled, perhaps Homer's *tradition* is rather nugatory and we can return unapologetically to Aristotle's poetics of *invention*.

Bibliography

Ancients

Apollonius Rhodius. *Argonautica.* Edited by H. Fränkel. Oxford: Clarendon Press, 1961.

Aristotle. *Poetics.* Edited by D. W. Lucas. Oxford: Clarendon Press, 1968.

"Demetrius." *On Style.* Edited by W. Rhys Roberts. Cambridge: Cambridge University Press, 1902.

Hesiod. *Theogonia, Opera et Dies, Scutum.* Edited by F. Solmsen. *Fragmenta Selecta.* Edited by R. Merkelback and M. L. West. 2d ed. Oxford: Clarendon Press, 1983.

Homer. *Opera.* 5 vols. Edited by D. B. Monro and T. W. Allen. Oxford: Clarendon Press, (*Iliad,* 3d edition, 1920; *Odyssey,* 2d edition, 1917; *Hymns,* etc., 1912).

"Longinus," *On the Sublime.* Edited by D. A. Russell. Oxford: Clarendon Press, 1964.

Plato. *Opera.* 5 vols. Edited by J. Burnet. Oxford: Clarendon Press, 1900–07.

Statius. *Achilleid.* Edited by O. A. W. Dilke. Cambridge: Cambridge University Press, 1954.

Vergil. *Opera.* Edited by R. A. B. Mynors. Oxford: Clarendon Press, 1969.

Moderns

Adkins, A. W. H. "Orality and Philosophy." In *Language and Thought in Early Greek Philosophy,* pp. 207–27. Edited by K. Robb. La Salle, IL: Hegeler Institute, 1983.

Alexanderson, B. "Homeric Formulae for Ships." *Eranos* 68(1970):1–43.

184   *Bibliography*

Aubignac, F. Hédelin, Abbé d'. *Conjectures académiques ou Dissertation sur l'Iliade* [1715]. Edited by V. Magnien. Paris: Hachette, 1925.

Austin, N. *Archery at the Dark of the Moon.* Berkeley: University of California Press, 1975.

———. Review of *The Epithets of Homer,* by P. Vivante. *Classical Philology* 80(1985):67–69.

Bassett, S. E. *The Poetry of Homer.* Berkeley: University of California Press, 1938.

Beaton, R. *Folk Poetry of Modern Greece.* Cambridge: Cambridge University Press, 1980.

Beattie, J. *Essays on Poetry and Music, as They Affect the Mind.* Edinburgh: Dilly, 1778.

Bentley, R. "Remarks upon a Late Discourse of Free-Thinking" [1713]. In *The Works of Richard Bentley,* Vol. 3, pp. 286–472. Edited by A. Dyce. London: F. Macpherson, 1836–38. Reprinted, New York: Ams Press, 1966.

Beye, C. R. *The Iliad, the Odyssey, and the Epic Tradition.* London: Macmillan, 1968.

Boisacq, E. *Dictionnaire étymologique de la langue grecque.* Heidelberg: Winter; and Paris: Klineksieck, 1916.

Bowra, C. M. "The Comparative Study of Homer." *American Journal of Archeology* 54(1950):184–92.

———. *Heroic Poetry.* London: Macmillan, 1952.

———. "Composition." In *A Companion to Homer,* pp. 38–74. Edited by A. J. B. Wace and F. H. Stubbings. London: Macmillan, 1962.

———. *Homer.* London: Duckworth, 1972.

Bréal, M. *Pour mieux connaître Homère.* Paris: Hachette, [1906].

Broccia, G. *La Questione omerica.* Florence: Sansoni, 1979.

Calhoun, G. M. "Homeric Repetitions." *University of California Publications in Classical Philology* 12(1933):1–25.

Chantraine, P. "Sur un trait du style homérique." *Revue de Philologie* 3(1929):294–300.

———. *Grammaire homérique.* Vol. 1: *Phonétique et morphologie.* Vol. 2: *Syntaxe.* Paris: Klincksieck, (1) 1958 and (2) 1953.

Combellack, F. M. "Homer the Innovator." *Classical Philology* 71(1976):44–55.

Croce, B. *The Philosophy of Giambattista Vico.* Translated by R. G. Collingwood. New York: Macmillan, 1913.

Dacier, A. (Lefèvre). *L'Iliade d'Homere traduite en françois avec des remarques.* 3 vols. Paris: Rigaud, 1711.

Dunbar, H. *A Complete Concordance to the Odyssey of Homer.* 2d ed. Edited by B. Marzullo. Hildesheim: Olms, 1962.

Düntzer, H. "Zur Beurteilung der stehenden Homerischen Beiwörter." In *Homerische Abhandlungen,* pp. 507–16. Leipzig: Hahn, 1872.

Ebeling, H. *Lexicon Homericum*. Leipzig: Teubner, 1885. Reprinted, Hildesheim: Olms, 1963.

Edwards, G. P. *The Language of Hesiod in Its Traditional Context*. Oxford: Blackwell, 1971.

Edwards, M. W. "On some 'Answering' Expressions in Homer." *Classical Philology* 64(1969):81–87.

——. "Homeric Speech Introductions." *Harvard Studies in Classical Philology* 74(1970):1–36.

Else, G. F. "Homer and the Homeric Problem." *University of Cincinnati Classical Studies* (Semple Lectures) 1(1967):315–65.

Erbse, H., ed. *Scholia Graeca in Homeri Iliadem*. 6 vols. Berlin: de Gruyter, 1969–83.

Farnham, F. *Madame Dacier: Scholar and Humanist*. Monterey, CA: Angel Press, 1976.

Fenik, B. Preface to *Homer: Tradition and Invention*. Edited by B. Fenik. Leiden: Brill, 1978.

Finley, M. I. *Aspects of Antiquity*. 2d ed. Harmondsworth: Penguin, 1977.

Finnegan, R. *Oral Poetry: Its Nature, Significance, and Social Context*. Cambridge: Cambridge University Press, 1977.

Foerster, D. M. *Homer in English Criticism*. New Haven: Yale University Press, 1947. Reprinted, Hamden, CT: Archon, 1969.

Fränkel, H. *Dichtung und Philosophie des frühen Griechentums*. 2d ed. Munich: Beck, 1962.

Garland, R. "The Causation of Death in the *Iliad*." *Bulletin of the Institute of Classical Studies* 28(1981):43–60.

Gehring, A. *Index Homericus*. Leipzig: Teubner, 1891.

Gennep, A. van. *La Question d'Homère: Les Poèmes homérique, l'archéologie et la poésie populaire*. Paris: Mercure de France, 1909.

Goldsmith, O. *The Vicar of Wakefield*. 2d ed. London: F. Newbery, 1766.

Hainsworth, J. B. "Structure and Content in Epic Formulae: the Question of the Unique Expression." *Classical Quarterly* 14(1964):155–64.

——. *The Flexibility of the Homeric Formula*. Oxford: Clarendon Press, 1968.

——. "The Criticism of an Oral Homer." *Journal of Hellenic Studies* 90(1970):90–98. Reprinted in *Essays on the Iliad*, pp. 28–40. Edited by J. Wright. Bloomington: Indiana University Press, 1978.

——. "Criteri di oralità nella poesia non omerica." In *I poemi epici rapsodici non omerici e la tradizione orale*, pp. 3–19. Edited by C. Pavese, C. Brillante, and M. Cantilena. Padua: Antenore, 1981.

Havelock, E. *Preface to Plato*. Cambridge, MA: Harvard University Press, 1963.

——. *The Literate Revolution in Greece and its Cultural Consequences*. Princeton: Princeton University Press, 1982.

————. "The Linguistic Task of the Presocratics." In *Language and Thought in Early Greek Philosophy,* pp. 7–84. Edited by K. Robb. La Salle, IL: Hegeler Institute, 1983.

Herder, J. G. *Abhandlung über den Ursprung der Sprache* [1772]. Edited by W. Pross. Munich: Carl Hanser, 1978.

Heubeck, A. "Homeric Studies Today." In *Homer: Tradition and Invention,* pp. 1–17. Edited by B. Fenik. Leiden: Brill, 1978.

Hoekstra, A. *Homeric Modifications of Formulaic Prototypes.* Amsterdam: North-Holland, 1965.

Janko, R. *Homer, Hesiod, and the Hymns.* Cambridge: Cambridge University Press, 1982.

Jebb, R. C. *Bentley.* London: Harper, 1902.

Jousse, M. *Le Style oral rythmique et mnémotechnique chez les verbo-moteurs.* Paris: Beauchesne, 1925.

Kirchhoff, A. *Die homerische Odyssee.* 2d ed. Berlin: Hertz, 1879. Reprinted, Hildesheim: Olms, 1973.

Kirk, G. S. "The Homeric Poems as History." In *Cambridge Ancient History,* 3d ed., vol. 2, pt. 2, pp. 820–50. Cambridge: Cambridge University Press, 1975.

————. "Formular Language and Oral Quality." *Yale Classical Studies* 20(1966):155–74. Reprinted in *Homer and the Oral Tradition,* pp. 183–200. Cambridge: Cambridge University Press, 1976.

————. *The Iliad: A Commentary.* Vol. 1: Books 1–4. Cambridge: Cambridge University Press, 1985.

Kullmann, W. "Oral Poetry Theory and Neoanalysis in Homeric Research." *Greek Roman and Byzantine Studies* 25(1984):307–23.

La Motte, H. de. *Oeuvres.* Vol. 2: *Discours sur Homere* [1714]. Paris: Prault, 1754. Reprinted, Bordeaux: Société Bordelaise de diffusion des travaux de lettres et sciences humaines, n.d.

Lang, A. *Homer and the Epic.* London: Longmans, 1893.

————. *The World of Homer.* London: Longmans, 1910.

Leaf, W., ed. *Iliad.* 2 vols. 2d ed. London: Macmillan, 1900–02. Reprinted, Amsterdam: Hakkert, 1960.

Lesky, A. "Mündlichkeit und Schriftlichkeit im homerischen Epos." In *Festschrift Kralik,* pp. 1–9. Vienna: Horn, 1954. Reprinted in *Leskys Gesammelte Schriften,* pp. 63–71. Bern: Francke, 1966. Also reprinted in *Homer: Tradition und Neuerung,* pp. 297–307. Edited by J. Latacz. Darmstadt: Wissenschaftliche Buchgesellschaft, 1979.

————. *Göttliche und menschliche Motivation im homerischen Epos.* Heidelberg: C. Winter, 1961.

Lloyd-Jones, H. "Remarks on the Homeric Question." In *History and Imagination: Essays in Honour of H. R. Trevor-Roper.* Edited by H. Lloyd-Jones. New York: Holmes and Meier, 1982.

Lord, A. B. *The Singer of Tales.* Cambridge, MA: Harvard University Press, 1960.

Marouzeau, J. Review of *Le Style oral rythmique et mnémotechnique chez les verbo-moteurs,* by M. Jousse. *Revue des études latines* 6(1928): 234–36.

Mazon, P. "L'Origine de l'Iliade." In *Introduction à l'Iliade,* pp. 137–299. Paris: Belles Lettres, 1942.

McLeod, W. E. Review of *Homeric Modifications of Formulaic Prototypes,* by A. Hoekstra. *Phoenix* 20(1966): 332–40.

Meillet, A. *Les Origines indo-européennes des mètres grecs.* Paris: Presses Universitaires de France, 1923.

Miller, D. G. *Improvisation, Typology, Culture, and "the New Orthodoxy." How "Oral" Is Homer?* Washington, DC: University Press of America, 1982.

Montaigne, M. de. *Les Essais de Michel de Montaigne* [1588]. Edited by P. Villey and V.-L. Saulnier. Paris: Presses Universitaires de France, 1965.

Monro, D. B., ed. *Homer's Odyssey: Books XIII–XXIV.* Oxford: Clarendon Press, 1901.

Murko, M. *Bericht über eine Reise zum Studium der Volksepik in Bosnien und Herzegowina im Jahre 1913.* Vienna: Hölder, 1915.

———. "Neues über südslavische Volksepik." *Neue Jahrbücher für das klassische Altertum* 22(1919): 273–96. Reprinted in *Homer: Tradition und Neuerung,* pp. 118–52. Edited by J. Latacz. Darmstadt: Wissenschaftliche Buchgesellschaft, 1979.

———. *La Poésie populaire épique en Yougoslavie au début du XXᵉ siècle.* Paris: Champion, 1929.

Myres, J. L. *Homer and his Critics.* London: Routledge & Kegan Paul, 1958.

Naber, S. A. *Quaestiones Homericae.* Amsterdam: van der Post, 1877.

Nagy, G. "An Evolutionary Model for the Text Fixation of Homeric Epos." In *Oral Traditional Literature: Festschrift for A. B. Lord,* pp. 390–93. Edited by J. M. Foley. Columbus, OH: Slavica, 1981.

Notopoulos, J. A. "Studies in Early Greek Oral Poetry." *Harvard Studies in Classical Philology* 68(1964): 1–77.

Ormesson, J. d'. *Le Vagabond qui passe sous une ombrelle trouée.* Paris: Gallimard, 1978.

Page, D. Review of *Ilias und Aithiopis,* by G. Schoeck. *Classical Review* New Series 13(1963): 21–24.

Paris, G. *La Littérature française au moyen age.* 5th ed. Paris: Hachette, 1914. 1st ed., 1888.

Parry, A[dam]. "Have we Homer's *Iliad?*" *Yale Classical Studies* 20(1966): 177–216. Reprinted in *Essays on the Iliad,* pp. 1–27. Edited by J. Wright. Bloomington: Indiana University Press, 1978.

———. Introduction to *The Making of Homeric Verse: The Collected Papers of Milman Parry*. Oxford: Clarendon Press, 1971.

———. "Language and Characterization in Homer." *Harvard Studies in Classical Philology* 76(1972):1–22.

Parry, A[nne Amory]. "Homer as Artist." *Classical Quarterly* New Series 21(1971):1–15.

Parry, M. *The Making of Homeric Verse: The Collected Papers of Milman Parry*. Edited by A. Parry. Oxford: Clarendon Press, 1971.

Pavese, C. O. *Studi sulla tradizione epica rapsodica*. Rome: Ateneo, 1974.

Perrault, C. *Parallèle des anciens et des modernes*. 4 vols. Paris, 1692–97. Reprinted, Geneva: Slatkine Reprints, 1979.

Pope, A. *The Poems of Alexander Pope*. Volume 7: *Translations of Homer*. Edited by M. Mack. London: Methuen; and New Haven: Yale University Press, 1967.

Prendergast, G. L. *A Complete Concordance to the Iliad of Homer*. 2d ed. Edited by B. Marzullo. Hildesheim: Olms, 1962.

Puech, A. *L'Iliade d'Homère*. Paris: Mellottée, [1932].

Reinhardt, K. *Die Ilias und ihr Dichter*. Göttingen: Vandenhoeck & Ruprecht, 1961.

Rousseau, J.-J. "Essai sur l'origine des langues." In *Oeuvres Postumes de Jean-Jaque Rousseau*. Vol. 3, pp. 211–327. Geneva: n.p., 1781.

Russo, J. A. "Homer Against His Tradition." *Arion* 7(1968):275–95.

———. Review of *Homeric Modifications of Formulaic Prototypes*, by A. Hoekstra. *American Journal of Philology* 88(1969):340–46.

Schadewaldt, W. "Die epische Tradition." In *Homer: Tradition und Neuerung*, pp. 529–39. Edited by J. Latacz. Darmstadt: Wissenschaftliche Buchgesellschaft, 1979.

Schmidt, C. E. *Parallel-Homer*. Göttingen: Vanderhoeck & Ruprecht, 1885. Reprinted, 1965.

Scott, J. A. "Repeated Verses in Homer." *American Journal of Philology* 32(1911):314–21.

———. *The Unity of Homer*. Berkeley: University of California Press, 1921. Reprinted, New York: Biblo & Tannen, 1965.

Shewan, A. *The Lay of Dolon*. London: Macmillan, 1912.

———. "Repetition in Homer and Tennyson." *Classical Weekly* 16(1923):153–66.

———. "The Homeric Repetitions Again." *Philological Quarterly* 8(1929):113–23.

Stanford, W. B. "Remarks on the Collected Works of Milman Parry." *Hermathena* 112(1971):36–51.

Stella, L. A. *Tradizione micenea e poesia dell'Iliade*. Rome: Ateneo, 1978.

Strunk, W., Jr. and White, E. B. *The Elements of Style*. 3d ed. New York: Macmillan, 1979.

Thérive, A. *Le Retour d'Amazan ou une histoire de la littérature française.* Paris: Le Livre, 1926.

Vivante, P. *The Epithets of Homer.* New Haven: Yale University Press, 1982.

Wade-Gery, H. T. *The Poet of the Iliad.* Cambridge: Cambridge University Press, 1952.

Whallon, W. "The Homeric Epithets." *Yale Classical Studies* 17(1961):97–142.

———. *Formula, Character, and Context.* Washington, DC: Center for Hellenic Studies, 1969.

Willcock, M. M. "Some Aspects of the Gods in the Iliad." *Bulletin of the Institute of Classical Studies* 17(1970):1–10. Reprinted in *Essays on the Iliad,* pp. 58–69. Edited by J. Wright. Bloomington: Indiana University Press, 1978.

———. Review of *The Flexibility of the Homeric Formula,* by J. B. Hainsworth. *Classical Review* New Series 20(1970):143–45.

———. "Ad hoc Invention in the *Iliad.*" *Harvard Studies in Classical Philology* 81(1977):43–53.

Wolf, F. A. *Prolegomena ad Homerum.* Halle: e libraria orphanotrophei, 1795. Reprinted, edited by R. Peppmüller, Hildesheim: Olms, 1963.

———. *Prolegomena to Homer.* Translated with Introduction and Notes by A. Grafton, G. W. Most, and J. E. G. Zetzel. Princeton: Princeton University Press, 1985.

Wood, R. *An Essay on the Original Genius and Writings of Homer.* London: Hughs, 1775. Reprinted, Hildesheim: Olms, 1976.

Young, D. C. C. "Miltonic Light on Professor D. Page's Homeric Theory." *Greece and Rome* 6(1959):96–108.

———. "Was Homer an Illiterate Improvisor?" *Minnesota Review* 5(1965):65–75.

———. "Never Blotted a Line? Formula and Premeditation in Homer and Hesiod." *Arion* 6(1967):279–324.

Homeric Index

191

Index of Names